Race, ethnicity and power

Donald G. Baker

Professor of Political Science and Sociology
Southampton College, Long Island University

Race, ethnicity and power

A comparative study

Routledge & Kegan Paul

London, Boston, Melbourne and Henley

First published in 1983
by Routledge & Kegan Paul plc
39 Store Street, London WC1E 7DD,
9 Park Street, Boston, Mass. 02108, USA,
296 Beaconsfield Parade, Middle Park,
Melbourne 3206, Australia, and
Broadway House, Newtown Road,
Henley-on-Thames, Oxon RG9 1EN
Set in IBM Press Roman by Columns, Reading

Printed in the United States of America

Copyright © Donald G. Baker 1983

Library of Congress Cataloging in Publication Data

Baker, Donald G., 1932-
Race, ethnicity, and power.
Bibliography: p.
Includes index.
1. Race relations. 2. Ethnic relations.
3. Great Britain – Foreign relations.
4. British – Foreign countries.
5. Power (Social sciences)
I. Title.
HT1523.B33 1983   305.8'00917'521   82-25492

ISBN 0-7100-9467-1

Contents

Acknowledgments

The research and writing of this study was aided by financial support from various institutions and the comments and criticisms of numerous individuals. Financial support was forthcoming from the University of Rhodesia and, later, the University of Zimbabwe, with appointments as Senior Research Fellow, and from St Antony's College, Oxford University, which provided funds for a series of seminars and lectures. Deepest gratitude is extended for their assistance and support to Professor Marshall Murphree, Director, Centre for Applied Social Science, University of Zimbabwe, and Professor Kenneth Kirkwood, St Antony's College. Financial support in the form of secretarial and photocopying services was provided in part by Southampton College, with special thanks due to Ms Joanne Alexander.

Numerous individuals provided comments or criticisms of earlier draft chapters or of seminars and lectures on which the chapters are based, and their criticisms were invaluable. Among those deserving mention in addition to Marshall Murphree and Kenneth Kirkwood are: John Stone (Goldsmiths' College, University of London), Robert Schrire (University of Cape Town), Heribert Adam (Simon Fraser University), Hasu Patel (University of Zimbabwe), Brady Tyson (American University), Frank Stevens (University of New South Wales), Joe Himes (University of North Carolina, Greensboro) and John Seiler. Special thanks are due to John Barrett who, as Director of the South Africa Institute of International Affairs, arranged what became a series of seminars and meetings in mid-1977 with Soweto high school students who had been expelled from school because of their participation in the 1976 demonstrations. Those meetings, as well as others with black South African leaders arranged under the auspices of the

SAIIA, the South African Institute of Race Relations and other organizations were particularly helpful.

Some of the materials in this study were presented as seminars or papers at various institutions (American University, Simon Fraser University, St Antony's, University of Rhodesia and University of Zimbabwe, University of Cape Town, University of Natal and Stellenbosch University) or appeared in earlier form as articles in books and journals, including, among others, *South Atlantic Quarterly*, *Canadian Review of American Studies*, the Australian *American Studies Bulletin*, *Journal of Ethnic Studies*, *International Review of Modern Sociology*, *Social Dynamics* and *Ethnic and Racial Studies*.

Introduction

These essays explore race and ethnic relations in the English settler countries: namely, the United States, Canada, Australia, New Zealand, South Africa and Rhodesia. Referred to by Hartz (1964) as 'Anglo fragment societies,' all six were settled either initially or subsequently by people of English descent.[1] Contemporary race and ethnic relations are the central concern, but earlier developments are considered, for only within a historical context can the character of contemporary group relations be fully understood.

These essays raise questions concerning intergroup relations, one major purpose that of prompting other comparative studies. Three underlying themes recur in the chapters. They are:

1 that contemporary race and ethnic relations are best understood when viewed from historical, comparative and, where possible, diverse disciplinary perspectives;

2 that comparative research of countries with somewhat similar cultural backgrounds provides a sounder basis for generating empirically testable hypotheses than do comparative studies of countries with widely disparate cultural heritages; and

3 that race and ethnic (or intergroup) relations, when shorn of extraneous factors, are best understood as types of group power contests.

It is the common English or Anglo heritage of what emerged historically as the dominant group that distinguishes these six countries, and cultural and power factors emerge as the major determinants of group relations. Situational and other factors, though significant, served essentially as intervening variables. Thus the analysis holds the dominant group cultural component constant,[2] and societies settled by the French, Spanish, Portuguese, Dutch or others are excluded. Studies of the latter societies are possible but are not considered here.

English settlers, supported for an extended period by the British metropolitan power, emerged as the dominant group in all six countries. Although French and Dutch settlers preceded the English in the colonies that later became Canada and South Africa, both ultimately came under British rule; and as incoming English settlers assumed power they shaped or determined the character of group relations in these and the other fragment countries. Two propositions concerning these countries can be posed:

1 English settlers and their descendants, despite variations in demographic, situational and other factors, used their power historically to control the major political, economic and social structures and shape the cultural policies of these countries; and

2 Ethnic and race relations, historically and more recently, are best understood by assessing the changing power capabilities of Anglo and non-Anglo groups. Changes in group relations are thereby the consequence of two major factors: (a) modifications in group power resources and capabilities and (b) changes in situational factors.

What emerged historically in these countries was a situation of Anglo dominance, structural as well as cultural. Variations and exceptions are evident, including the recent waning of Anglo dominance, but that group's tenacity in holding power is also evident. The persistence of Anglo dominance generates numerous questions, including the following:

1 How significant is power as a determinant of race and ethnic relations, be it in the past or at present?

2 What were the processes and techniques by which Anglo groups established and perpetuated their control over other groups?

3 What strategies and tactics have other groups employed to break Anglo control, and how, whether in the past or at present, has the dominant group responded?

4 What inferences can be drawn from the analysis of present group relations and power confrontations that provide clues to possible changes in group power capabilities and cultural politics?

Three factors emerge from these questions that need to be isolated and assessed:

1 The character of early contact situations between Anglo settlers

and other groups, including (a) indigenes, (b) other non-white groups (African slaves in the United States and Canada; Asians in all six countries), and (c) other European groups.

2 The processes and tactics by which people of Anglo descent acquired power and perpetuated their dominance.

3 The emergence of other factors which modified or transformed situations, group resources and group power capabilities, thereby precipitating changes in intergroup relations and cultural policies.

Historical developments in the Anglo fragments are traced more fully later, but a few preliminary comments are necessary. All six countries, whether settled initially or subsequently by English, remained under British metropolitan rule or control for an extended historical period. Consequently, it was the English settlers who determined the character of intergroup relations within each country, be it toward indigenous or other groups (Asians, Europeans and African slaves) who settled in these countries. All came under Anglo cultural and structural dominance.

Although the United States (1776) and South Africa (1961) declared their independence from Great Britain,[3] all six remained under British metropolitan control for an extended period. An uneasy English-Afrikaner alliance ruled South Africa for most of the period from 1910 to 1948, but at that point the Afrikaner Nationalist Party came to power. It has ruled since, Afrikaners being the majority white group. However, English-imposed institutions and cultural beliefs which prevailed previously still play a significant role, accounting for South Africa's inclusion in this analysis. Although Southern Rhodesia unilaterally declared its independence (UDI) in 1965, it technically remained a British Colony. In 1979 whites relectantly accepted black rule, and the analysis concludes at that point rather than the following year when Rhodesia returned to British rule briefly before becoming an independent Zimbabwe. Despite these and other variations, people of English descent, supported for a considerable period by the British metropole, exercised almost exclusive power in all six countries. Given that power they were able to control political, economic and social structures and thereby shape each country's cultural policies. Their policies, then, determined the character of intergroup relations.

This study's central concern is the character of group relations. Structuralist (or marxist) analysis, which emphasizes determinants such as class and the modes of production, is not discounted, but the argument here is that such variables as race, ethnicity and power have a saliency of their own. They cannot be so glibly dismissed as usually occurs in marxist analyses, for they are not simply dependent variables, epiphenomena or examples of false consciousness. Where most marxist analyses focus exclusively on economic structures and determinants, the structural analyses included here recognize political and social structures as systems of power (independent from and not simply secondary to economic structures) that significantly shape the character of group relations and behavior.

Analyses of ethnic and racial groups and their behavior must recognize three other factors. First, individuals, be it as individuals or members of groups, are not simply pawns or robots whose behavior is determined wholly by external (e.g. modes of production) or internal (i.e. irrational) forces of which they remain unaware or over which they exercise no control. Based on their perceptions, individuals evaluate situations and decide how to act. Their choices and behavior are decidedly influenced by what they consider to be beneficial to themselves. However, this does not imply that people are always rational or objective. Situations and, indeed, an individual's belief system screen his perceptions and judgments, and these, as well as other factors, may distort an individual's judgments. However, specific situations, events and encounters force individuals and groups to test their perceptions and beliefs against real-life situations, usually necessitating modifications in beliefs and perceptions that serve to bring their views into closer congruence with the real world. There do exist particular types of situations and belief systems that distort reality for individuals or groups and foster behavior that is not rational, and these are explored later.

Closely related is a second factor. Analyses of dominant-subordinate group situations often treat the subordinate group as a pawn that responds or reacts passively or automatically to dominant group actions. Subordinate group members, however, themselves assess situations and make choices, but their choices are usually circumscribed or narrowed by the superordinate group's power. Consequently, subordinate group actions may initially appear passive, but they may be clearly aware of and acting in a manner that protects or enhances their position. There are cases where subordinate group perceptions may be distorted by specific situations or beliefs, and conditions of deprivation, subordination and powerlessness may elicit in subordinate groups or individuals magical, utopian or irrational thinking. Subordinates should not be dismissed as simply pawns or puppets, for there is a give-and-take, a dialectic, that occurs in intergroup (including dominant-subordinate) relations.

The two preceding points raise still another. To speak of 'groups' acting is not to reify the group.[4] A 'group mind' does not exist, be it racial, ethnic or class, marxist assumptions notwithstanding. Class analysis presumes that underlying 'forces' compel groups to respond identically in an ineluctable or preordained manner. People are considered prisoners of their class, class wholly determining their behavior. Class is thereby reified as a group. However, individuals respond to situations as individuals, not because of a group mind. To the extent that individuals *appear* to respond together as a group, they may do so because they hold similar values or perceive a given situation alike. Even that does not fully explain similar responses, for other factors might also be present. Thus, to the extent that individuals' commitments or wishes are congruent with those of the group or to the extent that they feel compelled to conform to group pressures (whether real or imagined), they may respond in similar fashion to a given situation. Even where this parallelism occurs it should be recognized that: (a) variable responses of members are possible to group actions, ranging from intense or mild commitment to mild or intense opposition (or even rejection); and (b) even where participants appear to respond alike, different factors may motivate their behavior.

Consequently, the analysis of groups, be they racial, ethnic, class or otherwise, must recognize these variations. Groups are not monolithic. At any given moment cleavages may exist which, under different circumstances, could lead either to group fragmentation or solidarity. These conditions and characteristics are evident in the Anglo fragment societies, within dominant as well as subordinate groups, and they are explored in the subsequent analysis of the groups.

Implicit in these essays is a plea for cross-disciplinary and comparative research. Various social science disciplines can contribute significantly to an understanding of intergroup relations. Unfortunately, ethnic and race studies, particularly in the United States, have remained until recently largely within the domain of sociology. A few economists, historians and anthropologists have probed particular aspects of race and ethnic relations, but political science, until recently, has largely neglected the topic even though power is the fundamental determinant of group relations. Again, though mostly in the American context, psychology has focused almost exclusively on prejudice, ignoring the broader psychological issues of dominance and subordinance. There are exceptions to these criticisms, but what remains pronounced is the lack of cross- or interdisciplinary research.[5]

The following essays make a plea for comparative research. Although some comparative studies exist, few hold specified variables constant (such as similar cultural backgrounds or comparable development factors) as a means for exploring relationships. Consequently, it is difficult to draw from these studies even low-level propositions that can be tested empirically against still other types of group contact situations. Here it is the cultural component of the dominant Anglo group that is held constant, and the study traces similarities and differences in outcomes (in terms of group relations) that result from power, demographic and developmental variables. The approach taken is basically inductive, and it closely approximates that suggested by Schermerhorn in *Comparative Ethnic Relations* (1970). He proposed as an initial strategy the analysis of countries with similar cultural backgrounds, following which comparisons could be made of countries with different cultural heritages. This approach also closely parallels Hartz's (1964) analysis of 'fragment societies.' Comparisons of this type, Schermerhorn suggests, may generate low-level propositions which, when further refined and tested, might facilitate theory-building in race and ethnic studies.

These essays constitute an initial exploration into the character of race and ethnic relations. Some, though in substantially modified form, were previously published. That fact and the attempt to trace group relations from diverse viewpoints and disciplinary perspectives results in an overlap in some data and examples that could not be eliminated. The essays fall into three parts. Part I, composed of the first two chapters, provides a theoretical framework for the analysis of race, ethnicity and power. Part II, which constitutes the core of the study, traces developments in individual countries or compares group relations in different countries. Some of these chapters analyze race and ethnic relations from the perspective of a particular discipline or trace a particular theme or factor in group relations. Part III, the final chapter, serves as a conclusion to the study, exploring factors and low-level propositions that could be tested more fully and systematically in future studies, be it of these or other countries or cultural groupings.

The conclusions reached are, as a result, tentative and open to further exploration and evaluation. The essays represent a synthesis of (a) existing research by others and (b) the findings, based on extensive travel, research, and interviews in these countries by the writer. Research strategies, as C.P. Snow once suggested, are of two types: a strategy of discovery, based on the synthesis and exploration of existing data from which are derived tentative assessments or propositions that need to be subsequently tested; and a strategy of proof, where studies evaluate and test more systematically the propositions which emerge from the first type of study. These essays are of the first type, basically exploratory in character, their intent that of instigating research by others.

Given the scope of the study and the diverse purposes for which the original articles were written, there are gaps in the research and areas covered. These gaps indicate areas for future research. Greater attention, for example, is devoted to race than to ethnic relations. Although implicit in many of the studies, not enough attention is directed toward the dominant Anglo group, particularly its response to situations where its cultural beliefs and power were threatened. Likewise, too little attention is directed toward subordinate group perceptions and responses to dominant group actions. Some studies of the latter type exist, but only recently have scholars, often members of these subordinate groups, explored the historical responses of subordinate groups to these situations. This study suffers from these deficiencies. There are other limitations as well. For example, too little attention is directed toward Australia and New Zealand; development factors, implicit in some essays and the central concern of one, merit greater attention; and subsequent studies need to focus more fully and systematically on the questions and issues spelled out earlier in this introduction.

These gaps are readily evident, and more will undoubtedly occur to others. The essays suggest the need for systematic comparative research, and the study itself is part of a larger research project that commenced with *Politics of Race: Comparative Studies* (1975), a book the writer edited and co-authored. That book focused on these six Anglo countries and included articles by scholars whose research interests centered on the problems of race relations in the Anglo fragments. That collection, with this, provides the foundation for a forthcoming study that will explore more systematically some of the issues raised here.

Two brief points need to be raised in conclusion. South Africa, as noted earlier, is included even though Afrikaners assumed full control in 1948.[6] Its inclusion is based on the continued and extensive influence of English cultural beliefs and institutions. Moreover, the racial and cultural beliefs of people of Anglo descent in South Africa are significant, for their attitudes closely parallel those of their kin in Rhodesia. A second point needs brief mention: the problem of terminology. Designations for specific groups (e.g. Maori, Aborigine, American Indian, Asian, African, etc.) are generally used, but 'non-white' is often used when speaking about them collectively. That term is viewed by some members of these groups as pejorative, but because no other collective term is available it has been used though not in a negative or denigrative sense. Similarly, the terms 'native' and 'native group' have been employed, and no negative connotations are intended.

If these essays elicit responses or reactions, be it in agreement or disagreement, that prompt research by others, they will have served a primary function. Research is an ongoing and collaborative enterprise, a means by which ideas and propositions are tested and confirmed or discarded. One function of research is that of generating low-level propositions that can, when tested, assist in subsequent theory-building. Only through such steps, taken inductively and comparatively, will we gain a better understanding of how race, ethnic and power factors (among others) shape group relations and conflict.

PART I

Chapter 1
The comparative study of group relations

Race and ethnic relations are types of group power contests. Groups, be they racial, ethnic, class, religious or otherwise, constantly compete for control of the resources, power and privileges of society (Lenski, 1966; Wilson, 1973). Competition initiates the process that precipitates or intensifies the saliency of group identity, including racial and ethnic awareness (Noel, 1968), a fact that is evident in the six countries analyzed here: the United States, Canada, Australia, New Zealand, South Africa and Rhodesia. In these, the character of ethnic and race relations has been shaped historically and more recently by the interaction of cultural, demographic, situational and group power factors.

Three points are analyzed in this chapter: (1) the attributes of race, ethnic and group relations; (2) the cultural bases of comparative analysis; and (3) the major characteristics of the Anglo fragment societies. Demographic, situational and cultural bases of group relations are traced here while the role of power as a determinant of group relations is assessed in Chapter 2. Together these chapters provide a framework for the analysis of race and ethnic relations.

I Race, ethnic and group relations

Although their significance was earlier discounted or unrecognized, the importance of ethnic factors as determinants of group relations is now acknowledged (Burgess, 1978). Recent ethnic studies, taken in conjunction with those that focus on race, illustrate particularly three major aspects of group awareness and identity: (a) the character,

(b) the genesis, and (c) the situational bases of group identity. The three, though closely linked, are for analytical purposes evaluated separately.

I.1 Group identity

An individual is identified by himself and others by various attributes or 'markers,' including, among others, racial, ethnic, class, tribal, communal, corporate, nationalist or religious attributes (Barth, 1969). The more complex a society, the greater the number and possible combination of attributes by which individuals can be identified. These identities are often cross-cutting, and the importance of any given attribute for an individual (or group) is dependent upon numerous factors. Attributes of identity, whether real or imagined, significantly shape an individual's (or group's) perceptions of and behavior toward himself and others.

These characteristics are attributive, i.e. individuals and groups define themselves and are defined by others in terms of real or imagined characteristics, among which are: physical characteristics, such as color or physical features, defined as somatic, biological or genetic; cultural factors, such as language, values, beliefs (religious, political and otherwise) and modes of behavior; and other attributes, such as class or income. To the extent that individuals or groups attach importance to these markers, they become significant determinants of individual and group perceptions and behavior.

Group consciousness or identity occurs when a group recognizes itself as possessing unique attributes that distinguish it from others. That awareness may be (a) self-induced (b) emerge consciously as a consequence of the group's treatment by others, or (c) emerge when the group is defined analytically (e.g. by designations of class), even though in this latter case the group may not be aware of or be influenced by such criteria. The significance of these various designations is evident in marxist conceptions of class. Workers, Marx argued, can be analytically defined as a class. They may, however, not recognize or acknowledge their class basis, or they may mistakenly define themselves as middle class, this being an example of false consciousness. Only when workers recognize themselves as a class being exploited by capitalists, Marx contended, will they mobilize themselves to break the system of exploitation and oppression. The transition from non-awareness to recognition constitutes the essential step whereby a group moves from being a 'class in itself' to become 'a class for itself.' Only after that recognition occurs can a group mobilize its members to achieve a desired goal.

Group identity or consciousness assumes greater saliency when groups compete for scarce resources, power or other desired goods, but group awareness also emerges when groups perceive their valued attributes (e.g. culture, religion, language, identity) threatened by the actions of others, be that threat real or imagined. Group consciousness is awakened or sharpened under varied circumstances, including, among others, conquest, migration or other contact type situations. All may trigger a group's awareness of its own identity, and the consequent interaction of groups can exacerbate or diminish group consciousness.

Not all group contacts or encounters result in competition, threat or conflict, for some groups live together harmoniously. However, when resources or valued goods are scarce and groups compete for them, group differentiation usually results. Competition exacerbates the attributes by which groups differentiate 'we' from 'they' (Blumer, 1969), and groups generally impute positive values or attributes to themselves and negative ones to the opposing group. The greater the perceived threat of the other group, the greater the probability that this process of polarization will occur. A dominant group, whether threatened or not by the subordinate groups(s), may impute negative qualities to the latter. This is often simply a rationalization for domination and exploitation, but elsewhere it may derive from historical encounters where groups competed for power or situations where the dominant group fears a subordinate group may threaten its power in the future. What this indicates is that group conciousness is basically a psychological process, and the genesis of group identity should be viewed from that perspective.

I.2 The genesis of group identity
Group identity is basically a psychological phenomenon, situationally determined. As Connor (1978:379) claims, 'the essence [of group identity] is a psychological bond' based on 'self-awareness or self-consciousness' of the group's common attributes, be they of race, ethnicity, tribalism, communalism or nationalism. Group identity can be distinguished at two levels: that of individual or group *awareness* and that of individual or group *consciousness*. In terms of awareness, individuals or groups recognize their unique attributes or 'markers'

but do not regard these as meaningful bases for interaction with others, whereas with consciousness individuals or groups acknowledge their unique traits as a unifying basis for mobilizing members for interaction with others.

Diverse situations precipitate a group's movement from awareness toward consciousness. Awareness precedes that moment, but only with consciousness does the group achieve the potential for mobilization and action. Even then not all members do so. What occurs is that a few individuals initially achieve consciousness and labor to instill, though not always successfully, that consciousness in others. Thus the possibility for consciousness may exist for a group but remain dormant until particular situations or agents heighten that consciousness.

Geertz (1963) claims that 'primordial sentiments' (e.g. tribalism, communalism, ethnicity, etc.) determine people's behavior. These are not innate but emerge within people through socialization processes, and the sentiments persist as fundamental if not immutable determinants of behavior. Geertz's emphasis differs from that presented here, for the saliency of such sentiments is viewed here as variable and situationally determined. Sentiments remain dormant or insignificant until a group believes its identity or interests are threatened. Should such a threat occur and the group believe that preservation of the values threatened is important, group consciousness and mobilization will ensue. However, if the group or its members attach no special significance to the attributes being threatened, mobilization will not result. Geertz's viewpoint implies that mobilization is virtually inevitable under all conditions, and he plays down the precipitating force of situational factors.

More rudimentary than Geertz's concern are the issues of *why* such identity factors (or primordial sentiments) are important and whether or not group belongingness constitutes for individuals a basic psychological need. That is, do some or all people have basic needs that can be fulfilled only through identification with a group, cause or movement. Some psychologists (Maslow, 1954; Fromm, 1941) argue affirmatively. Among the basic needs of people, Fromm suggests, are those for belonging, for meaningful relationships, and for a belief system that transcends one's everyday existence, be it a religion or ideology. If such 'needs' exist, then it is these, not such factors as communalism, tribalism or ethnicity (as Geertz argues) that are the 'primordial sentiments.' What Geertz calls primordial sentiments are simply the *objects* to which primordial sentiments (such as Fromm discusses) attach themselves. If that is so, then under some circumstances it may be possible to transfer 'sentiments' from an object such as communalism or tribalism to another, such as nationalism. This does not discount the significance of group identity factors, but it does suggest that, contrary to Geertz's views, people can switch their allegiance from one object (ethnicity) to another (nationalism).

The possibility of reversions cannot be discounted, for group factors previously ignored may assume a new saliency because of changing conditions or circumstances. In the United States, for example, the re-emergence of Polish, Irish, Italian and other forms of ethnic group identification in recent years occurred only when these groups perceived their economic position and group identity threatened by increased black incorporation into economic and social structures. They are not necessarily 'unmeltable ethnics' (Novak, 1971; Glazer and Moynihan, 1974), an immutable force; rather, ethnic awareness evolved into ethnic consciousness because of circumstances, that consciousness a transient phenomenon having instrumental value. There are periods when ethnicity is important, but its variable saliency is situationally determined. That, however, points to the importance of underlying sociological and psychological factors.

Why some people embrace, hold stubbornly to or change values and particular cultural forms (i.e. the objects of the 'primordial sentiments') has sociological (particularly in terms of the socialization process) and psychological bases, but what determines the intensity or extent to which individuals embrace or reject particular values or belief system is psychologically determined (Rokeach, 1960). For example, one psychological factor that induces group identification and solidarity is threat perception. When individuals or groups perceive themselves as threatened, they mobilize to protect their common interests and identity. The degree of group cohesion is dependent upon individual commitments to the group as well as group pressures for conformity. The higher the perceived threat to the group, the greater the probability of group solidarity. Conversely, the less the perceived threat, the greater the possibility that group fragmentation will occur.

Group consciousness or identity, then, can be viewed from diverse perspectives. It may be generated by individual or group fears or the need for security and belonging. It may be prompted by material interests, where group unity is instrumental in protecting or enhancing the group's well-being. Or group identity may provide a cognitive map, a means whereby individuals and groups perceive and understand the world and their particular place within it (Kelly, 1963; Blumer, 1969). These motivations for group identity may remain dormant or latent, but crisis-type situations, precipitated by power contests, development factors, encounters that bring groups into competition, or threats that are perceived as emanating from another group, trigger the development of group consciousness and promote new forms of group mobilization, competition and interaction.

Viewed analytically, one can conclude that group identity is (a) situationally based, (b) psychologically determined and (c) the result of specific events or situations where groups become mobilized when their identity or interests are threatened. The factors noted above serve to increase the saliency of group identity and prompt new or ongoing group power contests. What emerges, then, is the significance of specific types of situations that precipitate group awareness and consciousness.

I.3 Situational bases of group consciousness

Three types of situations are particularly significant in precipitating group consciousness. They are: (a) group power contests, where threats to group interests or identity awaken or heighten group consciousness; (b) development situations, where industrialization, urbanization and related forces alter circumstances, create changes in the relative power capabilities of groups and, by so doing, generate new group power contests; and (c) crises, prompted by wars, depressions or major cultural changes which generate fears and prod groups into preserving or seeking changes in their position or status, thereby precipitating new group power contests.

Young's (1976) study of African politics illustrates the role of situational factors in generating ethnic consciousness. His study analyzes the triggering role of two specific types of situations: those where groups compete for power and scarce resources, and those where groups respond defensively because they believe their identity or culture is threatened. Hence it is the perceived threat to a group's identity (i.e. its culture, values, language, way of life, etc.) or its interests (i.e. its resources, power, privilege, opportunities, etc.) that serves as the precipitating factor for group consciousness. Such threats occur in specific types of situations. Group encounters, whether the consequence of conquest, migration, geographical border changes or other factors, represent a specific type of situation. If groups perceive a situation as threatening to their well-being (identity or interests), this can create stress for them and serve to sharpen inter-group differences, including the polarization of each group's perceptions of the other. Group competition will increase, and where the power capabilities of groups have been altered, power contests will assume a new intensity or new forms, the goal being control of structures or the determination of cultural policies for society.

Development factors play a crucial role in altering group power capabilities, thereby influencing the character of group contests. Among the major development factors are industrialization, urbanization and the often concomitant secularization of society and culture. Industrialization generates new occupations and opportunities, and previously excluded groups may share in these, thereby increasing their resources and organizational activities while generating new leadership. Urbanization often precipitates changes in a group's social organization and relations, prompting as well such cultural changes as the secularization of group attitudes and values. This process is not ineluctable, but where and when it occurs a previously disadvantaged group, strengthened by newly acquired group resources and newly developed mobilization capabilities and leadership, will more willingly mobilize itself to wrest additional power and opportunities from the dominant group. But development factors may have the opposite effect: namely, the exacerbation of group fears that secularization threatens its cultural identity. If that happens, a cultural crisis will occur and group members will respond defensively, transforming the group into a culture under siege. The siege group mobilizes itself, moves from awareness to consciousness, and seeks to achieve group solidarity as a means of defending its cultural identity. It is in these terms that Afrikaner nationalism, French Canadian nationalism and, more poignantly, the Iranian revolution can be explained.

Demographic factors also influence group relations and consciousness. The most striking example of this occurred where sharp population differentials between settlers and indigenous groups shaped group perceptions, values and power relations in the Anglo fragment societies. White settlers in North American (the USA and Canada) and Pacific (Australia and New Zealand) fragments early outnumbered indigenous groups, and the latter only briefly constituted a threat to settlers and white power. These fragments relied largely upon British and European immigrants, supplemented by African slaves and Asians where necessary, for development purposes. As a consequence the settlers isolated or relegated most native groups to reserves or reservations (Price, 1972), and few if any natives benefited from this type of uneven development. More significantly, they did not constitute a military or political threat to the dominant group. These subordinate groups were ultimately incorporated into the political systems but had little power or influence. In the African fragments (South Africa and Rhodesia), whites remained a small minority of the total population. Vastly outnumbered by indigenous groups, whites held tightly to power and manipulated the political system to prevent Africans from gaining power. However, the latter remained a potential threat to white power, culture, privilege and group identity. Because the influx of white settlers and immigrants was too limited for the country's development needs, Africans were utilized extensively though always in subordinate positions. Even this limited access prompted blacks to demand broader opportunities, political as well as economic, and this threatened white power. The result was a reaction in both countries: victories for the National Party (1948) in South Africa and the Rhodesian Front (1962) in Rhodesia, the basic goal of each that of preserving white power. Here the demographic or population factor significantly influenced and shaped the character of group relations along different lines than those evident in North American and Pacific fragments, but in each instance the struggle for power was at the root of group relations.

Uneven or unequal development also affects the character of group relations. Where there is uneven development (e.g. of industrialization), one group or region usually benefits more than others. When a disprivileged group believes its unique attributes (e.g. religion, race, ethnicity) are the cause of its unequal treatment, it will seek to mobilize its members to break out of that subordinate position. Uneven development, for example, contributed to the pre-1948 rise of Afrikaner nationalism and, more recently, to the emergence of French Canadian nationalism. Both groups were initially bypassed in the economic development of their countries, for most opportunities and benefits accrued to people of English descent. Feeling disadvantaged, both subordinate groups mobilized their members and sought to gain political power as a means of enhancing their welfare.

Development, including industrialization, urbanization and secularization, precipitates changes in values and generates new modes of communication. These, in turn, may lead to the rapid dispersion of new cultural forms and values. The changes are viewed by some groups as a threat to their culture, values and identity, and this precipitates cultural crises such as those noted below. Wars, along with economic, political, social and cultural problems, also precipitate crises that trigger group awareness, consciousness and cohesion. Even defeat in a war can generate a sense of group identity, solidarity or nationalism, as witnessed in the rise of German nationalism, following Napoleonic victories and Afrikaner nationalism following that group's defeat in the Anglo-Boer War. Economic crises, precipitated by depressions or economic deprivation, may prompt the emergence of separatist or nationalist movements, particularly when disadvantaged groups (for example, Welsh, Scots, Bretons or others) believe that the dominant group is discriminating against them.

Cultural crises also generate group awareness and consciousness. Both dominant and subordinate groups may fear that their culture or way of life is threatened by events or other groups, and this can initiate group awareness and solidarity. At various periods Boer-Afrikaner and French Canadian nationalism was initiated or exacerbated by English assimilationist pressures that threatened each subordinate group's culture and language. Both responded defensively in the nineteenth century, withdrawing into their rural enclaves or *laager*, but in the twentieth century they reacted in the opposite manner, politicizing and mobilizing their members as a means for wresting political (as well as economic) power from the dominant Anglo group. Both tactics, however, had the same goal: protection of the group's cultural identity.

Similar fears for their cultural identity can affect a dominant group. In late nineteenth- and early twentieth-century America, for instance, the dominant Anglo group (white Anglo-Saxon protestants, or WASPS), witnessing the massive influx of Asian and south European immigrants whose cultures were vastly different from the Anglo (or 'American') culture, feared for their cultural survival. The dominant group responded defensively, and it enacted measures that included 'Americanization' programs, restrictions on employment opportunities for aliens, the Prohibition Amendment, and restrictive immigration legislation. All of these measures, Gusfield (1966) suggests, were part of the dominant group's 'symbolic crusade' aimed at protecting the 'American (or Anglo) way of life' and 'ridding' the country of immigrant groups whose cultural differences were seen as threats to Anglo or Wasp cultural and structural dominance.

Groups, whether defined by themselves or by others as possessing unique attributes, usually coalesce and solidify when situations or events are seen as threatening their identity or interests. Such threats affect dominant and subordinate groups alike, for they initiate or increase a group's self-awareness. Group awareness, then, must be considered a *conscious* factor, i.e. it is a psychological process by which a group or some of its members acknowledge the attributes which distinguish it from others. What is significant, though, is that group awareness and consciousness are situationally determined. Thus, as Cohen (1974) has suggested, ethnicity is basically a politically (or situationally) determined and not a cultural phenomenon.

II The comparative study of societies

In earlier surveys of ethnic and race relations, Schermerhorn (1970) and Van den Berghe (1967) lament the paucity of comparative studies. This lack, Schermerhorn concludes, has restricted theory-building in ethnic and race relations, a view with which Van den Berghe concurs. Race relations research, the latter suggests, 'has come to resemble a theoretical no-man's land,' and this he attributes to the 'high degree of analytical isolation of race from its general context' (Van den Berghe, 1967:6). Blalock (1967:1), noting that race relations studies 'lack a logically interrelated system of general propositions that are close enough to the operational level to be directly or indirectly testable,' explored in his study a series of low-level propositions that could be tested.

These early observations remain largely valid. Most studies analyze societies with widely different cultural backgrounds, neglect to isolate comparable situational factors, or focus on one group or situation. Consequently, few of these studies provide a basis for comparative analysis, though some attempts have been made (Hall, 1979; Fredrickson, 1981). Comparative studies, Schermerhorn suggests, should hold cultural and situational variables constant and be based on inductive analyses of societies that display 'roughly similar historical sequence(s) and cultural relatedness' (Schermerhorn, 1970: ch. 5). From such studies it is possible to draw low-level conclusions and propositions that can be tested against studies of societies that have different cultural backgrounds but comparable historical sequences (e.g. developmental stages). Schermerhorn recognizes the existence of variations even among countries with similar cultural heritages, but these differences are less pronounced than exist where countries with widely different cultural heritages are compared.

Schermerhorn's cultural factor is roughly analogous to Hartz's (1964) 'fragment' notion. Hartz argues that the cultural traditions of early settlers continued to exert an influence in fragment societies, significantly influencing later developments. This holds true whether the fragment was French, Iberian or English. Early settlers brought with them the beliefs, institutions and practices of the metropole. These had to be modified to fit colonial circumstances, but the basic traditions persisted in most settler societies. The reason for this is fairly evident: in most cases the original settler group and its descendants continued to hold power historically, and given that power they shaped the culture and institutions of these societies.

The fragment notion has been criticized and modified, but this does not detract from its heuristic use for comparative purposes. Among the modifications or reservations concerning it are the following: (a) although the fragment culture had to be modified because conditions differed from those in the mother country, the basic cultural values remained if the fragment group retained power, control or dominance; (b) the physical environment of the new country generally forced some modification in the fragment itself; (c) the fragment group, as a consequence of its contact and relations with indigenous and, later, other groups sometimes had to modify its beliefs or practices toward these groups, particularly when the latter exercised a degree of power or possessed resources the dominant group needed; and (d) the fragment itself, especially where there was a rapid and massive influx of other immigrant groups, was modified to meet these new conditions.

Hartz considers among his case studies four of the Anglo fragments, including the United States, Canada, Australia and South Africa. New Zealand and Rhodesia were excluded, but they clearly meet his criteria for inclusion as fragment cultures. Hartz and Schermerhorn thereby provide the necessary rationale for an analysis of countries with comparable cultural backgrounds; and this analysis of demographic, situational and power variables illustrates the persistence of cultural factors as determinants of ethnic and race relations (cf. Smelser, 1973).

Schermerhorn, as indicated, proposes that societies (still holding the cultural factor constant) with roughly similar historical sequences be compared. These sequences constitute types of group contact situations — initial contacts, conquest, migration, developmental stages (e.g. industrialization) or other situations that bring groups into contact. For example, settler and sojourner societies (Price, 1963) can be compared. In the former, men took their families, settled permanently and established a replica of the mother society as in American colonies, Australia, South Africa, and elsewhere. In the sojourner society, such as the British West Indies, it was usually single men, inhabitants of a colony normally only for brief periods of time, who went there to make their fame and fortune. Liaisons with indigenous women were invariably of a transient nature, and many left behind them children of mixed racial background. These situational differences clearly influenced the character of group relations. Likewise, the frontier represented still another type of contact situation. Present in all Anglo settler societies, the frontier and its conditions influenced, along with cultural factors, the character of settler-native encounters and relations. Schermerhorn's historical and situational sequences, though, can be broadened to include still other types of contact situations, such as development or group contest situations. All of these situations can be compared, and if the type of contact situation is held constant, then ethnic, racial and power factors can be isolated and evaluated as determinants of group relations in the Anglo fragment societies.

III Anglo fragment societies

Given the differences evident from even a cursory analysis of the six fragment societies, doubts about their comparability can be raised. They were settled at different historical periods; the class and cultural backgrounds of the mainly English groups settling the countries were not identical; and historical, demographic and development factors differed from one country to another. They were all settler or frontier-type societies, but differences are immediately evident in the patterns of settler-indigenous relations. When the three fragment clusters (i.e. the North American, Pacific and African fragments) are compared, other distinctions emerge. Most pronounced are the demographic variations, for the North American and Pacific fragments are sharply different from the African fragments. Frontier conflicts occurred in all six countries, but only in South Africa and Rhodesia did settler groups remain a ruling minority surrounded by a numerically superior indigenous population. Settlers supplemented later by European immigrants, quickly became the numerical majority in North American and Pacific fragments. Settler-indigene population differentials decidedly influenced the character of ethnic and race relations in the two African fragments.

Major differences in political, economic and social structures characterize these countries (the United States, for example, early abandoned the parliamentary system), but the principles which rest at the foundation of the economic, social and political systems in the countries remain the same. That occurred because English settlers in each country shaped the institutions and culture, the British metropole supported them in their efforts, and people of English descent retained power for an extended period – despite the later influence of other groups.

A detailed historical documentation is not essential, but a few significant factors should be noted. English and other European groups settled the North American colonies, with most English groups settling in what would later become the United States, the French in Canada. Under the 1763 Treaty of Paris ending the Seven Years War, Paris ceded its Canadian colonies to Britain. That left Britain, except for Spanish claims, in virtual possession of North America. Canada remained a British colony, and its various settlements were brought together as one nation either under the British North American Act (1867) or subsequent legislation.

Following American independence, some English settlers emigrated to Australia and, later, New Zealand. A few settled in the Cape and Natal colonies in Africa, but most continued to emigrate from Britain to the United States because it was considered the land of opportunity. Settler-indigenous conflicts were most intense in what became the United States, but similar clashes and encounters occurred elsewhere in British colonies.

In what later became South Africa, early Dutch settlers fell under British rule when it annexed and retained the Cape colony during the Napoleonic wars. Opposed especially to British native policy, the Dutch, also known as Boers, fled inland, settling the Orange Free State and Transvaal. With its victory in the Anglo-Boer War of 1899-1902, Britain incorporated Cape and Natal colonies and the former Boer republics into South Africa in 1910. The Boers, or Afrikaners, outnumbered the English, but coalition Afrikaner-English governments ruled for most of the period until 1948 when the Afrikaner Nationalist party won the election. In 1961, confronted by increased British and world opposition to its racial policies, South Africa left the Commonwealth. Meanwhile, in 1893, under the leadership of Cecil Rhodes the colony of Southern Rhodesia was established, and the small white settler group gained virtual autonomy from British control after 1923. Following the breakup of the Central African Federation (Southern and Northern Rhodesia, Nyasaland), which lasted from 1953-1963, Southern Rhodesia, fearful of black rule, unilaterally declared its independence (UDI) in 1965 to preserve white power. Its independence was never recognized by Britain or the rest of the world, and it remained in that anomalous state until 1980. Whites in 1979 acceded to limited black rule, and in 1980 Rhodesia returned to British control briefly, gaining its independence that year as Zimbabwe.

Despite these historical differences, basic similarities characterize these countries, and they provide justification for the comparative studies that follow. Among the major similarities, some alluded to previously, are the following:

1 All six countries were settled initially or subsequently by English and controlled by them and the British metropolitan government. Power remained for an extended period with the metropole and settlers, the former usually retaining jurisdiction over native groups and foreign affairs for an extended period.

2 All were settler rather than sojourner societies, viewed as permanent 'little Englands' by the settlers, and entire families were settled. Land provided the major inducement for settlement, and this brought settlers into conflict with indigenes or other groups who defended or contested for control of the land.

3 In their policies and behavior toward indigenes and, later, other non-white groups, Anglo settlers often found themselves in disagreement with the metropole. However, when called upon by settlers caught in conflicts with native groups, the metropole usually came to the former's assistance, tipping the balance of power in the settler's favor, the settlers thereby becoming the dominant group in society. The metropole's control over settlers was limited, and when the two disagreed over policies affecting indigenous groups (even though the metropole usually retained control over native affairs), local settler policies usually prevailed.

4 English settler (and descendant) dominance over indigenous and non-white groups, whatever the techniques or means employed, was aimed at destroying or curtailing the power resources and resource mobilization capabilities of these groups, thereby assuring continued Anglo (hence white) control.

5 All six countries endured lengthy colonial experiences under British tutelage, and English cultural attitudes (of both the metropole and settlers) shaped the behavior of the white settler groups toward indigenes and other nonwhite groups.

6 Even after the metropolitan government withdrew, divested itself of or was divested of control, English settlers and their descendants retained control of the major political, economic and social structures. Given that control they were able to determine the cultural policies for the country.

7 Power, exercised by the fragment and Anglo descendant groups, was used to control structures, and that group's differential allocation of power, privilege and resources to itself and other groups was based on such criteria as ethnicity, race and culture, those of Anglo descent receiving preferential treatment.

8 Anglo settlers and their descendants, believing in the superiority of their own culture, used structural policy (whether as punishment or reward) to induce non-Anglo groups, white and nonwhite alike, to discard their own culture and accept the dominant Anglo culture.

9 The subsequent influx of other groups, white and nonwhite, often precipitated intergroup conflict, and that contributed to the intensification of discriminatory policies against the other group(s) by the dominant Anglo group.

10 Despite historical variations, all six countries retain to a considerable degree social, political and economic values and institutions, including the modified political system in the United States, which closely parallel basic British institutions and culture.

These factors, evident in all six countries, have served as determinants of cultural policies, thereby shaping the character of ethnic and race relations. English cultural values and attitudes shaped settler dominant group perceptions of and attitudes toward other groups.

Wherever possible, the Anglo group tried to anglicize or assimilate other groups, forcing the latter to discard their own cultural heritages. There were a few exceptions, discussed later, but the exceptions are attributable to power and development factors. These basic patterns persisted for an extended historical period, and only recently have there been movements away from Anglo cultural and structural hegemony toward cultural pluralism and the sharing of power in all six countries.

It is the cultural and power factors that are focused on in this study as determinants of intergroup, including race and ethnic relations. The cultural basis of group perceptions and behavior has received most of the attention in this chapter. Power, as a determinant of ethnic and race relations, is explored in the next chapter.

Chapter 2
Power and group relations

Power is the primary determinant of group relations. Racial and ethnic groups, whether in dominant, subordinate or equal positions mobilize their group resources and strive for control over the major political, economic and social structures of society, for it is within these structures that most policy decisions, including the allocation or reallocation of power, privilege and resources are determined (Lenski, 1966; Blalock, 1967; Katznelson, 1972; Himes, 1973; W.J. Wilson, 1973). Group power contests, therefore, occur within these structures, but when a group cannot or is prohibited from pursuing its goals within these structures, it may resort to other means (e.g. riots, rebellion, revolution or warfare) to achieve its aims. Its ultimate goal is that of gaining a voice in or control over the structures and institutions by and through which society allocates power, privilege and resources.

Group power contests take place primarily within political and economic arenas, and most crucial distributive decisions are made there. Two types of policy choices are particularly significant: (1) structural decisions and (2) cultural policy decisions. Structural decisions determine the degree of access to and incorporation within structures accorded a given group, and these decisions thereby determine the group's resources and power. Cultural policy decisions fall somewhere between two poles: one, a policy that leads toward the elimination of group cultures and loyalties through imposition of a more embracing 'national' culture; the other a policy of multiculturalism wherein society accepts the legitimacy of cultural diversity and leaves others, including racial and ethnic groups, with the right to their own cultural beliefs and practices. Multiculturalism may result because society believes in the principle of diversity or because no group has sufficient

power to suppress or eliminate the cultural beliefs and practices of other groups. The dominant group's structural and cultural decisions are very clearly influenced or determined by its racial (or somatic) and ethnic beliefs and attitudes.

The policy choices made by a society are evident in its legislative decrees and its behavioral norms and practices. Norms and practices are not always reflected in legislative decrees but are equally important as determinants of behavior. This combination of decree, norm and practice as well as racial beliefs shape the decisions society makes concerning cultural and structural policy, including how and the degree to which subordinate groups will be incorporated within political, economic and social structures.

Racial and ethnic factors invariably emerge as determinants of inter-group relations in plural societies (Rabushka and Shepsle, 1972; Van den Berghe, 1967; Young, 1976; Schermerhorn, 1970). Whether group contact results from conquest, migration or other factors, group relations are shaped by three factors: group ethnocentrism, intergroup competition, and the power capabilities of groups (Noel, 1968; Katznelson, 1972). Of these, power is the most significant, for stratification patterns, cultural and structural policy and the subsequent allocations of power resources are determined by the differential power of groups.

The power factor can be treated systematically in comparative analyses of ethnic and race relations. There are at least three possible ways in which it can be applied:

1 the analysis of race and ethnic relations as types of power contests, the outcome of each contest dependent upon such factors as group resources, capabilities and differential rates of group power;
2 the analysis of specific types of dominance systems, be they racial or ethnic; and
3 the analysis of racial and ethnic dominance systems from a historical and comparative perspective.

These approaches are not mutually exclusive, but their utilization helps answer two questions: first, do they clarify and explain the structure of group (ethnic and race) relations and how these evolved; and, second, do they provide a basis for understanding present and future patterns of intergroup relations?

I Power and group resources

One approach to the study of race and ethnic relations traces the role of group resources, resource mobilization capabilities and the strategies of actors as determinants of group power contests (Blalock, 1967: ch. 4). Differential group power is a basic determinant of stratification systems (Lenski, 1966: ch. 4), and the components of that power can be identified.[1] Power is usually defined as the ability of Group A to influence Group B, or vice versa, whether that influence is overt or assumes more subtle forms. An example of the latter is where B's behavior is influenced not by A's actions but by what B fears will be A's response unless B acts in a particular manner. The behavior of both A and B is based on two factors: an assessment by each of the resources and mobilization capabilities of (a) itself and (b) the other group. These judgments, along with how groups perceive a particular *situation*, determine the strategies each will pursue in its encounters with the other. Not all such perceptions and behavior are rational, for emotions, stress, threat and other factors can distort judgments, but in most instances an element of rationality is evident in the perceptions and behavior of the actors.

Analytically, Blalock (1967) distinguishes two major attributes of power: *resources* and the *mobilization* of these resources. He defines resources as properties of an individual or group, including, among others, a group's total numbers, physical and financial assets, social organization, culture and belief system, education and skills. Other less tangible but nevertheless significant resources include a group's prestige, authority and any natural or supernatural factors or beliefs that serve to strengthen the group. A group's mobilization capabilities are of a somewhat different character, defined more in behavioral terms. They include its morale, motivation, leadership, cohesiveness and ability to adapt to or cope with new or stress-type situations. One group may possess superior resources, but given ineffective leadership, lack of group cohesion or difficulty in coping with stress situations, it cannot effectively mobilize its resources against another group that possesses fewer resources but superior mobilization capabilities.

Two significant variables that Blalock tends to neglect are *additive resources* and the *strategies* employed by a given group. An example of an additive resource is the intrusion or incorporation of a third party on the side of either A or B, for this will significantly alter the outcome of their power contest. Schattschneider (1961) alludes to this as the 'socialization of conflict,' for a group may broaden the scope of conflict in order to incorporate other groups on its side. Strategies, too, are important. Based on their evaluation of situations, contesting groups adopt strategies they believe will strengthen their power capabilities and neutralize or weaken those of their opponent.

Because power contests constitute types of transactions between two or more actors, the resources, mobilization capabilities, perceptions and strategies of all actors must be assessed (Blau, 1964; Blumer, 1969). Whatever the power relationship (symmetrical where both groups are equal, asymmetrical where one is dominant), each group may initiate or respond to the acts or anticipated acts of others. Where the power capabilities of both groups are equal or nearly so, both groups possess various options. However, in extremely asymmetrical relations a subordinate group's options are sharply circumscribed. Even so, it can pursue options that range from opposition (extending from war or rebellion to more subtle forms of resistance or subversion) to compliance (extending from withdrawal or grudging acquiescence to 'emanation,' the latter a situation where the subordinate group discards its own identity and culture for that of the dominant group).

Intergroup relations can be viewed historically. Given changed circumstances, group power capabilities (measured in terms of group resources, additive resources and mobilization capabilities) alter over time, and this transforms the character of power relations. At any given moment in time (T_1) the power of A may be equal to that of B (symmetrical), at a later point (T_2) that of A may be superior to that of B (asymmetrical with A dominant), or at another point (T_3) that of A may be less than that of B (asymmetrical, with A subordinate). Thus the power capabilities of groups can be assessed at any given point in time, be it in terms of specific group encounters or of changing group power capabilities as reflected within specific political, economic and social structures (Nordlinger, 1968).

Three types of power analysis appear most feasible: (a) a static analysis of intergroup power relations within one society at any given moment in time (T_n); (b) an analysis of intergroup power relations within the same society at different moments in time (between T_1 and T_2, T_1 and T_3, etc.); and (c) the comparative analysis of two or more societies during the same period or during comparable stages of political and economic development. By using this analytical approach it is possible to compare ethnic and racial group contest situations and thereby isolate factors which contribute to similar or variable outcomes.

Race and ethnic relations are power contests in which competing or contesting groups seek to strengthen their own power resources while limiting or destroying those of an adversary group. This occurs in wars and in more peaceful contests pursued within political, economic and social structures (Rabushka and Shepsle, 1972). Groups seek control of these structures, for it is within them that allocative decisions are made which determine the distribution of power, privilege and resources. These decisions thereby determine the resources and mobilization capabilities of groups, and each group normally views the contest as a zero-sum game, i.e. what it wins or acquires the other loses.

In asymmetrical power relations, dominant group control of structures enables it to destroy, restrict or preclude subordinate group acquisition of resources and mobilization capabilities. But a subordinate group is not totally devoid of resources or mobilization capabilities. As Blalock (1967: 118-21) suggests, subordinate groups possess two types of possible power resources, *pressure* and *competitive* resources, both of which are important for opposing domination. Pressure resources refer to a group's ability to employ such disruptive tactics as strikes, boycotts, violence or even warfare for forcing changes on the dominant group. Subordinates may also possess competitive resources, including skills needed by the dominant group. These the subordinate withholds as a device for wresting concessions from the superordinate group. Thus, dependent upon its appraisal of the situation and the resources and mobilization capabilities available to itself and its adversary, the subordinate group may opt for those strategies it believes will break the prevailing pattern of dominance. The dominant group will, in turn, respond.

Group relations constitute a dialectical process, an ongoing power contest in which the outcome, whether temporary or permanent, is determined by group resources, mobilization capabilities and the strategies employed by the contestants or actors as they seek to maximize their own power and position vis-à-vis other groups. The analysis of these contests can be static, focusing on a specific moment or event, or dynamic, analyzing these contests as an ongoing process in which changes are constantly occurring on group power resources and strategies. Both types of studies are essential for an understanding of ethnic and race relations.

II Systems or types of dominance

A second approach to the study of race and ethnic relations focuses on specific types of dominance systems. Three types can be distinguished: (a) military and coercive dominance, (b) structural dominance, and (c) psychosocial dominance. Although the three overlap, there are characteristics that distinguish each, be it in Anglo fragment or other societies.

II.1 Military and coercive dominance

Settler-indigenous relations were shaped by the relative power capabilities of contesting groups. Where indigenes were more powerful, settlers sought to negotiate treaties of amity even though conflict, precipitated especially by land disputes, often ensued. When that occurred, settlers enlisted additional support from native groups who joined with them against other natives or from the metropole which sent troops to assist in frontier conflicts. With these additive resources settlers quickly subdued indigenous groups and gained military superiority. Thereafter they normally moved to subjugate completely the indigenous groups, including those with whom they were previously allied.

Settler-indigenous conflicts persisted for prolonged periods, marked by wars, rebellions and uprisings. Settler efforts during and following these conflicts were aimed at the systematic destruction or curtailment of indigenous power resources, be they political, economic or social. Once military dominance was achieved, whites relied upon coercive, structural and psychosocial means for maintaining their control. Numerous techniques were employed. Defeated groups were deprived of their weapons; their leaders or potential leaders were removed or imprisoned; and subordinate economic and political systems were destroyed by dispossessing the people of their land and cattle or by isolating them on reserves where close military surveillance curtailed organizational efforts and possible uprisings.

When a group's economic system is destroyed it must rely upon the dominant group for food, work and other essentials for survival. By withholding these the dominant group can usually coerce compliance from recalcitrant subordinates. Military or civilian control thereafter can be direct or indirect, and coercion and deprivation can be used to maintain domination. The impact of these measures on morale should not be discounted, for together these various techniques of military and coercive dominance help destroy the social system and cohesion of a subordinate group, making dominant group control much easier. But other techniques must also be used by a dominant group to maintain control, be it over indigenous or other subordinate groups. Their control of the major structures provides them with this means.

II.2 Structural dominance

Through its control of political, economic and social structures a dominant group makes distributive decisions that determine the power resources available to itself and other groups. It also has the power to impose its structures upon or simply destroy subordinate group structures. Moreover, given its power the superordinate group can determine how and the extent to which subordinate groups will be structurally incorporated. It is this factor that determines the resources available to the subordinate group, and dominant group decisions are often based on its ethnic and racial beliefs.

Economic structures are of particular importance. The major resources of a pastoral/agricultural society are its land, cattle and manpower. If a group is deprived of its land and cattle, or if its labor is controlled by others, it is forced into a dependent and powerless position since it must offer its labor to the dominant group. A person's labor power is his major resource and means of livelihood. Thus in an industrialized society the dominant group can restrict the resources and mobilization capabilities of subordinate groups in at least five ways: (1) it can deprive the subordinate group of its land, thereby forcing the subordinate to labor for the dominant group under wages and conditions set by the latter; (2) it can restrict the education of subordinates, assuring that they acquire only skills which limit their job opportunities and advancement; (3) it can restrict the types of jobs available to subordinates through job reservation and job fragmentation; (4) it can establish wage scales for specific industries and other positions, thereby making sure that there is no competition for workers which would drive up wages and enhance subordinate group competitive resources; and (5) it can control or prohibit workers from organizing, thereby making sure that jobs and positions are not turned into competitive-type resources by the subordinate group. Moreover, by keeping labor unskilled or semi-skilled, especially when there is a surplus labor population, or by keeping subordinates as migrant labor, the dominant group can skillfully curtail and control the economic power of the subordinate group.

Social structures can be used for preserving the dominance of one group over another. Of significance in this context are: (a) the modes of cultural integration of groups, (b) the social relations of groups, (c) the impact of dominance on subordinate group social organization, and (d) the role of education, including socialization processes, in perpetuating dominance.

Every group embraces a cultural norm image (CNI), i.e. a belief system based on what it considers as either acceptable or unacceptable and good or bad in terms of values, religion, beliefs, behavior norms, and physical and somatic characteristics.[2] Likewise, each group embraces a somatic norm image (SNI), i.e. a set of beliefs of what it considers acceptable or repugnant physical and 'racial' features. How groups treat each other is influenced by their cultural and somatic perceptions of each other and by their relative power capabilities. Where one group is dominant, it can determine cultural policy for the society, and its cultural/somatic norm images are thereby important. Cultural policy falls somewhere between the two poles noted earlier, of monoculturalism or multiculturalism (Weiner, 1965). With monoculturalism the dominant group seeks to eliminate subordinate group cultures and loyalties through the imposition of a national culture which is normally that of the dominant group. Multiculturalism exists where the dominant group accepts diversity as a principle or tolerates its presence because it has insufficient power to eliminate other cultural forms. Dominant group cultural/somatic attitudes also determine the degree and type of structural incorporation of subordinate groups. Generally, the closer the congruence between the subordinate group culture and that of the dominant group, the greater the probability of the former's structural incorporation by the latter.[3] This principle also usually applies in terms of somatic congruence of the two groups.

Negatively viewed subordinate groups suffer in still other ways. If the dominant group considers the subordinate group's cultural or somatic characteristics to be inferior, it may force the latter to shed its cultural characteristics if it desires structural access or opportunity. However, a group cannot shed its physical or somatic attributes, and it is these by which whites have historically defined some groups. Moreover, whites also attempted historically to instill in nonwhites a belief in their supposed inherent inferiority, a tactic explored more fully later.

Dominant groups generally establish a social relations 'etiquette' that creates hierarchical patterns in intergroup relations (Doyle, 1937). Both dominant and subordinate groups are socialized and expected to play specific roles vis-à-vis each other, and infractions of these rules precipitate coercive sanctions. For example, segregatory legislation concerning housing, work relations and other group contact situations was enacted in the late nineteenth century American South to preserve racial practices that were being eroded or contested by blacks (Van den Berghe, 1967). Legislation seeks to make explicit what were previously common practices that are now being eroded or threatened.

Given its control of political structures, the dominant group can determine the fate of subordinate group social organizations. These it may ignore, tolerate or destroy. In some settler societies, for example, the imposition on indigenous groups of social workers, missionaries and administrators as well as the prohibition of subordinate group religious, marriage and other cultural or social practices was specifically aimed at destroying indigenous cultures. This deculturation, in conjunction with other factors, precipitated instances of social disorganization within indigenous groups that severely hampered their ability to protect their cultural identity.

Education and socialization processes thereby play a key role in keeping a group powerless and subordinate.[4] By limiting subordinate group educational and vocational training opportunities, the dominant group restricts the former group's employment opportunities. But education is also used for the purpose of indoctrination, i.e. as a means to inculcate within subordinate groups a belief that they are inferior to the dominant group and, therefore, incapable of governing themselves. Beyond this, education can be used to destroy a subordinate group's culture or, in other instances, to emphasize differences among subordinate groups' cultures as a device for keeping them hostile to and isolated from each other. In all of these cases education is used for the purpose of subordination rather than liberation (Carnoy, 1974; Freire, 1974).

In still other situations a superordinate group may incorporate subordinate groups though only at lower structural levels, restricting thereby the latter's acquisition of power resources. Where necessary, the superordinate will 'buy off' or co-opt subordinate group leaders, this co-option helping maintain the status quo. Elsewhere, the dominant group will isolate a subordinate group, then negotiate with the latter's leaders as a device for maintaining control by indirect means. At the apex of this total control system, then, are political structures.

The major distributive decisions are made within *political structures*. Through its control the dominant group decides how to allocate resources between itself and others. Four specific ways can be traced by which a dominant group involves or incorporates subordinate groups within political structures. Under the first two forms the subordinate group has *no direct participation*. In the first of these, characterized by slavery or a reservation system, the dominant group has complete control and determines what is best for the subordinate group. In the second there is indirect representation, i.e. the subordinate group may: (a) through its own leadership make recommendations or requests to government departments (e.g. 'native' or indigenous affairs) that control them; (b) through some type of council that represents them make representations to the dominant group; or (c) select not their own but members of the dominant group to 'represent' them within dominant group structures.

Under the other two forms the subordinate groups are *more directly incorporated* within political structures, but this occurs in such a way that the subordinate group has little or no power. Under the first of these the subordinate group participates within the political structure, but requirements for the franchise (education, financial assets, etc.) are so restrictive that few of its members can vote or the electoral system is so manipulated (i.e. gerrymandered) that few of its members can be elected to political office. Under the second the subordinate group is fully represented, but being a minority group it can elect few members. Consequently, those elected are virtually powerless to prevent enactment of legislation that impinges on their rights or opportunities. However, since the group is included in the system, the decisions reached are considered legitimate by the dominant group.

Subordinate groups have little ability to influence policy in any of these situations. Should they protest against conditions, their leaders could be banned or incarcerated, thus preventing the subordinate group from mobilizing its members to challenge dominant group control. The latter has at its disposal the coercive powers of the state, and these it employs in conjunction with security legislation for silencing opposition. Thus the dominant group preserves its control especially through political structures, and it makes decisions that strengthen its own power resources while restricting those of others.

The dominance of one group over another is not preserved solely by structural means. Morale, group identity and cohesion, leadership, motivation and the acceptance or rejection of domination or a subordinate status are, ultimately, psychological factors or states of mind. Where a dominant group wishes to retain its position of power it may utilize other, primarily psychological means, for inducing behavioral acceptance of subordination within those it wishes to dominate.

II.3 Psychosocial dominance

Three categories of psychosocial dominance are evident. These psychosocial states can be classified as compliance, dependency and thought control. They result from innumerable factors, including a group's perceptions and experiences, most of which occur or evolve under structures of dominance. The 'meanings' that situations, events and relations have for people are largely determined by their experiences, including their interactions with others, and their psychological needs (Barbu, 1960; Blumer, 1969; Maslow, 1954; Knutson, 1972). Their experiences take place largely within political, economic and social structures; and the meanings people derive from these experiences, in the form of values, assumptions and even perceptions *in part* determine their behavior.[5] The examples of psychosocial dominance and subordinance given below typify the more extreme racial forms, but they are also evident, though in lesser degree, in ethnic situations where one cultural group is dominant over another.

In terms of *compliance*, the first category of psychosocial dominance, the superordinate group uses its coercive/reward powers for maintaining control. It relies primarily upon the application within structures of 'carrot and stick' methods to gain obedience from the subordinate group. Psychologically, the subordinate group responds in terms of the pleasure/pain principle, its perceptual field and the meaning it attaches to dominant group actions construed in terms of (a) deprivation, denial and punishment, or of (b) relief, opportunities and the absence of pain and deprivation. For the subordinate group there is a limited perceptual field, i.e. the immediate consequences of dominant group actions are more readily recognizable than are its possible long-range effects. Thus pleasure/pain and immediacy serve as significant determinants of subordinate group behavior, and the latter directs little effort towards the long-range development of its resources and mobilization capabilities.[6]

Tactically, the dominant group, wary of nascent or developing discontent within the subordinate group, may attempt to 'buy off' that disgruntlement by granting the group minor concessions or privileges, co-opting in the process subordinate group leaders and members. However, the dominant group must utilize large numbers of personnel, be it in security, administrative or other capacities to maintain subordinate group compliance. This can be a costly enterprise, and as a result less expensive modes of dominance are utilized.

The second category of psychosocial dominance, *dependency*, includes a number of distinct types. Fundamental to all these types is the inability (whether real or presumed) of the subordinate group to cope with situations. Whether that inability results from dominant group actions or other factors, the subordinate group's difficulties in coping leaves it increasingly impotent against superordinate power. Three types can be distinguished within this dependency category: the first is psychological but structurally derivative while the other two are more clearly psychological. With the structural type the dominant group so deprives the subordinate group of resources (e.g. land, cattle, food, jobs, etc.) that coping is difficult. Thus the latter must rely on the dominant group for its physical survival, and this leaves it psychologically vulnerable to the dominant group's use of coercive/reward powers.

The second and third types of dependency are also psychological. With the second, the subordinate group says in effect to the dominant group: 'We cannot cope; we are confused and uncertain; we rely upon you to tell us what to do.' Within this type three subtypes are evident: (a) expertise, (b) symbiotic and (c) authoritarian. Under the first, the subordinate group defers to the dominant group because the latter is seen as having an expertise the former does not possess. Mannoni (1964) defines the symbiotic subtype as a form of dependency behavior based on a group's inferiority feelings, while the third subtype is the authoritarian submissive form described by Fromm (1941). In the latter, the subordinate group says: 'We do not know what to do; we are incapable; we need a leader; please lead us.'

The third type within the dependency category includes two subtypes. These are psychological states that develop because of a group's almost total inability in coping with situations, be these the result of conquest or other factors. Psychosocial disorganization constitutes the first subtype, its characteristics including within individuals or groups high levels of alienation, mental illness, alcoholism, drug addiction and divorce as well as other types of individual, family and group disorganization (Leighton, 1959). All of these usually result from the difficulties that individuals and groups experience in coping with high stress situations. The second subtype, anomie, has even greater disintegrative effects, sometimes resulting in psychological or physical suicide. Unable to cope with uncertainty and stress, individuals commit suicide. This stress manifests itself in various forms. For example, it became pronounced in primitive societies following European contact and conquest, the consequence reflected in the increased practice of infanticide, suicide and abnormally high death rates among people who no longer had the will to live. This then resulted in a rapid decline in the group's population (Pitt-Rivers, 1929; A.G. Price, 1972).

The third major category of psychosocial dominance, *thought control*, has been variously referred to as cultural imperialism, deculturation, brain-washing and emanation (Carnoy, 1974; Halpern, 1970; Lifton, 1961). Its major principle is that the culture and identity of the subordinate group must be destroyed and be replaced by that of the dominant group. This imposition results from two factors: dominant group efforts to impose these changes and, more importantly, the acceptance of this new identity by the subordinate. Deculturation is followed by the implanting of the new culture: the subordinate sheds his own identity for that given him by the dominant group, a process and situation that Halpern (1970) referred to as 'emanation.' Fanon (1970: 137) described this as 'cultural imposition.' However, he criticized Mannoni's (1964) thesis that people were readily colonized because they had a dependency need that the colonizer filled, claiming rather that the colonizer had the power and used it to do two things: first, to destroy the language and culture of the subordinate group and, second, to instill in the latter an inferiority complex.[7]

The result of this process was threefold: first, the denial of the subordinate's separate identity; second, the inculcation within the subordinate of a belief that his own culture and identity were inferior to that of the superordinate; and third, the acceptance by the subordinate of the identity and values of the superordinate. Its consequence is described by Fanon (1970: 137): 'After having been the slave of the white man, he [the subordinate] enslaves himself' by accepting these notions and beliefs about his own inferiority.

By relying upon psychosocial means, the dominant group has less need to utilize coercive/reward powers for controlling subordinate groups. As a consequence of emanation or thought control the subordinate group controls itself. It behaves as the superordinate group desires because it has internalized, a consequence of the socialization process, the same belief system. The subordinate group members reject their own individual and group identity. This, then, can be considered the most sophisticated form of psychosocial dominance. Although this represents an extreme form of psychosocial dominance, it differs primarily in degree from the process of assimilation or anglicization directed against other groups by the dominant Anglo group in the fragment societies.

III Comparative analyses of dominance systems

The forms that ethnic and racial dominance take are determined by both the character of power contests and how the participating groups adapt to changing circumstances and conditions. Group strategies and actions, although rational and preconceived in some instances, are more often the pragmatic response of groups to specific events. As a consequence of factors noted in the preceding chapter, situations change. Because of this, the relative power capabilities of groups themselves change and prompt new intergroup power contests. It is these changes that suggest a third possible approach to the study of ethnic and race relations: the comparative analysis of dominance systems sequentially.[8]

Comparisons of the recurrent patterns of intergroup power contests reveal the diverse types of control that characterize each sequence, for it is this control component that determines how the dominant group acquires and preserves power. The three major types of control include:
1 the establishment and perpetuation of dominance by one group over another through the use of coercive and reward techniques (coercive/reward control);
2 the establishment and perpetuation of dominance by one group over another by making one group dependent or making it feel dependent upon the other group (dependency control); and
3 the establishment and perpetuation of dominance by one group over another through the destruction of the latter's cultural identity (thought control).
At specific moments, and particularly when circumstances and

conditions change, a subordinate group may confront the existing power imbalance and mobilize its resources to break the prevailing pattern of dominance. When this occurs, and when the subordinate group is successful, what appears to happen is a *reversal* of the sequences by which the dominant group earlier acquired its power. This suggests that the subordinate group's confrontation must be directed at the highest sequence level that characterizes the existing situation. For example, where dominance is based on thought control, to be successful a subordinate group must move first to destroy that control, i.e. by rebuilding its own cultural identity. Should it instead seek to break dependency control (which in all likelihood is also present), thereby ignoring the more sophisticated level of thought control, the probability of its success decreases. Where all three types of control are present, the subordinate group must pursue strategies that confront all three sequences, but its major thrust must be directed against the higher level sequence. Successful confrontation at one sequence level means that greater attention can thereafter be directed toward the other sequences. What in effect happens is that the subordinate group continues to build its resources and mobilization capabilities in a manner similar to Smelser's (1963) value-additive process.

It is possible to trace briefly the development of these forms of control in the Anglo fragment societies. There were and are, of course, exceptions to these patterns, but the parallels are quite pronounced. Reward and coercive techniques were utilized extensively and initially by dominant Anglo groups to control others. Whatever means it used to gain power and control, the Anglo group thereafter relied on coercive/ reward tactics to assure its continued dominance. In the case of indigenes: (a) the dominant group instituted a reserve/reservation system or isolated the subordinate group in a manner that brought the latter under military or civilian rule; (b) dispossessed of their lands, indigenous groups were left economically dependent upon the white society; and (c) the whites' police power effectively suppressed up-risings and forced subordinate group compliance. Rewards, if only in the form of food and clothing, were used to preserve order, for these rewards could be withdrawn if subordinate groups did not abide by white rule.

Similar tactics were employed when necessary against other sub-ordinate groups, be they slave or immigrant, particularly in situations where subordinate groups were forced or compelled to live in ghetto areas that could be readily controlled by the superordinate. Together, the reservation and ghetto, in conjunction with the evolving welfare system, created a dependency system with power in the hands of the dominant group military, police and civilian administrators. Native groups, for instance, deprived of lands and economic resources, were forced to rely upon the government for assistance and employment. Laws controlled their social and economic life, and restrictions were often placed on their physical movement within designated geographical areas. Moreover, if indigenes committed infractions of white-imposed rules, they found themselves at the mercy of a legal system they seldom understood. Dependency behavior also occurred when indigenous cultures and social structures were shattered, for the social disorganization that resulted left subordinates even more dependent upon the dominant group. What clearly emerged, then, was a form of dependency control.

New forms of dependency that critically affected subordinate groups evolved with the advent of urban and industrial society. Of greatest significance were the dominant group's control of employment opportunities and the emergence of a social welfare system which, while providing subordinate groups with assistance, simultaneously left them more dependent than previously.[9] Dependency roles were effectively established or inculcated through diverse means, including, among others: (a) the prevailing social ideology or cultural belief system, (b) the social system and the etiquette of race-ethnic relations, (c) employment, housing and living conditions, and (d) the educational system.[10] Political, economic and social structures were geared toward the establishment of dependency behavior particularly within subordinate groups whose culture and physical appearance differed most sharply from that of the dominant Anglo group. Because they recognized that coercive/reward tactics necessitated constant and close supervision and dependency controls or techniques were less costly but still had limitations, dominant groups moved to preserve their control by a more sophisticated means: namely, thought control.

The ultimate form of control is that of the mind. If people can be indoctrinated to believe they and their culture are inferior and their subordinate position is thereby justified, or if they believe they must reject their supposedly inferior culture and accept that of the dominant group, then the subordinate group builds its own prison and becomes, simultaneously, prisoner *and* warden. The group's chains are in part forged by itself. Society can use structures to prevent a group from building its power resources, but a group that accepts the notion that it is inferior restricts its own development of power resources. Historically, not all subordinate groups or their members accepted these beliefs or the subordinate positions assigned to them. Some rebelled, some isolated themselves from the dominant group, and some conformed rather than face possible punishment or the withdrawal of rewards.[11] Others, however, by rejecting their own cultural identity became supporters of the system.

A major transformation has occurred since the 1960s, for members of numerous subordinate groups have reasserted their cultural identity, an essential first step for a group struggling to develop its resources and mobilize its members. This affirmation of group identity occurs when a group seeks benefits for itself or defends the position it holds. Whatever the motivation, group affirmation (be it race or ethnic) constitutes an initial and essential step for a group seeking to break the thought or cultural control exercised by the dominant group.[12]

The processes or sequences noted appear most clearly in racial situations but also exist in modified form in ethnic and cultural group situations where the dominant group, viewing its culture as superior, has tried to impose its culture on others. The earlier cited examples of Afrikaners and French Canadians best illustrate this, but persistent efforts to anglicize other immigrant groups in these Anglo societies suggests the pervasiveness of these pressures.

The approaches explored above illustrate how power can be assessed as a determinant of ethnic and race relations. Group relations are power contests in which groups develop and mobilize their resources and pursue diverse strategies to gain influence or control over the major societal structures within which the power, privilege and resources of society are allocated. These allocative decisions, in turn, determine the relative power capabilities of groups. Power analysis, then, when applied to the study of group relations, helps clarify the dynamics of intergroup relations, and the chapters that follow trace the relationship of race, ethnic, power and situational factors in the six Anglo countries.

PART II

Chapter 3
Race relations: North American and Pacific fragments

I

In a strident though provocative study of racism in the United States, Kovel (1971) concludes that the roots of white racism are deeply embedded in western culture. Given its emphasis on property, order and self-control, the culture, Kovel contends, virtually compels people to de-emphasize human relationships and treat themselves and others as objects to be manipulated and used. He concludes that racism is pervasive in America, a view supported by the earlier Kerner Commission *Report* (Kerner, 1968). That study, commissioned by the United States government to determine the causes of massive 1967 race riots, pinpointed racism as the cause. Racism permeates all aspects of American life, the *Report* suggests, and 'white institutions created it, white institutions maintain it, and white society condones it.' As a consequence, discrimination and the denial of equal opportunity to black Americans created anger, resentment and hostility, the 1967 riots a culmination of that seething anger. The studies of Hartz (1964) and his colleagues, though not directly concerned with racism, lend credence to this view, for they conclude that the racism they uncovered in their studies of the United States, Canada, Australia and South Africa derived from their common British or Anglo heritage.

Although these studies focus on countries settled by the British, other studies document how a broader European racism contributed to the oppression and exploitation of native groups throughout Europe's colonies. Historically, European nations conquered and controlled or settled vast areas of the Americas, Asia, Africa and the Middle East, bringing indigenous groups under their rule. Whatever the initial motivation, colonialism was invariably justified by such rationalizations of racial superiority as 'the white man's burden,' 'civilizing the native,' 'the superiority of white civilization' or 'survival of the fittest.' Although these served as rationalizations for European domination, their roots can be discerned in European cultural beliefs that envisaged non-Europeans as inferior.

With the discovery of the New World, there emerged in sixteenth- and seventeenth century Europe a utopian or Edenic literature, one that envisioned a new paradise on earth. The New World provided the setting for that literature, and indigenous groups were transmogrified into an idyllic model of man, the 'noble savage.' As Baudet (1965: 28) suggests, 'the dominant sentiment regarding the Indian — the savage *par excellence* — was one of admiration and esteem.' Later that image changed when the 'noble savage' refused to give up his land, for most Europeans were less interested in a new Eden than they were in such tangible assets as gold, land, minerals and trade. Whatever form colonization took, be it settler (permanent) or sojourner (temporary),[1] the consequence for the native was invariably the same: loss of his freedom and land. As Price (1963: 51-2) suggests, European colonization was

> in most regions, a brutal age: an age in which swarms of savage
> invading males slew, raped, plundered, and enslaved the natives
> or decimated them with exotic diseases, after which they replaced
> them in some instances by hardier and more complacent slaves.

Elesewhere Price (1972) compares British or Anglo encounters with native groups in the United States, Canada, Australia and New Zealand, and he reaches similar conclusions. Price discerned three discrete stages in settler-native relations: first, a period of invasions and conquest when whites subjugated and controlled indigenous groups; second, a relatively more humane period later in the nineteenth century when philanthropic and religious groups prodded American and British governments (the latter retained control over 'native affairs' for an extended period in Canada, Australia and New Zealand) into curtailing settler aggression against indigenes; and a third period, commencing in the 1930s, when governments reassessed and revised programs for indigenous groups.

During the initial period white settlers, by conquest, negotiation or guile took possession of native lands. Native populations declined drastically thereafter, and native religions, cultures and societies were destroyed. Early nineteenth-century philanthropic-humanitarian groups pressured British and American governments to abolish slavery, prompting the British government to abolish slavery in its possessions and curtail settler hostilities toward indigenes. Governments encouraged missionary activities among indigenes, and though these activities were originally considered humanitarian, they contributed to the destruction of native cultures and traditions.[2] By the mid-nineteenth century, however, the Manchester movement pressured the British government into cutting costs for maintaining its colonies by withdrawing some British troops. Natives were as a consequence left increasingly at the mercy of settlers. The metropole's restraining influence was partly removed; and native groups, often powerless and despite the odds, rebelled and opposed settler aggrandizement. Settlers then demanded that the metropole, be it Britain or the American federal government, send troops to quell the uprisings. Subjugation ensued, and most native populations were transformed into wards of the state, isolated on reserves or reservations. Largely ignored or neglected, native populations thereafter declined. New Zealand's Maoris and Canada's Indians suffered somewhat less than did indigenes in the United States and Australia, but there were parallels in settler behavior toward native groups in the four countries.

Tracing the development of Indian policy in the United States, Price, whose study was completed shortly after the Second World War, concluded that new policies initiated in the 1930s would significantly influence the direction of policies elsewhere. This new stage, he surmised, emerged from a recognized need for more scientific, humane programs that encouraged native cultures and brought indigenes more fully into the development and administration of policies that directly affected them.[3]

Aside from Price's there are few comparative studies of settler—native relations in British or non-British societies. The studies that exist focus generally on slavery rather than settler—native relations,[4] and Hartz's (1964) is one of the few that compares settler societies which have different cultural backgrounds. His study, along with others of a more fragmentary nature, document differences, attributable in part to cultural factors, in intergroup relations within Iberian and Anglo settler societies.

There is evidence that the treatment of indigenes and non-white groups in Iberian colonies was somewhat less harsh than in Anglo countries. That is in part attributable to such factors as religion, class notions, missionary activities and possibly prior historical experiences of Spanish and Portuguese with non-whites, especially the Moors. Religious factors were particularly significant. More than Anglican or other Protestant churches, the Catholic church accepted the native and nonwhite as a *person*. It upheld the principle that the slave was, first of all a person, who possessed certain inherent rights. Although often ignored in practice by Spanish and Portuguese settlers (Tannenbaum, 1968; Hanke, 1970; Hoetink, 1967), the principle existed and priests attempted to enforce it. Within Anglo countries, however, the slave was viewed as *chattel*, and neither Anglican nor Protestant churches seriously questioned that premise. Moreover, in Iberian-Catholic areas the church insisted that slave-owners bring their slaves to church and that slaves be christianized. As Hoetink (1967: 9) notes, under Catholicism the slave 'was a person — juridically and morally — and not, as in the American and British areas, a chattel.'[5]

The Catholic church specified the rights of natives and slaves in its codification of 1789; and though settlers often ignored these proscriptions the church served as a tempering influence in Iberian settler treatment of native and slave.[6]

The linkage of economic and religious views also contributed to variations in Anglo-Iberian treatment of indigenes. Hoetink, Hartz, and others isolate as significant the universalistic, hierarchic beliefs of Catholicism contrasted with the individualistic, less-hierarchical religious beliefs of Anglo and protestant missionaries and settlers. These, they contend, contributed to differences in perceptions of and behavior toward indigene and slave. Where the Catholic church retained relatively firm control over its members, Protestant churches exercised little control, particularly in dealings with native groups. The studies of Tawney, Weber and others note that under Protestantism each individual was somewhat isolated, unsupported by a church hierarchy, more responsible for making his own way in the world and less encumbered by church restrictions or controls. This meant that the individual was significantly freer in the economic realm, and acquisition of money, property and material goods, the core of capitalism, became the primary goals for which individuals struggled. Property, wealth and power, in the form of influence and control, were coveted, and in the process, as Kovel (1971) and Fromm (1941, 1947) suggest, individuals viewed themselves and others as objects to be manipulated and used for acquiring wealth and power.

These factors converged particularly in Anglo culture and practises. Hartz suggests that Iberian countries adhered to a feudalistic, rigid class structure whereas in England the class system became more fluid or open with capitalist development and the emergence of a middle class. This greater degree of 'openness,' whether of class, religion or elsewhere, influenced the individual psychologically, leaving him feeling relatively isolated and alone as he struggled to find his 'place' in society. Not all individuals were influenced by these forces, but some were, and they construed life in terms of competition and struggle (cf. Barbu, 1960). This openness led to other assumptions, one of which was that individuals should be considered initially equal, measured by their achievements rather than class standing. However, Hartz suggests, the individual who accepted this 'classlessness' premise would have to judge indigenes and nonwhites by that same principle or standard. In the Iberian feudalistic class structure, native or nonwhite were designated lower class and thereby presented no threat to other classes. However, given his cultural beliefs, particularly concerning color, the Anglo could not accept indigenes or nonwhites as equal. The latter had to be left *outside* the social system. What thereby emerged in Anglo settlements was a *segmented* society, one composed of distinct and mutually exclusive social groups, caste-like, with the movement of native or nonwhite members into the Anglo class structure virtually impossible (Hoetink, 1967). Color, then, became the distinguishing characteristic for a segmented society, nonwhites considered 'outsiders' (cf. Fredrickson, 1981; Huttenback, 1976).[7]

Still another factor shaped settler—native encounters. North American and Pacific fragments were settler rather than sojourner societies, and whites settled permanently, becoming, in Hartz's terms, 'fragments' of the larger mother society. Settlers brought their families, acquired and worked the land, perceived themselves as permanent settlers and associated little with indigenous groups. The Iberian settlements were also permanent, but because the Spanish and Portuguese governments often sent men without women or families they cohabited with or married and had children by indigenous women, leading to the emergence of racially mixed societies. This seldom occurred in the Anglo settler societies but did in the sojourner ones. In both Anglo and Iberian fragments contests for control of land and resources generated hostilities and shaped settler attitudes toward indigenes. When short of labor, settlers imported slaves, justifying their domination with racial and cultural rationalizations. As Eric Williams (1966: 7) notes, 'slavery was not born of racism: rather, racism was the consequence of slavery.' Despite differences in Anglo and Iberian cultural traditions, native and slave were exploited in both societies. Where there were differences in the treatment of subordinate groups, that was partly attributable to these cultural variations.

Another factor that mitigated against the settlers' repressive treatment of native and slave groups was the 'outside power,' be it the Catholic church or imperial government. Both the church and government in Spain intervened to curtail settler hostilities toward indigenes and slaves; and the British government, by stationing troops in its colonies and retaining control over native affairs, acted as a buffer between settler and indigene. When the metropole withdrew, however, indigenes were at the mercy of the settlers. Usually the less powerful the indigenous group, the greater the rapacity of settlers. When weak native groups fought settlers, as did numerous American Indian groups and the Tasmanian Aborigines, they were virtually exterminated. Where indigenes possessed considerable military power, as did the Maoris who fought settlers and British toops to a virtual stalemate, settlers grudgingly acknowledged some of the indigenes' land claims and rights.

II

Group power differentials were the main factor shaping the character of settler-native relations. This is illustrated in the US and Canadian cases. Despite earlier efforts aimed at converting and 'civilizing' native groups, settlers invariably viewed Indians as obstacles to their quest for land. The massive influx of European immigrants into colonies and the United States propelled settlers westward, and they constantly battled Indians for possession of the land. Supported by superior weapons and metropole troops, first British and then US military, settlers reacted ruthlessly against the Indians. The Indians responded in kind, and that prompted a policy of Indian extermination. The policy recognized the tragedy of the situation but rationalized the Indians' extermination as the consequence of purportedly inevitable 'forces of progress' (Kraus, 1949; Pearce, 1965).

Power clearly played a role in this. Where whites perceived Indians as powerful or potentially powerful, they negotiated treaties or sought peaceful accommodation. Indian uprisings were feared, and, given the military weakness of the newly independent nation, Congress proposed at one point the establishment of a separate Indian state that would send representatives to Congress. Nothing came of the proposal. However, when Indian groups sought to consolidate and oppose further settler encroachments on Indian lands, the US military retaliated quickly. Indian forces were dispersed and defeated between 1811 and 1813. That effectively destroyed the power of the Indians and earlier proposals for an Indian state were abruptly dismissed, federal (and settler) policy thereafter aimed at the Indian's destruction (Horsman, 1967; Prucha, 1962).

Prior to Andrew Jackson's presidency (1829-37), the United States government sought to protect Indian lands from settler encroachment, though it had difficulty controlling settlers. Jackson's policies were blatantly anti-Indian. He refused to enforce Supreme Court decisions protecting Indian rights and supported the 'Indian removal' policy that expelled Indians from lands east of the Mississippi. Pushed westward during subsequent decades and decimated by military encounters, diseases and starvation, Indian tribes dwindled rapidly. There were sporadic uprisings, most of which were ruthlessly suppressed by the military. No longer a threat and short of resources and power, the Indian, as traced in the following chapter, became a ward of the state. Thereafter the government relied upon military, coercive-reward, dependency and thought-control techniques for keeping indigenous groups in a state of subjugation (Gurian, 1975).

Historically, the Canadian Indian fared better than the United States Indian, both power and development factors contributing to that difference. Among these factors were Canada's original settlement by the French, the role of the Catholic church, the subsequent role of the British government in protecting Indians, and a more limited influx of Europeans which meant less pressure from settlers for Indian lands. Early French settlers included fur-trappers, traders and farmers, many of whom came without families. They mingled freely with and often married Indian women, from which emerged a 'mixed breed,' the Metis, who during the nineteenth century constituted a sizeable percentage of the total population. Successful in its efforts to convert natives in eastern Canada, the Catholic church also managed during the French period to acculturate Indian groups.

Political factors influenced Britain's policy toward Canadian Indians following its 1763 takeover of the country. Because the American war of independence threatened its control of Canada, Britain curried favor with Indian tribes. It negotiated with and paid them tributes in return for their loyalty and use as a buffer against the United States. This policy continued thereafter, for neither the British nor Canadians fully trusted an expansionist United States. Besides the treaties that provided Indians with annual gifts and stipends, Britain protected Indian lands from settler encroachment and retained control over Indian affairs until that responsibility was turned over to the new central Canadian government under the British North American Act (1867).

Only as settlers increased late in the nineteenth century did the Dominion government, as earlier the United States federal government, find itself caught between settler land demands and the protection of Indian territory. But there were fewer settlers than in the United States, and Indian power remained a potential threat. There were sizeable numbers of Metis in the west, and they joined disgruntled Indian tribes in the abortive Riel Rebellions of 1869 and 1885, conflicts that focused attention on Metis and Indian land rights. Nevertheless, as in the United States, Indians ultimately found themselves relegated to reservations, but in contrast to the United States most Canadian reservations were on lands originally occupied by Indians. In British Columbia, however, Indian land rights were seldom recognized. As elsewhere, Canada's indigenous population declined in later decades, and government and missionary efforts to convert and assimilate western Indians contributed to their cultural and social disintegration (LaViolette, 1961; Melling, 1967; Patterson, 1972, 1975). Their position, too, is explored more fully in the following chapters.

Settler—native encounters in Australia, although on a smaller scale, paralleled intergroup relations in the United States. Because there were fewer Aborigines than American Indians, white Australians easily pushed Aborigines from desired lands. The British government recognized the land claims of North American Indians but totally ignored Aboriginal claims and declared as Crown Lands all Australian lands not previously claimed by settlers. Initially under the British government's protection, Aborigines, except in Western Australia, were turned over to state government control in the 1850s. Bowing to settler pressures, these governments ignored Aboriginal claims and forced the latter onto reservations where many still remain. Unlike the North American Indians, Aborigines made few attempts to organize, and as a consequence they remained powerless politically and economically. Their condition has changed little despite some efforts to organize an indigenous Black Power movement (Rowley, 1972; Stevens, 1972). In contrast to the United States and Canada, where indigenous groups have a power base in their reservations and support from white liberals, there are few groups who support the Aborigines. Consequently, Aborigines have had only limited success in eliminating discrimination or in changing social policies (Lippmann, 1970, 1973; Pittock, 1975).

Power capabilities and differentials also shaped settler–native relations in New Zealand. White traders and settlers exploited Maoris early in the nineteenth century, but Maoris, who exchanged staples and other goods for weapons, quickly retaliated. Skirmishes and conflicts, the consequence of land disputes, culminated in the 1840 Treaty of Waitangi whereby Britain recognized Maori land rights, guaranteed protection of Maori lands from white purchase, and stipulated that Maori lands could only be sold to the British government which would then subdivide and sell to settlers. Nevertheless, settler land encroachments continued, precipitating new conflicts and warfare during the 1860s. Prodded by religious and humanitarian groups into protecting native rights, the British government found itself enmeshed in settler–native wars, including that which now exploded in New Zealand (Sinclair, 1961; Williamson, 1967; Mellor, 1951; J.D.B. Miller, 1966; Dalton, 1967).

Maori military strength was evident in their ability to fight settler and British troops to a virtual standstill; and when Britain tired of the costly war, it threatened to withdraw its troops, leaving settler forces to fight the Maoris. That prodded settlers into acknowledging the power capabilities of the Maoris, and although the latter were nearly defeated, they were given seats in Parliament. Even so, a period of disillusionment set in, and Maori population rapidly declined before increasing during the twentieth century (H. Miller, 1966).

Following the war's termination, most Maoris withdrew to their farmlands, shying from contact with whites. Christianity lost much of its influence, for it was suspected as a 'white man's religion.' By the turn of the century a grass-roots movement emerged aimed at improving Maori conditions, but it had only limited success (J. Williams,

1969). More recently, Maoris, who constitute approximately 8 per cent of the population, have moved to urban centers seeking employment. There they have encountered discrimination, and they are poorly educated or equipped to compete successfully with whites in an urban, industrialized society. The prejudice and discrimination they experience precipitated development of a Brown Power movement, its aim that of bringing Maoris equal opportunity within society (Schwimmer, 1968; Metge, 1964; Mol, 1966; Pocock, 1965; Forster, 1975).

III

Beyond group power resources and differentials, three other power factors shaped settler–native relations: (a) perceptual and motivational factors; (b) the role of the metropole government; and (c) the process of domination and dependency.

Interpersonal behavior is significantly influenced by images that individuals or groups hold of each other (Deutsch, 1970). These images derive from at least three sources: prior conceptions that each holds of himself and the other, particularly assumptions about one's own and the other's culture and power capabilities; factors (e.g. the desire for land) that motivate or prompt group encounters; and new perceptions of self and the other that emerge from intergroup encounters.

Previously held cultural beliefs shape the perceptions that actors have of each other. Most groups hold ethnocentric views and see themselves, including their culture and physical appearance, as superior to others. The Englishman (and European in general) usually concluded from contacts with native cultures that his own was infinitely superior. Indeed, the Anglo cultural tradition regarded the color white as purity and black as evil, and this was applied to skin color and somatic characteristics.[8] In general, Anglos and Europeans viewed non-Europeans as inferior in color and culture, and their military subjugation and domination over native groups confirmed to them their presumed superiority. This is reflected in their 'white man's burden' and 'survival of the fittest' (i.e. white superiority) notions. Conquest and control also affirmed for the European the legitimacy of his actions and domination.

Motivations shaped settlers' perceptions of and behavior toward native groups. The desire for land or for 'civilizing' indigenes usually ran counter to native wishes, and the latter's response shaped subsequent relations. Usually, the more intense the settler land desires and the greater the indigenes' resistance, the more hostile the confrontation. That solidified the negative images each held of the other and influenced their behavior.

To the extent that settlers viewed natives as objects, comparable to the physical environment and capable of thwarting realization of their goals, settlers responded aggressively. Natives, unlike the weather, could be dealt with by extermination or removal. If indigenes were too powerful or capable of expelling him, the settler negotiated, temporarily accepting the indigenes' power parity or superiority, as in treaties with American Indians prior to 1811 or Maoris prior to the 1860s. This did not preclude conflicts, but these were usually resolved by negotiation. When settlers achieved or believed they held military superiority, they disregarded prior agreements and sought to subjugate and wrest from the native his land. If settler perceptions were wrong and native groups proved too powerful, settlers quickly demanded metropole assistance, e.g. British troops in the American colonies and New Zealand or United States federal troops on the American frontier.

The more intense the settlers' desire for land and the greater the natives' resistance, the more readily did settlers perceive indigenes as savages whose extermination was justified (Pearce, 1965; Kovel, 1971). Once settlers achieved military superiority, the indigene, regarded as less than human, was 'removed' to reserves or reservations, his cultural and somatic characteristics considered repugnant to whites. In South Africa and Southern Rhodesia, however, a labor shortage and acute development needs necessitated the use of indigenes. Even so, they were usually placed on reserves or in compounds, far removed from whites except in the case of domestic labor. Extermination rather than removal of indigenes was favored by many settlers, but metropole intervention normally prevented implementation of the former policy.

The further removed in distance and level the government from the settler, the less intense were pressures on it for satisfying settler demands at the expense of indigenes. The British government's dealings with colonies illustrates this. In North America the metropole issued the 1763 Proclamation which prohibited settlers west of the Appalachians. Its purpose was to keep settlers and Indians separate, but the

Proclamation angered settlers because they coveted the Indians' rich Ohio valley lands. Settlers saw the Proclamation as a denial of their freedom. Where earlier they welcomed British troops who assisted in defeating hostile Indian tribes, they now perceived the metropole and its troops as a tyrannical imposition. Thus the Proclamation helped precipitate the American Revolution.

Under the Articles of Confederation and Constitution the federal government attempted to protect Indian lands, but it had little more success than the British government. Settlers ignored government prohibitions and took Indian lands, then demanded that federal troops crush Indian uprisings and reward settlers with additional Indian territory. Under President Jackson settler pressures were eminently successful, and thereafter the metropole became a supporter of settler greed rather than a defender of Indian rights. That policy prevailed for most of the nineteenth and twentieth centuries.

British policy elsewhere illustrates the metropole's importance in protecting indigenes. Having pressured the British government into abolishing slavery, nineteenth-century humanitarian and religious groups demanded that it take up the 'aboriginal question' and protect native rights. This Parliament did, and it moved to protect natives from settler encroachments in Canada, New Zealand, South Africa, Southern Rhodesia and, to a lesser extent, Australia. For a period the metropole rebuffed settler protests and protected natives, stipulating that only the Crown could purchase lands from native groups. These lands were then sold to settlers. Despite that, settler–native conflicts continued, particularly in New Zealand, South Africa and Southern Rhodesia. Colonial governors called for assistance from British troops, and the troops sometimes served as a buffer between settlers and natives. Elsewhere, though, wars normally resulted in the defeat of indigenous groups. The metropole did try to protect natives in various ways. For example, it negotiated treaties that protected native lands, established buffer zones or native territories that curtailed settler land encroachments, and, as indicated previously, restricted the sale of native lands to the government.

By the 1860s other forces compelled a metropolitan retrenchment and withdrawal from the internal affairs of the colonies. The Manchester movement, aimed at cutting costs to British taxpayers, demanded that colonies be self-supporting. The government was forced to curtail its overseas, including military, expenditures, a step it accepted since settlers themselves were restive and threatening possible independence if the metropole did not relax its control over native affairs. Britain retained limited powers, including a veto over settler policies affecting natives, but that power was seldom exercised. British weariness, too, at the continued use of its troops overseas to police colonial conflicts prompted its retrenchment. Later in the century, however, it was compelled to send troops to protect settlers who precipitated conflicts particularly in South Africa and Southern Rhodesia.

Dominant group racism, resulting from cultural beliefs, rationalizations and group encounters, can be reinforced by a dependent or subordinate group's behavior. Dependency behavior, as Mannoni (1964), Memmi (1965) and others suggest, elicits specific dominant group responses, although as Fanon (1967) argues, dependency behavior itself usually has been instilled or inculcated in the subordinate by the dominant group. In some cases Anglo military prowess generated magical forms of thinking in indigenous groups, particularly when they saw their power waning vis-à-vis whites. The actions of American Cherokees and New Zealand's Maoris reflect this. Believing that settlers derived power from their political institutions, the Cherokees adopted a constitution similar to that of the United States while the Maoris established a king, emulating the British political system in hopes of gaining power with which they could repel the settlers. Elsewhere, both prior to and following their subjugation, native groups in the United States, Canada, New Zealand and South Africa enthusiastically embraced messianic movements. These were led by self-proclaimed prophets or messiahs who believed they possessed divine or supernatural powers that would help them drive the white invaders from native lands (Lanternari, 1963).

Ultimately, though, whites prevailed, and native groups, subjugated by military and coercive measures, became powerless as new forms of dependency and thought control were imposed, whether in the United States, Canada, Australia or New Zealand. Following military defeat or subjugation, native groups usually underwent a period of disillusionment and decline, prompted in part by government policies, disease, starvation and, quite often, the individual or group's loss of a will to live. Messianic movements provided momentary hope, but their failure simply increased despondency, reinforced negative feelings and precipitated social disorganization and disintegration within groups.

The example of the United States, although the most extreme, illustrates this process. There were exceptions, but a pattern emerged. Whether the consequence of military defeat or treaty, most Indian groups were removed from their lands and placed on reservations which disrupted their economic and social organization, forcing them to rely on the military for food and other essentials. Deprived of food and without weapons for hunting, Indians became wards of the military. By withholding these essentials military or government officials could coerce compliance from native groups. Indians were left in a position of dependency, and missionary or government activities aimed at assimilating Indians further destroyed indigenous cultures and created havoc with their social systems, particularly since educational and other programs were aimed at making Indians believe that their own culture and way of life were inferior to that of whites.

The breaking of native resistance and the process of domination that ensued had a traumatic and disintegrative impact on native populations. The processes were roughly comparable in other Anglo fragments, and societal and individual disorganization and disintegration usually occurred. Characteristic disintegration patterns, evident in individuals and groups, included: the breakdown of personal and family relationships and community values; a high incidence of alcoholism and promiscuity; increased hostility directed against self and others; increased poverty; the disintegration of cultural value systems; increasing isolation of the individual; and the decline of traditional authority and leadership (Leighton, 1959). Powerless, deprived of resources, and their leadership ineffectual, removed or co-opted, native groups increasingly became wards of the state, numerous individuals within the group reflecting such behavioral or attitudinal attributes as dependency, docility, resignation, self-doubt and even self-hatred.[9] The internalization of these characteristics resulted from dominant group techniques and measures of control, and where such attributes were internalized by subordinate group members the dominant group found it much easier to control the subordinate than where it had to rely exclusively on military and police powers.[10] Although changes have occurred recently, particularly in the last decade, these patterns still prevail in some instances.

IV

The treatment of other nonwhite groups further illustrates how race relations are shaped by cultural and power factors. This is evident in the case of Asians present in all four countries and those of African descent found in the United States and Canada. Substantial numbers of Asians, especially Chinese and Japanese, settled in these countries.[11] Most came during the second half of the nineteenth century, brought in as indentured workers or lured by employment opportunities. Africans, however, were brought unwillingly as slaves to the North American colonies. Confronted by labor shortages, either the host country or the British government initially encouraged this influx. Wherever he settled the Asian encountered opposition from white workers who viewed him as an economic threat. That hostility was also expressed toward free blacks in the northern United States before and after the Civil War, and southern whites were similarly hostile toward free blacks as well as the few Asians who settled there (Litwack, 1961; Voegeli, 1967; Berwanger, 1967; Berlin, 1974; G. Barth, 1964).

Nearly 3,000 Chinese 'coolies' were in Australia by the 1840s as contract labor, but few more arrived there or elsewhere until the 1850s. The response of white Australian workers was immediate. Fearing the competition from cheap Chinese labor, whites rampaged against the Chinese, reflecting sentiments that prevailed there and elsewhere (C. Price, 1966). However, the shortage of farm workers and general laborers, the demand for miners following gold discoveries from the 1850s onwards in California, British Columbia, New Zealand and Queensland, and the scarcity of railroad construction workers commencing in the 1870s all created acute labor shortages in these countries and prompted the introduction of Chinese labor.

Governments initially encouraged this immigration. In 1852 California's governor welcomed the Chinese and called for legislative approval of land grants to serve as an inducement for Chinese settlement. White workers were less receptive. They reacted negatively, and violence against the Chinese broke out in California, British Columbia, New Zealand and Australia. Thereafter the Chinese sought jobs that would not threaten white workers, but they were continually made scapegoats during economic crises.[12] The response of whites to the Chinese in all four countries was similar. The first large wave of Chinese came during the 1850s, to California, British Columbia, Victoria and

New South Wales. Worker violence followed, and local governments enacted legislation barring or discriminating against the Chinese. Prompted by new gold discoveries yet another wave of Chinese arrived in the 1870s. Again violence flared, and this time local, state and national governments ignored Chinese government protests and enacted discriminatory or exclusionary legislation.[13]

Following the exclusion of Chinese, Japanese immigrants flooded into California and British Columbia in the late nineteenth and early twentieth centuries, precipitating 'yellow peril' fears and renewed outbursts of anti-Asian violence. The Japanese government protested vehemently. The United States, British and Canadian governments attempted to placate Japan and their own citizens, doing so by negotiating 'gentlemen's agreements' with Japan whereby the latter voluntarily restricted the emigration of its citizens. Thereafter, the United States, Canada, Australia and New Zealand all enacted measures restricting further Asian immigration. Even so, anti-Asian sentiments persisted, and during the Second World War the United States and Canada incarcerated Japanese, whether they were aliens or citizens of these two countries, in concentration camps (Young and Reid, 1939; LaViolette, 1945, 1948; TenBroek et al., 1968; Maykovich, 1975). To a considerable degree there has been an abatement in the racism that characterized these countries earlier, this attributable to numerous factors.[14] Australia, however, retained until the 1970s what was a 'whites only' immigration policy, and the United States, Canada, New Zealand and now Australia have immigration laws that only indirectly limit Asian immigrants.

There is a common thread of beliefs that permeate the earlier white attitudes toward Asians, attitudes that are applied to other nonwhite groups as well. There was a real or presumed threat of Asian labor competition that exacerbated white animosities, but underlying that were cultural biases. Asians, for example, were viewed as untrustworthy, dishonest, corrupt, evil and immoral; and they were depicted as sexual perverts who, given the opportunity, would corrupt the virtue of white women. Underlying this was a fear that Asians wanted to assimilate with whites and intermarriage would lead to miscegenation and the 'pollution' or 'mongrelization' of the white race. This racial view was also applied to blacks. All of these factors contributed to hostility toward Asians. Given their lack of power, political as well as economic, the Chinese were especially defenseless against these prejudices and practices. In the case of the Japanese it was somewhat different. Japan, having defeated Russia in the 1904-5 war, was recognized as a world power, and when it vigorously protested about the treatment of its citizens, United States, Canadian and British governments (the last retained a degree of influence over its colonial governments) responded quickly with measures to placate Japan (and their own citizens). However, as in the encounters of settlers with indigenous groups, the metropole could not always control its local citizens. But the image of Japan as a powerful nation, in contrast to that of China, prodded these governments to act.

Black North Americans, too, must be considered in this context. In its study of racism, the President's Commission on Civil Disorders (Kerner, 1968) reported that prejudice and discrimination were pervasive, permeating all aspects of American life. Historically, blacks have been discriminated against in the United States and Canada, first as slaves and then as second-class citizens. Canada had fewer slaves and they were freed earlier by British proclamation. Despite that, and even though the Underground Railroad for escaping southern slaves had its terminus in Canada, blacks, whether in Nova Scotia, urban centers, the midwest provinces or British Columbia have encountered discriminatory treatment (Scott, 1975; Winks, 1971).

The transformation of white ethnocentric views into racist beliefs can be traced during the development of the American colonies (Jordan, 1969; Kovel, 1971). African slaves were initially accorded an ambiguous status, somewhat comparable to that of white indentured workers. That changed rapidly. Given the acute scarcity of labor in the south, notions of permanent servitude quickly evolved. Blacks, as traced more fully in the next chapter, were powerless, more so than indentured white servants, and rationalizations quickly emerged justifying their continued subjugation and exploitation, these rationalizations based on cultural notions of the black man's assumed inferiority (L. Williams, 1975). These ideas persisted long after the abolition of slavery, and they were used to justify the continued subordination of Afro-Americans in both south and north (Jordan, 1969; Gossett, 1965; Stanton, 1960; Newby, 1965; Genovese, 1969; Wilson, 1973).

Thus emancipation brought freedom but not equal treatment or opportunity. Following withdrawal of northern troops and the termination of Reconstruction, white southerners wrested and used power to disfranchise blacks. Terror was systematically employed to achieve that end; legislation was enacted that deprived blacks of any semblance of economic or political power; and other discriminatory measures were implemented by state and local governments. Socially isolated, most Afro-Americans were exploited economically and forced into a hopeless poverty. The federal government ignored this discriminatory treatment, and federal courts condoned the repression when they declared unconstitutional federal civil rights laws and interpreted other legislative measures in a manner discriminatory to blacks.[15] This process, commencing in the late nineteenth century, continued, reaching its apex under President Woodrow Wilson (1913-21). Where previously blacks were moving into relatively important federal positions, Wilson instituted discriminatory measures that restricted black opportunities. Moreover, previously integrated federal public facilities, including cafeterias, restaurants and lavatories, were segregated, the federal government implementing the 'separate but equal' principle the Supreme Court upheld in Plessy v. Ferguson (1896).

Labor shortages, along with threatened black protests prior to and during the Second World War, prodded federal and some state governments into establishing or enacting equal employment measures, but thereafter civil rights issues lay dormant until the 1960s when an increasingly organized and vocal black minority demanded termination of their second-class status in American society (Himes, 1973, 1975; Wilson, 1973, 1978). Earlier, the movement was given impetus by Supreme Court decisions that struck down discriminatory measures in housing, education and other areas, the most notable case that of Brown v. Board of Education (1954) which declared 'separate but equal' measures in education, the core of racial discrimination, inherently unequal and unconstitutional.

In terms of race relations, what appears most evident is that groups in these four countries whose cultural and physical characteristics differ sharply from those of the dominant Anglo group have borne the brunt of discrimination. This has been especially true of indigenous and nonwhite groups, including two others in the United States not previously mentioned, Puerto Ricans and Mexican-Americans. When deprived of power, as were indigenes and slaves, or possessing little in the way of power resources, as Asians or blacks, the various nonwhite groups have been isolated, exploited and treated discriminatorily. Only recently have these groups mobilized their limited power resources and membership to contest against their unequal status. By so doing they have initiated the process of breaking out from their subordinate position in society. The interaction of the critical factors that account for this pattern of race relations, color, culture and power, are traced in the next chapter. The examples used are those of Indians and blacks in the United States and Canada.

Chapter 4

Color, culture and power: the USA and Canada

I

Observing that the 'first Americans – the Indians – are the most deprived and isolated minority in our nation,' President Nixon in 1970 proposed major revisions in national policies affecting native Americans. Similar conclusions were reached a few years earlier by an observer of Canadian Indians (Melling, 1966: 383), who noted that they suffered from neglect, prejudice and discrimination, remaining largely 'out of sight and out of mind of most white Canadians.' Nixon's appraisal of Indians in the US holds true for Canadian Indians: 'On virtually every scale of measurement – employment, income, education, health – the condition of the American Indian ranks at the bottom' (*New York Times*, 9 July, 1970; Melling, 1966, 1967). The major indices which illustrate the disparities between Indians and other citizens include: a life expectancy one-third shorter than the national average; a higher incidence of deaths at birth; higher rates of tuberculosis, illness and alcoholism; a higher suicide rate; lower educational achievement levels; higher unemployment levels; and a higher percentage living on welfare and under extreme conditions of poverty and destitution.

Multiple factors, historical and otherwise, shaped Indian–white relations in both countries. There are similarities as well as differences. Despite somewhat dissimilar historical developments, contemporary Indians in both countries find themselves in virtually parallel positions. Two of the major factors that historically account for their contemporary condition, *color* and *culture*, have received considerable attention, but a third, *power*, although alluded to in numerous analyses of intergroup encounters, has received little attention. Color and culture alone cannot explain the configurations of Indian–white relations;

power must be taken into consideration, for the three are closely linked.

The color or racial factor was evident in early meetings of white and red men, but it was not initially the most significant factor shaping the perceptions and behavior of each toward the other. Only later, Jordan (1969) suggests, did color become paramount, when there developed a 'European predilection for dividing the world's population into "white men" and "colored" peoples' (ibid.: 253). Even then, white colonists usually viewed red men (in terms of color) in less denigrative terms than black men. However, color cannot be totally discounted as a factor in the shaping of Indian—settler relations, as Gossett (1965) and others indicate.[1]

The color or racial factor is explicitly or implicitly seen in some studies as having shaped white—Indian conflicts. 'Race' is used in its sociological sense, i.e. to define the 'existence of groups presenting certain similarities in somatic (biological or physical) characteristics which set them off from any other group' (Comas, 1958: 18), color being one identifying attribute. Elsewhere race is defined as a 'human group that defines itself and/or is defined by other groups as different from other groups by virtue of innate and immutable physical characteristics' (Van den Berghe, 1967: 9; cf. Jordan, 1969: 583-5). Each group has particular somatic (including color) characteristics that it views as ideal, and these constitute part of a 'somatic norm image.' In Hoetink's (1967: 126) terms: 'Each "race" has, in theory, its own somatic norm image, and it considers its members aesthetically superior to others.'[2]

Racism is that situation where one group, believing its somatic (including color) characteristics superior to those of another group, accepts and uses these differences to justify the use of power to dominate over, discriminate against and/or in other ways exploit or deny equal treatment or opportunities to the group it regards as inferior (Van den Berghe, 1967; Wilson, 1973).[3] Thus, some whites, believing themselves superior to nonwhites, be they brown, black, red, or yellow, utilized power to dominate and exploit these groups.

Several studies previously cited emphasize the racial factor in Indian—settler encounters. MacLeod (1928), for example, focuses on that factor in a chapter he entitled 'War of the Races;' Hanke (1970) subtitles his analysis, 'A Study in Race Prejudice in the Modern World;' and Josephy (1958) portrays settler—Indian clashes as 'racial conflicts.'

As Hanke (1970: x) suggests, the 1550-51 debate in Vallodolid, Spain, between Las Casas and Sepulveda centered on the racial question. 'For the first time ... in the modern world we see an attempt [by Sepulveda] to stigmatize a whole race [the New World Indians] as inferior, as born slaves according to the theory elaborated centuries before by Aristotle.' Las Casas's defense of Indians' rights was partly successful, and the Spanish Crown intervened to protect them, but the racialist belief that Indians were inferior received increased support thereafter, vying with the opposite view that portrayed the Indian as a 'noble savage' (Baudet, 1965).

English settlers increasingly viewed Indians as 'savages' and 'inferior people,' and King Philip's War in 1675-6 is described by Josephy (1958: 40, 43, 53) as an 'absolute racial war.' There is some question about his interpretation, however, for he overlooks the fact that some Indian groups fought *with* the settlers. That factor brings into question the 'racial contention,' but it can be explained by the power factor: namely, the willingness of settlers to join momentarily with Indians whom they regarded as inferior but whose support they needed to put down the uprising. That 'almost forgotten colonial war,' Josephy (ibid.: 35) claims, 'set a cruel pattern of racial conflict that was to continue along a westward-moving frontier for two centuries.' As soon as the colonists landed, concludes Gossett (1965: 3), the English colonists 'encountered one race "problem" in the Indians,' and he characterizes settler—Indian clashes as examples of 'explicit racism.'[4] This racism, he argues, shaped white attitudes and behavior towards indigenous groups thereafter. The 'anti-Indian racism ... declined in volume and virulence' by the end of the nineteenth century, Gossett (ibid.: 237) contends, only because the Indian was now powerless and whites possessed most of the land.

Vaughan (1965: 63) cautions against viewing Puritan—Indian relations as color or racial encounters. In the Pequot conflict and King Philip's War, many Indians aligned themselves with settlers, and the encounters were not simply red man versus white man. Jordan also cautions against focusing solely on the color factor in early settler—Indian relations. Settlers did emphasize the *African's* color, for the color black was a symbol viewed in highly negative terms (Jordan, 1969: 7, 19-20). But settlers placed 'much less emphasis upon the Indian's color than upon the Negro's color,' and during the seventeenth century settlers did not view Indians as different from Europeans 'except in religion and savage behavior.'[5] That did not mean Indians were the European's equal; rather, Indians were considered superior to blacks but inferior to whites, a classification which, for instance, is clearly reflected in James Fenimore Cooper's novels.[6] Culture, rather than color, was the factor or characteristic which at that time distinguished Indians from whites.

Color and culture, though, often merged as factors, and even Jordan recognizes this in his analysis of white attitudes toward blacks and Indians. For instance, 'the colonists' initial sense of difference from the Negro was founded not on a single characteristic but a congeries of qualities,' among which were religion, color and culture. Significantly, 'the specific religious difference was initially of greater importance than color.'[7] By the late seventeenth century, colonists de-emphasized the terms 'Negro' and 'African' and identified slaves as *blacks*, now referring to themselves (where previously they identified themselves mostly as 'Christians') as *English* and *white*. Thus, a transition occurred from the use of 'Christian' and 'Negro' for contrast purposes to, as enslavement proceeded, the terms 'white' and 'black.' Indians were usually referred to as 'savages' or 'heathens,' settlers referring to themselves as English when the two groups were being discussed or contrasted (Jordan, 1969: 95).

There is a significance in the distinctions. Having enslaved the African by the late seventeenth century, colonists used the *color* designation to define slaves. As Jordan and others conclude, the color black elicited negative images and overtones of subhuman beings who were, among other things, considered 'brutish' and 'bestial.' The *cultural* designation was used to identify Indians, 'savage' employed interchangeably with the term 'uncivilized.' Some settlers initially believed that Indians could be 'civilized' if they accepted the European's religion and culture, but that belief waned as settler–Indian clashes intensified.

Whatever the forces prompting their New World settlement, English colonists' awareness of their cultural heritage was heightened by their encounters with contrasting indigenous cultures. Thrown into a strange, often hostile, environment, the colonist turned to his culture, including his religion, as a source of refuge, identity and security. It also served as a stabilizing force. The colonist became acutely aware of his Englishness, especially his beliefs, values, customs and modes of behavior and thought (ibid.: 46). This awareness of one's English identity was sharpened by encounters with other European cultures as well. As Jordan (ibid.: 86) suggests: 'Englishmen possessed a view of other peoples which placed the English nation at the center of widening concentric circles each of which contained people more alien than the one inside it.'[8]

As English or English-descended people gained political control over the colonies and eventually the nation, they were able to shape the society's culture and institutions. Given the pressures, or acceding to them in order to broaden their opportunities within society, other European settlers were anglicized, assimilated and 'Americanized.' By becoming anglicized or Americanized, most Europeans 'disappeared' into society, becoming one of the masses with no readily identifiable characteristics that set them apart from people of English descent. But Indians and Africans faced a virtually impermeable barrier to assimilation: their color. The African was enslaved, the consequence of the Anglo's color and culture predispositions and his power. The Indian, though considered a savage and uncivilized, was initially thought capable of being civilized if he accepted the Anglo's religion and culture. His culture, settlers contended, was inferior and had to be discarded. Vaughan (1965: 208) acknowledges this Anglo cultural ethnocentrism among Puritans: 'Indians were encouraged to forsake their tribes and join in Puritan society,' but English 'were forbidden to forsake advanced society for the lure of the primitive life' (cf. Jordan, 1969: 12-13, 89-94, 211). Vaughan (1965: 20-1) suggests: 'there was no doctrine of racial inferiority to blind the Puritans to the desirability of civilizing and Christianizing the American aborigines. To be sure, the Englishman looked on the red men as culturally inferior, but this could be overcome by exposing the native to the benefits of European civilization.' As indicated, however, even this exposure to or acceptance of Anglo culture did not help Indians during settler—indigenous group conflicts or when settlers wanted Indian lands.

Colonists considered religion the ideal means for civilizing the Indian. Once converted, they thought, the Indian would readily discard his own and accept the white man's culture. He would settle down, become a farmer, and accept English beliefs, including English notions of property. That, in turn, would open vast new tracts of 'uninhabited' former Indian lands for settler use.[9]

Even when he was converted and 'civilized,' the Indian was not trusted or accepted as equal. Whites suspected his 'civilization' was only 'skin deep' and feared he would 'revert to savagery.' Vaughan, whose sympathies rest with the Puritans, confirms this. During King Philip's war, he notes, settlers distrusted Christian Indians living in 'Praying Towns,' and they were rounded up and incarcerated or restricted to specified areas. Some were deported to Deer Island, particularly those the settlers feared might revert to 'savagery' and turn on them (Vaughan, 1965: 315-19). Thus conversion and acculturation did not accord the red man equal treatment; he was still considered an outsider. Some Christian and other Indians fought with the settlers against King Philip, but thereafter the colonists 'tended to consider the Indians as a race apart' (ibid.: 319). With that statement Vaughan nearly contradicts his earlier rejection of Josephy's claim that the conflict set a 'pattern of racial conflict' for subsequent centuries.[10]

Ambivalent white attitudes toward Indians continued during the eighteenth and early nineteenth centuries. Efforts to civilize and convert the Indian into a farmer competed with settler efforts to expel him and expropriate his lands. Some settlers viewed Indians as animals who should be exterminated (Gossett, 1965: 229-30; Jordan, 1969: ch. 12; Prucha, 1962: ch. 9; Horsman, 1967: chs 4, 7), but others such as Jefferson believed 'the Indian then to be in body and mind equal to the whiteman' (quoted in Jordan, 1969: 453). Jefferson advocated the 'Americanization' of the Indian, by which he meant transforming the Indian into a red Englishman (ibid.: 477-81). Were that to occur, he concluded, white and Indian would freely intermingle and live in peace. Jefferson's notions were not widely accepted, particularly by settlers who coveted Indian lands. In Georgia, for instance, Cherokees accepted Jefferson's earlier proposal to settle down, farm the land and accept the white man's culture. But landhungry white Georgians prodded state and federal governments into ousting the Indians. The consequence, given President Jackson's hostility toward Indians, was inevitable: the federal government, ignoring the Cherokees' civilized status and treaty rights to the land, used its power to expel them. Although they were acculturated they were still regarded as inferior (Prucha, 1962: ch. 9; Foreman, 1953).

Thus, Indians and blacks, although for different reasons initially, were classified as inferior to white men. The black was regarded so because of his color; the Indian, for his culture. Where originally some whites believed Indians could become equal by accepting the white man's religion and culture, Indians who followed that advice quickly realized the hollowness of these statements. Their stigma was that of being 'uncivilized' and 'savage,' characteristics which, whatever they did, they could not escape, just as the black could not escape his color. For whites increasingly considered 'savageness' to be a cultural trait that was *inherited* and thereby immutable.[11] Consequently, Indian and black alike were 'locked in,' damned, as Gossett (1965: 229) argues, by supposed biological 'facts.'[12]

Pearce's (1965) study of white images of Indians in colonial and nineteenth-century American literature reinforces this thesis. The Indian was viewed as locked in to his culture, biologically incapable of becoming civilized. Thus he fell victim to the ineluctable 'progress' of civilization, a process which compelled his ultimate destruction since, it was argued, he could neither adjust nor adapt to a 'superior' white civilization. Pearce traces this notion through the novels of James Fenimore Cooper and others. The white man, moving relentlessly forward, wresting the land from the Indian, was seen as simply fulfilling his historical destiny and an inevitable 'law of progress.' The Indian had to give way to a superior white culture that was, in reality, a superiority in weapons, manpower, organization and military power. As Pearce (ibid.: 212) concludes:

> The truth for writers of fiction, as for other Americans who thought seriously about the matter, was that the Indian might well have been a noble savage but that his nobility, inferior to civilized nobility, could not survive the pressures of civilization. Their task came to be to put this truth down imaginatively, at once publicly to admit that the Indian had been cruelly destroyed and to satisfy themselves and their readers that the destruction was part of a universal moral progress which it was the special destiny of America to manifest.

Whites thereby absolved themselves of guilt for exterminating the Indian and taking his land. White superiority, and particularly the role of power in this, was put most bluntly by Jackson. In ousting the Cherokees from Georgia, he rejected their treaty claims, suggesting that the settlers' earlier willingness to sign treaties 'had grown out of [white] weakness and special circumstances and [was] not based on any rights acknowledged to be possessed by the Indians' (quoted in Prucha, 1962: 234). Indians, initially viewed as temporarily inferior because they were 'uncivilized' (but thought to be civilizable), were increasingly viewed as permanently inferior as they lost their ability to oppose the white man's military power.

In his appraisal of racial thought in America, Ruchames (1969: 15) briefly alludes to this power factor:

> The white man's enslavement of the African Negro, as a being obviously different from himself, and his ability to do so with impunity, were the basic factors in the origin of prejudice and discrimination toward the black man.

Where Ruchames speaks of 'differences' he is alluding to color and culture; where he speaks of the ability to enslave 'with impunity' he is referring to power, the relative power capabilities of whites and blacks. The white man, perceiving his color and culture superior, used his power to enslave the black man and destroy the red man. His notions of superiority, centering on his color and culture, were confirmed for him by his increasing power; and his ethnocentric beliefs about color and culture were employed as rationalizations for his exploitation of and domination over other groups. Through all of this, the power factor emerges as highly significant. Indeed, it, more than color, culture or other factors, accounts for similarities in the condition of contemporary Indians and blacks in the USA and Canada.[13]

II

History is, in part, an accounting of ethnic and racial group encounters, resulting from, among others, incorporation, migration, conquest or settlement. In many respects, each society's encounters are unique; in other ways there are observable similarities, patterns and comparable sequences.[14] Settler rather than sojourner societies, Canada and the US witnessed an influx of Europeans, mostly Anglo-Saxons who wrested the land and control from indigenous groups, a pattern repeated extensively wherever Europeans went. The patterns that emerged in these encounters were paralleled elsewhere, and initial friendly relations were usually followed by tension, conflict, indigenous efforts to expel or stop the 'intruders' and ultimate settler hegemony (Shibutani and Kwan, 1965: 122-5).

Settler–native group clashes were 'stages on which struggles for power and privilege' took place (Lenski, 1966: 17), representing 'inter-group power contests' (Blalock, 1967: 109) that occurred at three distinct levels: (a) for possession of the desired objects (land, resources and other riches); (b) for power itself, i.e. for enhancing one's own power resources and capabilities while curtailing or destroying those of the other; and (c) for control of the political, economic and social structures within which allocative decisions concerning the previous two are made. Early settler–Indian contests focused on the first two levels, for Indians had no voice in settlers' institutions. Following settler conquest, however, decisions affecting indigenous groups were made at the third level, and the Indian had neither voice nor power within these structures.

In the United States, the indigenes' demise prompted Congress to assert absolute dominion over Indian affairs, and it enacted legislation during the 1870s and 1880s that legitimized its control. In 1871, for example, Congress declared in a resolution: 'hereafter no Indian nation or tribe within the territory of the United States shall be acknowledged or recognized as an independent nation.' Although Congress recognized previous treaties, it now claimed full power to treat all Indians as 'wards of the state.' The government, it stated, knew what was best and good for Indians. This policy was broadened in the Dawes Act (the General Allotment Act) of 1887. It divided Indian lands into individual plots which Indians were supposed to farm, but the Indian lands left over after that allocation (millions of acres) were retained by the government and made available to white settlers. The Act also proffered citizenship to Indians who would abandon their tribe and adopt 'the habits of civilized life,' its major thrust that of coercing Indians into becoming assimilated. Its consequence, however, was that of stripping Indians of their 'excess' lands which settlers coveted. In the enactment of the legislation, Indians were not consulted even though the Act aimed at destroying indigenous cultures. By its actions, Congress asserted a wardship or trusteeship over Indians, and thereafter it dictated to and often selected Indian leadership, proscribed particular Indian religious and cultural practices it disliked, imposed its own religious and cultural beliefs and practices on indigenes, and assumed the right to 'civilize' or assimilate Indians without considering their own wishes.

Indian–settler encounters in Canada, explored more fully later, followed a somewhat less brutal path than in the USA, yet whites in both countries gained total control almost simultaneously. The Canadian government, too, prodded by settler pressures, dispossessed

Indians from their lands and pursued paternalist policies, including the adoption of practices specifically aimed at destroying and replacing Indian cultures with the dominant white culture. Here, too, it forced these changes on resistant Indian groups (LaViolette, 1961), a policy which it, as its US counterpart, could pursue because of its power.

Power, or *macht* in Weber's terms, 'is the probability that one actor within a social relationship will be in a position to carry out his own will despite resistance' (Weber, 1947: 152), or in Blalock's (1967: 110) terms: 'Power is the actual overcoming of resistance in a standard period of time.' Power issues are concerned with who has the capability, by persuasion or other means, including physical force, to make or implement allocative decisions concerning the distribution (and to whom) of society's rewards and resources, including power itself. Indian–settler historical encounters constituted a zero-sum game, although at different periods power relationships were symmetrical or asymmetrical. But the objective correlates of power (resources, mobilization capabilities, etc.) were not the sole determinant of relationships, for the character of these relations and how the participants acted or reacted toward each other was influenced by their perceptions, including their assumptions about the power capabilities of themselves and their opponent(s).

The power of a group, as specified in Chapter 2, can be isolated in terms of group resources and mobilization capabilities. Resources (e.g. manpower, weapons, money), unless mobilized or mobilized improperly, are of limited value in power contests. Resources are significant, but if they cannot be mobilized properly because of disorganization, ineffective or indecisive leadership, low morale or other factors, then it is possible for a group with more limited resources but superior mobilization skills to succeed in power contests. For example, Indian manpower usually surpassed that of settlers on the frontier, but Indian tribes, be it in Canada or the USA, seldom (or only too late) rallied other tribes to support them in conflicts with settlers and military forces. Moreover, the settlers occasionally enlisted other Indians on *their* side, providing an additive resource that tipped the balance of power toward them. What emerges, then, in the assessment of settler–indigene conflicts are two sets of factors: settler resources and mobilization capabilities, and indigenous group resources and mobilization capabilities (cf. Blalock, 1967: ch. 4).

The power factor is most explicit in the US experience. From the earliest days colonists 'ignored any Indian rights to sovereignty or land' (Price, 1972: 11), thereby exacerbating tensions and conflict (Josephy, 1958: 110, 139-42, 182; Washburn, 1959; Prucha, 1962: chs 2-4, 7-9). Indian power, whether real or imagined by the settler, sometimes tempered his land aggrandizement, but ultimate settler superiority in resources and mobilization skills destroyed native power. Alcohol, the white man's diseases and the social disintegration of indigenous cultures resulting from contact with the white man, all contributed to the Indian's demise (Price, 1972; Josephy, 1958; Vaughan, 1965; MacLeod, 1928). Where settlers perceived indigenes as powerful, they restricted their behavior and negotiated accommodative arrangements prior to and following American independence. Indian indifference or presumed weakness invariably prompted new settler encroachments, and at that point Indian reprisals led settlers to call for metropole military support. That tipped the power balance in favor of settlers, even though their and the metropole's aims were often at odds with each other. Early in the new nation's history the federal government, recognizing its military limitations and the Indians' legitimate claims, sought to restrict settlers and placate Indians through treaties, peace offerings and gifts (Prucha, 1962: chs 3, 5-6; Horsman, 1967: chs 4-9; Josephy, 1958: ch. 5). It tried to protect Indian lands but settlers brazenly ignored their own government and took the lands, precipitating new conflicts. Although settlers accused the Indians of savagery, Prucha (1962: 199) concludes: 'The frequency of offenses committed against Indians by the frontier whites – among which outright murder was commonplace – was shocking. It was often a question of who was more aggressive, more hostile, more savage – the Indian or the white man' (cf. Horsman, 1967: ch. 4).

Fear of Indian power influenced even Congress, and during early decades of the republic it seriously considered establishing a separate Indian state that would send representatives to Congress (Abel, 1907). The proposal received serious consideration, but the crushing of Indian power east of the Mississippi (1811-13) terminated serious consideration of the proposal (Josephy, 1958: 147-73). Even so, the proposal lingered on and surfaced again during Georgia's dispute with the Cherokees in the 1820s. Southern slave state congressmen, fearful that a 'red' state would set a precedent for a subsequent 'black' state, 'took opposition on the color line' and 'announced themselves as opposed on principle to a prospective Indian State, and declared a Negro State would be just as proper to them and just as [un] acceptable' (Abel, 1907: 97).

The role of the metropole, be it British or American, in protecting native rights needs additional comment. Whatever its motivation, be it protection of the native, settler and/or the prohibitive cost of troop support, the metropole pursued diverse strategies to preserve peace. In 1755, for instance, the British government took steps to 'remove Indian affairs from the incompetent hands of the colonists' who were aggravating conflicts with the Indians. That policy failed, and British troops were called in because of settler–Indian conflicts. That resulted in the Proclamation of 1763, separating Indians from settlers by restricting the latter to lands east of the Appalachians. As noted previously, settlers resented the prohibition, and it and subsequent British colonial measures precipitated the revolution. Later, the US federal government sought to restrain settler aggressiveness, but its efforts also encountered settler circumvention (Prucha, 1962: 45-50, 143-86, 191-203). Federal policy changed following the Indians' defeat, 1811-13, and Jackson's 'Indian removal' policy signaled two significant factors: first, that the white–Indian power struggle had changed decisively, the whites now possessing vastly superior power; and second, that the metropole, which previously recognized Indian rights, now under Jacksonian democracy would cater to settler demands.

As a consequence, Indian–settler conflicts continued, but federal troops and state militia crushed Indian 'uprisings.' By the 1870s, despite a few subsequent encounters, Indian power was effectively destroyed. This shift, as previously suggested, was symbolized in the 1871 congressional resolution whereby Congress rejected Indian tribes as independent nations and claimed they were wards of the state. Under the 1887 Dawes Act, the government divested Indians of millions of acres of lands previously protected by treaties, doing so under the guise of 'land allotment.' They also initiated policies aimed at destroying Indian cultures and imposing upon indigenes the white man's culture. This constellation of factors – harassment, conflict, military defeat, disease, starvation and military wardship – precipitated social disintegration within various Indian groups, contributing to their subordination. Shorn of his resources and military power, the Indian became a ward of the state. At that point, too, the dominant group sought to impose its own cultural values on the Indian.[15]

Initially somewhat different, the Canadian experience had by the twentieth century come to parallel that in the US. French settlement and control of Canada until 1763 contributed to early variances, and intensive Catholic church efforts to convert Indians were in marked contrast to English settler efforts at Indian conversion. Similarly, the lighter influx of French settlers and the seigneurial system of land tenure limited friction between the two groups. Fewer settlers also meant that Indian power capabilities were relatively stronger, settlers recognizing the foolhardiness of alienating indigenous groups. Relations, however, were not always peaceful. Indeed, early seventeenth-century French settlements encountered hostile Indians; and the Iroquois plagued French trappers and settlers until the late seventeenth century. The French, in contrast to the English, maintained fairly amicable relations with most indigenous groups, and by the late seventeenth century even the Iroquois had been pacified. Thereafter, strict metropolitan control over trapper and settler activities contributed to fairly peaceful settler—Indian relations (Eccles, 1969; Bailey, 1969; Kennedy, 1950; Jenness, 1932; McRae, 1964; Parkman, 1902).

Early French penetration of Canada was by trappers rather than settlers, although the latter followed shortly thereafter. Trappers and Indians intermixed and married, and racial admixture, the offspring of whom were called Metis, was fairly common. That was not so in the British colonies. Wary of the British to the south, the French pursued a policy of befriending and cultivating the Indians' favor with annual gifts and bribes. This proved beneficial in maintaining intergroup harmony and it contributed to Indian support for France in its conflicts with Britain (MacLeod, 1928: 359-61; McRae, 1964: 220-5; Josephy, 1958: 100-4). Prior to ceding Canada to Britain, France actively encouraged Indians to convert to Catholicism and become farmers, a policy sharply in contrast (except for the Praying Towns) to the British colonies. Consequently, there was a higher degree of settler—Indian cultural and racial mixture. Later, British trappers in Canada followed their French counterparts in mixing with Indians, the result being the emergence of Metis of British—Indian as well as French—Indian parentage. Many of the Metis were in or emigrated to what would later become the western provinces where they settled and farmed.

Following French practice, the British prior to and following the American Revolution befriended Canadian Indian tribes, enlisting their support against the Americans and using them as a buffer between Canada and the US. Through treaties, annual gifts and other inducements the British cemented their friendship with numerous tribes. Aware from their earlier experience with American colonists of settler efforts to wrest away Indian lands, Britain retained in Canada tight control over 'native affairs' as well as sole right to acquire Indian lands. It later turned these powers over to Canada's Dominion government. Britain refused to be swayed by settler pressures, but the Dominion government had more difficulty doing so. As settlers moved into the western provinces, they came into conflict particularly with Metis, who had earlier occupied some of the lands, and Indians.

French and British trappers, along with the Metis, earlier emigrated west and settled in the Red River valley area. English settlers moved into the area during the 1860s and questioned the legitimacy of the land titles held by the earlier settlers, touching off the 1869 and 1885 rebellions led by Louis Riel. Himself a Metis, Riel rallied his followers, Metis and Indians, in protest against the newcomers' threat to their lands. Because of this Metis-Indian combination, the rebellions were not construed simply as a settler versus Indian conflict. The new settlers called for assistance from the metropole, which put down the rebellions, and thereafter power shifted to the white settlers and away from the Metis and Indians. From that point on Indians were forced on to reservations or into assimilating with whites, although the ones who attempted the latter were discriminated against. Lacking power, Indians became the target of dominant group cultural practices, including efforts to destroy Indian cultures (Stanley, 1960; Melling, 1966; McRae, 1964: 254-64; LaViolette, 1961: chs 1-4).

The experience of US and Canadian Indians has been quite similar in the twentieth century despite these earlier differences in historical developments. The Indian was deprived of his lands; his culture and social institutions were disrupted by encounters with whites, including missionaries; and an alien culture was imposed upon him. Some Indians resisted, but their lack of political and military power as well as the coercive/reward powers used by the dominant group to force compliance with their policies made resistance difficult if not impossible. The Indians' right to self-determination was severely circumscribed. Social disintegration, as previously indicated, often ensued,[16] and efforts to destroy Indian cultures and replace them with the dominant group culture had a shattering impact on Indian life (Price, 1972; DeLoria,

1970: ch. 5). Politically powerless, the Indian became the object of white society's color and cultural biases, prejudices which whites, because Indians lacked power to retaliate, could readily translate into discriminatory behavior towards indigenous people.

III

In late 1541 the Frenchman Jacques Cartier established the first Canadian settlement along the St Lawrence River, but by the following spring adverse conditions and hostile Iroquois Indians necessitated a French withdrawal. Not until the following century did France earnestly attempt to settle Canada, and the Iroquois were an ever-present danger until a peace treaty was later negotiated (Goldstein, 1969; Parkman, 1902). British and French experiences were similar in that sense: Indian power was an omnipresent factor, one that could not be ignored. Until the late nineteenth century Indian power had to be reckoned with (Billington, 1967).

Power as a variable emerged in numerous guises: in the resources and resource mobilization activities of settlers and indigenes; in the role of the metropole; and in the linkage of color-culture-power factors. During colonization and subsequent frontier periods, Indians in both countries possessed superior resources, particularly in numbers as they encountered settlers and federal troops. Seldom, though, did they mobilize their resources sufficiently. Numerous factors contributed to this: difficulties in getting intertribal co-operation to fight settlers or troops; the geographical dispersion of indigenous groups; the lack of sustained co-operation even when Indian groups did combine to oppose whites; and the willingness of some Indians to ally themselves with whites rather than their fellow Indians in these conflicts. All these factors detracted from indigenous group resources and mobilization capabilities. French, British and Americans were thereby able to prevail in most situations, although often they needed additive resources, be it Indian allies or metropole troops.

Defeat or the fear of defeat prompted settlers to demand metropole intervention, and troops from the latter swung the balance of power in the settlers' favor. Indian—settler clashes were ongoing, including periods of stalemate and open warfare. Settler encroachments on Indian lands destroyed the game on which Indians survived, and this, too, forced them westward. Indian power was vitiated by numerous factors: wars with settlers and metropolitan troops; intertribal conflicts, sometimes instigated by settlers; the scourge of the white man's diseases; and the relentless westward push of settlers. Ultimately it was the white man's superiority in weapons and mobilization capabilities that brought about the Indian's demise.

Superior white power and the increasing powerlessness of Indians allowed the latent ethnocentrism and cultural prejudices, based on color and culture, to surface in the dominant group. Indians were viewed as inferior, and confirmation of this for whites was the Indian's subjugation. What this indicates, then, is that racial beliefs are not in all cases simply rationalizations, post-facto techniques for justifying domination and exploitation. Rather, they can be cultural beliefs (i.e. somatic and cultural norm images) that are latent, which surface when given the opportunity or when exacerbated by particular conditions or situations. Or, if not present initially, such beliefs emerge from group contact situations, particularly conflict or stress-type situations. In either circumstance these beliefs are more apt to surface when a group has power, particularly if it can implement its beliefs against another group that lacks countervailing power. Not all groups espouse ethnocentric beliefs, but research on intergroup relations indicates that such beliefs are present in most groups. Whether or not they surface, however, is dependent on numerous factors, particularly a group's power vis-à-vis other groups and in certain types of conflict situations. It is power, then, or the relative power capabilities of groups that serves as a corrective against each group's implementation of ethnocentric, racist or other negative beliefs.

Given their power, settlers were able to put into practice their ethnocentric cultural and somatic beliefs. These included their racist beliefs, the implementation of which resulted in 'racism' (Van den Berghe, 1967). This racism manifested itself in white perceptions of the Indians' supposedly 'inferior' culture, a view that increased as Indians lost power. Where initially Indians were considered temporarily inferior because they were 'uncivilized,' a condition that could change if they accepted the white man's culture, they were now seen as permanently inferior because their 'uncivilized' nature was innate and unchangeable. That change in assessment occurred, as Pearce (1965) indicates, as Indians lost power. In Schermerhorn's (1970) terms, this represented a shift from minimal to maximal racism.[17] A somewhat comparable process occurred with blacks in both countries. In that case color rather than the cultural factor served as the basis for discriminatory treatment and domination. Thus domination, i.e. the power of white over nonwhite, whether justified by color or culture rationalizations, was seen as 'proof' of the Indian's and the black man's inferiority. Domination, in the final assessment, was based on the factor of power.

Chapter 5

Race and power in South Africa and Rhodesia

I

Race relations in South Africa and Rhodesia can be viewed as ongoing group power contests, Europeans and Africans historically vying for power and control of resources. Following a period of conflict, whites, as in other Anglo settler societies, wrested control and used it to deprive Africans of their power resources. Whites also subordinated other nonwhite groups, including Indians and Coloreds, but the emphasis here is on black—white relations.

Historically, whites in both countries were wary of African power, potential or actual, and the postwar emergent African nationalism transformed whites into siege groups, as described in the following chapter. The siege perceptions (i.e. the threat of Africans) of whites shaped the character of race relations in both countries. The historical juxtaposition of diverse racial groups, whatever the cause, invariably precipitates group struggles for power and resources, the contests serving to accent group differences (Chapter 1). Whether contests are of a military nature or take place within political, economic and social arenas, the victor makes cultural and structural policy decisions that determine the allocation or reallocation of power resources.

Cultural policy choices, as previously noted, determine whether there will be in society (a) the elimination of subordinate group cultures and the imposition of a 'national' culture (usually that of the dominant group) or (b) the acceptance of polyculturalism, that decision resulting from acceptance of group diversity or the inability of a group to impose its culture over others. Cultural factors influence structural policy decisions: namely, how and the extent to which the dominant group will structurally incorporate the subordinate group(s). These decisions are based on three factors: (a) dominant group attitudes toward subordinate groups, (b) power differentials of dominant and subordinate groups, and (c) the development (primarily economic) needs of society. The dominant group, for example, may extend or restrict a subordinate group's structural incorporation contingent upon the latter's rejection of its own and acceptance of the dominant group culture. If, however, group power capabilities are nearly equal or economic needs require incorporation of subordinate group labor, dominant group policy choices are narrowed. However, should the dominant group believe its power or way of life is threatened, it will seek to destroy the subordinate group's power resources regardless of economic or other consequences to itself. The Afrikaner National Party (1948) and Rhodesian Front Party (1962) electoral victories illustrate how quickly siege groups emerge when members believe their group identity and security are threatened. Although the two groups pursued different strategies, their goal was the same: the thwarting of African nationalism and the 'modernizing' (H. Adam, 1971a) of white racial dominance systems.

Power as a determinant of race relations was traced in Chapter 2, the emphasis there on resources, mobilization capabilities, additive resources and the strategies utilized by groups in power contests. Race relations are usually asymmetrical, as W. Wilson (1973: 18) suggests:

> ... there are no known cases in which the relationships between racial groups have been based on complete equality of power. Differential power is a marked feature of racial-group interaction in complex societies; the greater the power discrepancy between subordinate and dominant racial groups, the greater the extent and scope of racial domination.

Wilson's statement is applicable to South Africa and Rhodesia. Historically, whether by military force or other means, whites assumed a dominant position. Coercive power was utilized whenever necessary, but other techniques were also employed. Indeed, whites controlled and transformed structures in a manner that forced Africans into a position of dependency, economic and otherwise, and that facilitated the emergence of still another, more sophisticated form of control: psychosocial dominance. Numerous parallels are evident in the South African and Rhodesian experiences. For example, whites in both countries (a) destroyed or deprived blacks of power resources, (b) curtailed the strategies blacks could use to ward off subordination, (c) used their control of political, economic and social structures to keep Africans powerless and (d) modified and modernized their racial dominance systems in order to rebuff African nationalism. Most significant in accounting for continued white hegemony was the reliance on three particular types of dominance: coercive, structural and psychosocial.

I.1 Coercive dominance

Conflict situations, be they wars, rebellions, riots or otherwise, are contests in which adversary group resources, mobilization capabilities and strategies determine the outcome unless additive resources (e.g. entry of a third party on one side or the other) shifts the power balance. Frontier encounters and wars during the eighteenth and nineteenth centuries in South Africa and 1893 and 1896-7 in Southern Rhodesia brought defeat to African groups (Elphick and Giliomee, 1979; Walker, 1957; Macmillan, 1963; Gann, 1965; Ranger, 1967, 1970). Whites thereafter moved to deprive Africans of their power resources, and subsequent African stirrings of discontent, such as the 1906 Zulu uprising in South Africa, were quickly suppressed (Marks, 1970). The convergence of white military and police power with policies aimed at curtailing African power resources assured continued white rule. Their military powers circumscribed, black opposition thereafter surfaced in muted or masked forms, ranging from millennial religious movements to nascent political opposition, all signaling black hostility to white domination (Lanternari, 1963; Sundkler, 1961; Mafejo, 1975; Ranger, 1966, 1970).

Whether white rule resulted from conquest or treaty, subsequent African subjugation evolved from white policies that destroyed or restricted black resources and mobilization capabilities. The basic resources of an agricultural/pastoral society are its land, cattle and labor. Once whites acquired power, they expropriated African lands and cattle, forced indigenes on to lands generally of an inferior quality, and disrupted their economy and self-sufficiency. Thus conquest, disruption of tribal economies and imposition of white rule, whether direct or indirect, disoriented African societies, leading to social disorganization and shattered group morale and cohesion. All of these factors made it exceedingly difficult for African groups to resist or contest against white dominance.

Assured of control through their military and police power, whites solidified their dominance by enacting policies that further destroyed or curtailed African power resources. Whites thereafter resorted to various modes of structural dominance to keep control over Africans.

I.2 Structural dominance

Through its control of political, economic and social structures, a dominant group makes allocative decisions that determine the distribution among groups of power, privilege and resources. Subordinate structures may be retained or discarded, but in either instance the subordinate remains under the control of the superordinate group.

Economic structures are of critical importance. As noted previously, an agricultural/pastoral society's major resources are its land, cattle and labor. If deprived of these resources, the group is virtually helpless. Whites, by dispossessing Africans of their land and cattle, sharply restricted the latter's resources. Subsequent land appropriations further curtailed African resources. Some Africans were allowed to remain on lands held by white farmers or the government, but they were forced to pay rent. Later, as white farming expanded, Africans were expelled and forced to move to reserves or seek employment within the European sector.

Land appropriations continued into the twentieth century, the major allocation (there were later minor modifications) and demarcation of European and African lands set out in South Africa's Native Land Act (1913) and Southern Rhodesia's Land Apportionment Act (1930). Whether they remained on European lands, where they paid rent, or moved to African reserves, blacks had difficulty surviving. This was attributable to various factors. Africans initially sustained themselves on these lands though they were invariably of inferior quality to those owned by whites. Within the reserves, Africans held lands in communal ownership, but elsewhere a few Africans were allowed to purchase non-reserve private lands if they had the financial resources. In cases where Africans purchased European farms and momentarily competed successfully against whites in the market economy, they were quickly rebuffed.

Three factors contributed to the African's increasing impoverishment in the twentieth century: first, as the African population grew, reserve lands were inadequate to sustain the group's economic needs; second, land pressures increased as Africans were ousted from European lands; and third, the land shortage forced Africans to overuse and overstock their lands, resulting in soil depletion and reduced productivity. Unable to survive on reserves, numerous Africans were by the 1930s forced to seek employment within the European sector, usually at below-subsistence wages. Pauperization of the African was the direct result of white land policy (Horwitz, 1967; chs 4-6, 9-10; Arrighi, 1967, 1970; Clarke, 1974a, 1974b).

African farmers experienced difficulty in competing with white farmers. In general, African reserves or purchase lands were far removed from road or rail transport, whites having taken possession of the prime lands more accessible to transport. Despite these difficulties, some Africans managed to compete successfully with white farmers and thereby build up their economic resources. Threatened by this, white farmers demanded government assistance for themselves. From the 1920s onwards, governments in both countries devised marketing arrangements and agricultural legislation that clearly favored Europeans (Horwitz, 1967: chs 4-5; Moyana, 1974; Palmer, 1968). Funds for improving agricultural skills and production were made available to white but not black farmers, and governments prohibited any further encroachment of blacks in 'white areas.' Blacks, whites argued, had a lower standard of living than whites and could sell their commodities at lower prices. That was unfair competition, whites claimed, and they demanded government measures which clearly discriminated against Africans (Horwitz, 1967: 46ff, 130-40).

Because Africans resisted working for European subsistence wages, both governments enacted measures that virtually forced them into the wage sector. For example, hut and other taxes were imposed; Africans were ordered to pay their taxes in cash rather than agricultural produce; and marketing arrangements were initiated that made it difficult for Africans to sell their surplus produce. As African agricultural production fell and their needs increased, Africans were forced to seek employment to pay their taxes. Whites utilized other tactics as well. Laws prohibited Africans from squatting on unused European or government lands: squatters had to pay rent or be expelled. Expulsion meant they had to return to unproductive and overcrowded reserves or seek employment in the white economy. So acute were labor shortages in both countries that whites recruited non-indigenous Africans. However, as a means of preventing mines from competing for scarce labor and thereby driving up African wages, whites established hiring boards that recruited labor and set wages.

The wages paid to Africans seldom met the expenses of unmarried labor and were totally inadequate for the married man with family. Because of this, laborers were forced to leave their families behind on reserves, thereby breaking up the family for extended periods. The migratory labor system had a decidedly destructive impact, particularly social (broken families, wives left behind to operate farms, social problems, social disorganization), be it within the reserves, the mining compounds or the urban areas. Work conditions and wages were deplorable, precipitating numerous strikes (Phimister, 1971; Ranger, 1970; Horwitz, 1967: chs 11-14). Bad conditions and inadequate wages were usual in agricultural, domestic, mining and other sectors. Despite labor shortages, whites were determined to keep African wages low. By the 1930s impoverished conditions in the reserves compelled Africans to seek employment, and that momentary labor surplus also kept wages low. Some Africans moved into the industrial sector, but job reservation and job fragmentation locked them into unskilled and low-paying positions. African economic resources were as a consequence at a minimum.

The preceding factors severely restricted African mobilization capabilities. The male exodus from reserves to seek employment in the European sector forced women into agriculture, and their lack of agricultural experience seriously curtailed agricultural productivity. Three factors made it difficult for African laborers to organize or strike against working conditions and wages: (a) given the transient character of labor, most laborers worked for only brief periods before returning to the reserves, making efforts to organize them difficult; (b) non-indigenous African workers usually refused to organize or strike for fear of losing their jobs; and (c) the fear that dissidents or potential strikers might be fired (despite labor shortages, management discharged workers rather than tolerate organizational activities aimed at strengthening labor's bargaining position) kept many from organizing. However, the momentary labor surplus during the 1930s meant that strikers could be easily replaced. Consequently, African workers, whether in mining, agriculture, domestic service or elsewhere, were at the mercy of employers who could set their own wage and working standards (Rex, 1971). The mobilization capabilities of workers were thereby circumscribed by the insecurities of their position (Harris, 1974: chs 2-3): first, there was the insecurity of tenure, for most were unskilled and could be easily replaced; second, there was the uncertainty of tenure in terms of housing, for without employment an African (in South Africa) could be sent back to the reserves; and third, there was the insecurity of wages, for despite the inadequacy of wages a person could not quit since he needed the funds to support his family in the reserves. An African accompanied by his family was even more insecure, for his added responsibilities made it more difficult for him to organize for wage increases or better working conditions. As a result, worker and employer power differentials were vast.

The numerous restrictions upon African resources and mobilization capabilities perpetuated white dominance. Deprived of land and cattle, thwarted in efforts to compete in the market economy, forced by economic circumstances to work for whites and constrained by conditions from organizing to better his wages or working conditions, the African was transformed into a pauperized and virtually powerless person (Macmillan, 1940: 118-20; Van der Horst, 1942). He was restricted from developing skills, for as an unskilled worker he could be easily replaced. Moreover, his position as a migrant laborer contributed to his powerlessness (Meer, 1971; F. Wilson, 1972; Arrighi, 1970). All told, the African's economic impoverishment kept him powerless.

The use of *social structures* to maintain dominance can be viewed from such perspectives as: (a) the national or cultural integration of groups; (b) the social relations of groups; (c) the impact of dominance on subordinate group social organization; and (d) education and domination. Although it is more difficult to trace how social structures deprived subordinates of resources and mobilization capabilities, their impact is significant.

Cultural policy within society is influenced by group power differentials. Both Boer-Afrikaner and Anglo groups assumed they were culturally superior to Africans. Afrikaners originally viewed Africans as innately or biologically inferior, incapable of becoming civilized, and born to be 'hewers of wood and drawers of water.' Cultural assimilation or structural incorporation of Africans except as subordinates at the lowest of levels was rejected (Moodie, 1975; Van Jaarsveld, 1964; Walker, 1957; MacCrone, 1937). Anglo settlers usually held that Africans were culturally but not biologically inferior to the English and thereby capable of being 'civilized', i.e. anglicized. English policy was, in principle, directed toward the cultural assimilation and structural incorporation of Africans. In practice, however, the English were paternalistic, and the cultural assimilation and structural incorporation of Africans was limited (Thompson, 1960; Stone, 1973: chs 4, 6-8; Macmillan, 1963). Nevertheless, English racial beliefs threatened Afrikaner beliefs, and the latter were fearful that English cultural beliefs spawned black nationalist demands for equality.

Both Afrikaners and English dissociated themselves from tribal or uneducated Africans, but readily employed Africans as domestic servants or in other capacities. As the African urban population expanded in the nineteenth and twentieth centuries, both white groups upheld social segregation for Africans except for their domestic servants. As a result, three distinct societies emerged: Afrikaner, English and African. Black—white social contacts were usually limited to master—servant relations or the market place, giving both South Africa and Southern Rhodesia the characteristics of a 'plural' society (Kuper and Smith, 1969; Rabuska and Shepsle, 1972). There were limited contacts between educated blacks and whites (mostly English), but a 'race relations etiquette' (Doyle, 1937) evolved wherein each racial group followed prescribed roles and modes of behavior in their racial contact situations. The 'etiquette' necessitated that Africans defer to whites in a manner that acknowledged their subordinate position.

Conquest, white control, westernization and the migrant labor system contributed to the disorganization and even disintegration of African tribal society. Western culture was a divisive force in some cases, for groups and even families split along religious (indigenous vs. Christian) and cultural (tribalist vs. modernist) lines, destroying tribal unity and morale. Moreover, the migratory system had a disintegrative impact on family life, and often those who could not find employment resorted to lives of vice or crime. Tribal society was jeopardized by these conditions and European influences, for they undermined African attempts to mobilize and oppose white rule (M. Wilson, 1961; M. Wilson and Thompson, 1969, 1971; Schapera, 1967; Carstens, 1966).

Until recent decades virtually the only education Africans received was in missionary schools. The purpose of that education was to christianize, westernize and thereby 'civilize' Africans, for most missionaries considered African life and culture inferior to western culture. The motive of most missionary education was clear: Africans should be 'de-cultured,' i.e. their old way of life should be replaced by western beliefs and behavior, a form of 'cultural imperialism' that helped destroy the African's cultural identity. There were exceptions, and not all Africans accepted or embraced European beliefs, but those who desired employment within the European sector readily recognized the necessity for becoming acculturated. Because of this cultural indoctrination some Africans came to *believe* they were inferior to whites, and those who did so were easier to control. The black who believed that he was inferior to the European in effect imprisoned himself, for he presumed he was incapable of competing with whites or making choices for himself. However, education often had unintended consequences (Murphree, 1976), for some Africans, recognizing their own capabilities and believing in Christian pronouncements of brotherhood and equality, protested against the African's subordination. Indeed, black Christian ministers were in the forefront of protest and nationalist movements. Meanwhile, governments in both countries limited the 'academic' education that mission schools provided Africans, maintaining that blacks should receive only technical training. Following the election of Nationalist and Rhodesian Front parties, South African and Rhodesian governments brought African education under their exclusive control. South Africa did so with the Bantu Education Act (1953), and in 1971 the Rhodesian government assumed control of most mission-operated African primary schools. Thereafter, both governments used education to indoctrinate Africans with dominant group racial beliefs concerning society (K. Adam, 1971; Dickie-Clark, 1971; Dorsey, 1975).

It is within *political structures* that the major distributive decisions of society are made, and group power differentials, in terms of access to and control over these structures largely determines the decisions reached. In both South Africa and Rhodesia the African's access to these structures was non-existent. Historically, within the Cape Province and Southern Rhodesia, Africans who met specified property and/or educational requirements were eligible for the common voting roll.[1] However, white governments constantly modified franchise requirements to restrict the number of eligible African voters. The low wages paid and the limited schooling received by most Africans assured that few could meet the franchise requirements. Since reserve lands were communal property (the franchise stipulated private ownership of land), Africans living on reserves could not use land to qualify for the vote (Tatz, 1962; Leys, 1959; Bowman, 1973).

The presence of Africans on the common voting roll was opposed by many whites. Thus, in 1936 the few enfranchised South African blacks were removed from the common voting roll. Thereafter they could only elect whites to represent them in parliament. Following the National Party victory (1948), even that form of representation was abolished (1956) and Africans were restricted to voting for their homeland leaders under the Bantu Self-Government Act (1959). Through the manipulation of franchise requirements white Rhodesians consistently restricted the number of Africans on the common voting roll. Under the 1961 Constitution a complicated two-tier voting system was introduced. It purportedly gave Africans greater representation but in reality 'guaranteed nothing but indefinite white rule' (Bowman, 1973: 40). Later, under RF rule, new constitutions were introduced in 1965 and 1969, their purpose specifically that of guaranteeing continued white rule.

Within political structures, therefore, Africans had virtually no voice. Even within tribal society Africans did not control their own destiny, for through native commissioners or administrators both governments exercised direct or indirect rule (Holleman, 1969; Weinrich, 1971; Brookes, 1974). Africans could select their tribal leaders in most instances but white administrators could depose or replace African leaders who did not heed their dictates. Moreover, major decisions affecting African groups were made by the white native administrators, not tribal leaders. The consequences were of two types: first, tribal political organizations were effectively emasculated, and second, a dependency relationship evolved between administrator and African wherein Africans grew apathetic or indifferent or allowed the white administrators to make decisions for them. They became wards of the state, and administrators used coercive/reward powers to maintain control.

By these tactics white society controlled Africans and denied or deprived them of political resources, including among others: limited or no voice in political decisions affecting them, removal of black leaders who might mobilize supporters and threaten white rule, and curtailment of the power of tribal organizations. If black leadership did emerge, it could be deposed, co-opted, detained or imprisoned. A few Africans were co-opted by the government, some serving as teachers or administrators of native affairs. Whites could always utilize coercive/police powers, and black leaders considered dangerous were silenced or incarcerated under various security laws. The military and police were relied upon to suppress strikes, riots and uprisings.

In summary, whites manipulated and used economic, political and social structures historically to destroy or impede the development of African power resources, relying upon the techniques described. These structures of dominance proved highly effective, but dominance was not preserved solely by structural means. Morale, group identity and solidarity, leadership, motivation and the acceptance or rejection of dominance are all, ultimately, psychological states of mind. Thus the group that wishes to retain power must utilize other means for inculcating a proper state of mind, i.e. of subservience, in those it wishes to dominate. These psychosocial means constitute another, more subtle and effective form of power or dominance.

I.3 Psychosocial dominance

The three categories of psychosocial dominance that can be analytically distinguished, compliance, dependency and thought control, were discussed in Chapter 2 and need only brief elaboration here. Human behavior derives from innumerable factors, including one's belief system and psychological needs. These factors, along with the situation or given historical milieu, shape a person's perceptions (Barbu, 1960: chs 1-3). Whether the person is or is not aware of these factors, they shape his perceptual field. Moreover, his behavior and interaction with others is based on what he perceives as reality. The 'meanings' that people attach to situations and events are largely the consequence of their experiences, most of which transpire within political, economic and social structures. The structures themselves are thereby significant in determining the 'meaning' of experiences, for they serve as socialization agents, shaping, at least in part, the psychological predispositions and perceptual field of the individual. This does not imply that the individual is simply a robot of socialization forces, for as an actor he determines for himself the meanings of these things (Blumer, 1969; Kelly, 1963) and acts in response to his interpretations. Consequently, the significance of structures in socializing and shaping the psychological perceptions of individuals cannot be discounted.

As noted previously (Chapter 2), the first category of psychosocial dominance is that of *compliance*, the dominant group relying upon its coercive/reward powers to elicit from the subordinate group desired forms of behavior. The preservation of dominance through coercive/reward techniques is costly although it is generally effective, but its costs prompt dominant groups to utilize other control devices. Among these is the second category of psychosocial dominance, *dependency*, of which there are three types. Fundamental to all is the inability of a subordinate group to cope with situations, be that condition structurally or psychologically induced. The structural type of dependency, discussed more fully in Chapter 2, evolves when the superordinate deprives the subordinate of his economic resources or means of livelihood, thereby making survival itself difficult. In this situation the subordinate must rely upon others for the basic necessities of life, including food, shelter, clothing and employment. The second type of dependency is more directly psychological, for the subordinate group, believing itself unable to cope with situations, relies for leadership and direction upon the dominant group, the subtypes including expertise, symbiotic and authoritarian forms. The third type within this dependency category constitutes a form of psychosocial disorganization, the first subtype characterized by individual or group disorganization (e.g. alienation, mental illness, alcoholism, drug addiction, divorce and other types of individual or group social disintegration), the second by anomie, which manifests itself in forms of self-destructive behavior, including suicide.

The major consequence of these diverse forms of dependency behavior was that individuals and groups, unable to adapt or cope (for whatever reasons) with the situation in which they found themselves, were virtually immobilized and prevented from developing their resources or mobilization capabilities. Indeed, given their structural or psychological state of dependency, Africans were relatively easily controlled by the dominant group. This dependency type of control proved more effective than coercive/reward techniques, but even dependency control had its limitations. That prompted development of more sophisticated forms of control.

The third category of psychosocial dominance, *thought control*, proved most effective. Under it, the superordinate proceeded to destroy the subordinate's cultural beliefs and identity, instilling within the African the belief that his own culture and even physical appearance were inferior to that of the superordinate. When this deculturation process is followed by the subordinate's acceptance of the dominant group's values as superior, the result is that he thinks and behaves like the superordinate. In so doing, he in effect says: 'I am only worthy when I am like you; my own identity is nothing; only in being like you can I be somebody.' In replacing his own cultural identity with that of the dominant group, the subordinate destroys his own identity. Thus, by identifying with the superordinate, the subordinate does not recognize his own exploitation and oppression. Rather, he sees the impoverished condition of his own people as the consequence of their being 'uncivilized,' concluding that that accounts for their wretched condition. When this process occurs, the dominant group has little need to use its coercive/reward powers to control the subordinate group, for they control themselves.

A dominant group maintains its control over others by diverse means, including structural and psychosocial techniques. It does not begin by rationally or deliberately employing these control devices; rather, they evolve historically in response to situations, the superordinate modifying and adapting new tactics when its power is threatened. Historically, whites in South Africa and Southern Rhodesia used diverse strategies for preserving their power. Following the Second World War, the character of white-black relations changed in both countries. Their power, privilege and way of life threatened by black nationalism, whites supported the National and Rhodesian Front parties who promised to preserve white hegemony. The methods they employed are described below.

II

Successful in their electoral bids, the Nationalists and Rhodesian Front modified structures and pursued new tactics to destroy African nationalism and power resources. In the postwar period especially, economic development and changing political circumstances contributed to the rise of black nationalism. Black resources and mobilization capabilities increased and, encouraged by the rise and success of anti-colonialism elsewhere, blacks protested against racial systems in the two countries.

Fearful that white power was endangered, Nationalist and Rhodesian Front parties contested the elections, warning that existing policies would lead to black majority rule. The influx of Africans into 'white' urban areas and their franchise demands would destroy 'white civilization,' Nationalists claimed, and only total racial separation, or apartheid, would protect white rule (Carter, 1962; Rhoodie, 1969; H. Adam, 1971a; Brotz, 1977). Similarly, the structural incorporation of black Rhodesians, accelerated by the country's participation in the Central

African Federation (1953-63), threatened white power. Basing its campaign on 'black peril' fears, the RF demanded new policies that would preserve European rule (Barber, 1967; Bowman, 1973). Elected in 1948 and 1962 respectively, the Nationalists and the Rhodesian Front moved quickly to secure white hegemony. They utilized existing legislation and structures where possible but pursued new policies as well. Given Afrikaner cultural beliefs, the Nationalists responded more vigorously in reshaping structures. Each, however, moved initially to blunt and then destroy African power resources.

South Africa
White dominance characterized race relations historically in South Africa. The National Party, however, envisaged apartheid as a fundamental modification of prior policies which rested on the partial segregation of races (Neame, 1962; Mansergh, 1962; Macmillan, 1963; Welsh, 1972, 1973). Historically, Britain had established African reserves as a means of control. Though Britain espoused the principle that 'civilized' Africans should have the right to vote, that right was severely circumscribed in the Cape and ignored in Natal, while the Afrikaners in the Orange Free State and Transvaal rejected African political participation. As President Reitz of the Orange Free State claimed in 1891, the Boers would 'maintain steadfastly, that there shall be no "equality" between the aborigines of South Africa' and Europeans either then or in the future (Welsh, 1972: 37). English settlers and the metropole professed that 'civilized' (i.e. anglicized) Africans should be accorded the same rights and opportunities as Englishmen, but even so the structural incorporation of educated Africans was restricted. A few Africans were granted the franchise; some, if westernized, moved upward within the economic sector; but few were accepted as equals in social relations (Van den Berghe, 1964; Neame, 1962).

Economically impoverished because of government policies, Africans sought employment in urban areas during the 1930s depression and the war years. There they encountered poor Afrikaners who likewise had fled the land, and the two groups competed for jobs.[2] Economic competition and black nationalism appeared as a direct threat to Afrikaner power and culture. Fear for their cultural survival was not new, for since British annexation of the Cape Afrikaners had been forced to rebuff Anglo assimilationist pressures. Afrikaner and African experiences were in some ways similar: both were moving from rural, more traditional ways of life into an urban, industrial setting in which the Anglo language and culture prevailed. For the Afrikaner, who viewed Africans as biologically inferior, the similarity in their condition and their juxtaposition in a competitive context created extreme stress. Apartheid offered salvation to the Afrikaner and his culture.

Fear for Afrikaner cultural survival motivated Nationalist politics (Rhoodie, 1969: 80, 100-9). Nationalists recognized that white-black relations were a power contest (ibid.: 81) and that blacks, if economically incorporated, would have a legitimate right to demand the vote. That would put them in the majority and threaten the Afrikaners' future (ibid.: 100, 105). Thus, as Rhoodie (ibid.: chs 4-5) suggests, apartheid and, later, separate development — with the geographical separation of the African homelands (the reserves or bantustans, as they were earlier called) from 'white' South Africa — was a logical outcome. The homelands would be established as 'independent' nations with close economic ties to South Africa (H. Adam, 1975, 1971a). This is precisely what has happened, with the granting of 'independence' to Transkei, Bophuthatshwana and Venda. Rhoodie (1969: 65) describes this relationship in the following terms:

> In White South Africa the Black worker will always be regarded as a temporary sojourner — a visitor — someone whose presence in the White areas is primarily motivated by his desire to sell his labor, but exercising his rights as a citizen within the geo-political jurisdiction of his ethnic homeland.

Initially, apartheid did not envision independence for the homelands, for Afrikaner leaders viewed them as dependencies still under direct government control. However, the Tomlinson Commission report (1956) warned that unless there was complete separation black political incorporation would lead to black majority rule (Rhoodie, 1969: chs 3-5). Hence Prime Minister Verwoerd's 1957 policy of homeland self-government under white guardianship was changed in 1959 to a policy calling for homeland independence. That was a radical step, Verwoerd acknowledged, but it was necessary if 'white South Africa' was to survive (ibid.: 67-8). As one Afrikaner spokesman indicated: 'We would rather choose a smaller South Africa with political power in the hands of Whites than a larger South Africa with political power in the hands of non-Whites' (ibid.: 84). Thereafter government policy was directed toward ridding South Africa of its homelands, leaving South

Africa composed of whites, coloreds and Indians. The blacks remaining within South Africa would be transients, migrant workers whose home and citizenship rights are in the homelands (H. Adam, 1975). South Africa continues to implement this strategy, and it is reflected in recent (1979-83) efforts to establish new political structures that include Europeans, coloreds and Asians but exclude Africans.

Afrikaner ideology has in part taken precedence over economic development and profit (Horwitz, 1967), as evident in the Physical Planning and Utilization of Resources Act (1967) which stipulates that future industrial development dependent upon African labor must be in the homeland border areas, thereby limiting the African influx into white urban areas. The importance of ideology is confirmed in a survey of Afrikaner elite (H. Adam, 1971c) who claimed that preservation of white power and beliefs should take precedence even if that meant sacrificing profits. However, the economy is built on unskilled (and, increasingly, semiskilled) black labor, and nearly 80 per cent of the manufacturing labor force is African (H. Adam, 1971a, 1975). Although Nationalist policy has attempted to restructure society and separate the blacks, lax implementation of apartheid policies, due in part to white desires to use blacks for maintaining white privilege, has undermined the implementation of apartheid (Brotz, 1977). Africans remain in white areas and are an integral part of the economy, apartheid having never been fully implemented.

The Nationalists modified *political structures* to curtail African power resources. Their goals have been: (a) to deprive blacks of political resources and power; (b) to establish black political substructures in the homelands that are indirectly white controlled or, later, with independence, cannot become antagonistic because of their economic dependence upon South Africa; and (c) to devise security measures that effectively silence white and black opposition.

Where previously Africans and coloreds were elected to the Cape Parliament, the Representation of Natives Act (1936) removed Africans from the common voter roll. Thereafter Africans could only elect whites to represent them in that body. On coming to power, Nationalists sought to remove both groups, but the Separate Representation of Voters Act (1951) was declared unconstitutional. Through a series of legislative and constitutional manoeuvers, the government ultimately succeeded, and coloreds and Africans were totally removed from white political structures in 1956 (Tatz, 1962; Carter, 1962; Brotz, 1977).

Deprived of parliamentary seats, both groups were deprived of an effective means of protesting against apartheid policies.

Africans, government claimed, were represented by tribal leaders in the reserves, where white administration has wavered historically between direct and indirect rule (Brookes, 1974). Under the Native Administration Act (1927), for example, the government accorded greater recognition to African custom and law (Welsh, 1972), but because the government was fearful that chiefs might become leaders in African nationalist movements, it limited their powers (ibid.: 45). From the Depression onwards Africans migrated to urban areas, and the Smuts government overlooked and, indeed, tolerated this gradual incorporation of Africans in the economic sector (Horwitz, 1967: ch. 17). This policy frightened Afrikaners, and once in power the Nationalists moved quickly to stop the influx and arrest the detribalization and westernization of Africans. The Bantu Authorities Act (1951) restored some of the powers of chiefs, established a hierarchical structure of tribal, regional and territorial authorities, and sought to re-establish African custom and law. Under the Native Laws Amendment Act (1957), the government provided additional support for African customs, cultures and the teaching of native languages, the Act's intent that of curtailing the westernizing influences that encouraged detribalization and, indirectly, black nationalism.

By emphasizing tribal, cultural and ethnic differences, the government sought to divide and separate African groups. Group diversity was encouraged as a means of undercutting black nationalist efforts to unite and solidify the African masses. Hence government policy was directed toward three goals: (a) the removal of Africans (and others) from white political structures, thereby curtailing effective means of opposition; (b) the fragmentation of African groups through the re-establishment of African customs and tribal life, the purpose that of curtailing the influence of western political ideas (e.g. democracy) and African mobilization efforts; and (c) the reintroduction of the authority of tribal leaders who could be easily manipulated and controlled by government. If, however, blacks remained part of South Africa, they could demand political rights. The Tomlinson report indicated the way to resolve that: granting 'independence' to the homelands. All blacks became citizens of those states, not of South Africa. They would be transient migrant workers in a 'white' South Africa, and as migrants they would have no political rights in South Africa.

The first major step toward implementation of separate development was the Bantu Self-Government Act (1959). It designated eight 'national units' or homelands; and blacks, as citizens with political rights in the homelands, lost their political rights within white South Africa. To accent tribal and cultural differences of the homelands (presaged in the 1957 Native Laws Amendment Act), the government initiated still other measures, including: the Urban Bantu Councils Act (1961) which established tribal 'ambassadors' who, acting on behalf of homelands chiefs, served as representatives for blacks in the white urban areas; the Bantu Investment Corporation Act (1958) and Bantu Homelands Development Corporation Act (1965), whose function it was to assist in the development of new industries along homeland borders; and the Physical Planning and Utilization of Resources Act (1967), which stipulated that future industrial development relying upon African labor must be near the homeland border areas. Some of these policies were geared toward homeland economic development, but the government allocated only limited funds for that purpose. Indeed, industry continued to develop in 'white' areas, attracting additional African migrant labor. In 1970 the government enacted the Bantu Homelands Act which gave Africans dual citizenship, as citizens of their homeland, exercising political rights there, and as citizens of the Republic of South Africa under international law. All of these measures were aimed at depriving blacks of their citizenship and political rights in South Africa (Horrell, 1973). Thereafter, the Transkei, Bophutathswana and Venda sought and obtained their independence. They, in turn, were followed by still others.

These policies, aimed at curtailing the Africans' power and depriving them of South African citizenship, created a flurry of opposition, white as well as black. The government responded with numerous 'security' measures. These included; the Suppression of Communism Act (1950), whereby the government could ban meetings and organizations or arrest those it claimed were communists (the term was broadly defined, and it also used the older Riotous Assembly Act for the same purpose); the Criminal Law Amendment Act (1953) which meted out severe penalties to those who broke the law as a means for protesting against other laws; the Public Safety Act (1953) whereby the Governor-General could claim a state of emergency and suspend all laws except elections and the functioning of Parliament, that allowing the government to rule by decree (applied during the 1960 disturbances); the Criminal Procedure

Act (1955) which allowed for detention without trial; the Unlawful Organizations Act (1955) which outlawed African political organizations, including the African National Congress (ANC) and the Pan African Congress (PAC), and gave the government authority to outlaw groups thought to be dangerous to the country; the Sabotage Act (1962) which defined sabotage so broadly that most political activity could be construed as falling under its definition, the individual arrested having to prove his innocence; the numerous Detention Acts (1963 and thereafter) which permitted the detention of individuals for periods of 90-180 days without trial; the establishment of a Publications Control Board (1963) for censorship purposes; the Terrorism Act (1967) which provides for unlimited detention or house arrest without trial; and the Prohibition of Political Interference Act (1968) which prohibits multiracial political parties and makes 'interference' by one racial group in the politics of another a punishable offense, thereby preventing whites and blacks from working together. Moreover, by withholding passports, applying administrative measures or other restrictions, and through the use of pass laws and influx control, the government has severely curtailed most organized opposition to its policies. In 1968 a Bureau of State Security, subsequently renamed, was established that brought other security branches under its control and gave the Bureau the right to forbid use in court trials of evidence it claimed would create a threat to state security. All of these measures along with others, curtailed the development by Africans and white opposition groups of resources and means for opposing government measures.

White and black opposition to National policies after 1960 was largely ineffective, but spontaneous black workers strikes in Durban in 1973, the 1976 Soweto riots, boycotts of schools by colored and African students and new industrial strikes during 1979 and 1980 demonstrate increased opposition to white rule. To placate some of these pressures, the government proposed constitutional revisions that would grant limited political power to coloreds and Indians (but not Africans) but not endanger white control. These proposals were rebuffed by the two communities, but the coercive powers available to the government indicate that it can preserve its position for an extended period of time regardless of internal and external pressures (Johnson, 1978; Adam and Giliomee, 1979).

Fears for the Afrikaners' cultural survival, exacerbated by increased black-white social contacts resulting from the blacks' economic incorporation and movement into urban areas, prompted Nationalists to move quickly following their election to revamp *social structures* and curtail racial contacts. The government moved in four broadly defined areas: (a) inter-personal relations; (b) social and spatial relations; (c) education; and (d) the cultural area.

White-black contacts throughout South Africa's history were usually of a superordinate-subordinate character. The Boer/Afrikaner, holding that Africans were biologically and culturally inferior, treated blacks accordingly. A major fear was that of miscegenation, particularly since sexual liaisons had occurred earlier. Numerous attempts were made historically to separate the races — pass laws, segregation in housing, immorality laws and other measures (Welsh, 1972; Neame, 1962; Swanson, 1968). Opposition to intergroup relations increased during the twentieth century, as evident in legislation: the Native Land Act (1913) demarcated African and European lands and living areas; the Native (Urban Areas) Acts of 1922 and 1930 delineated urban 'white areas' and controlled (through the use of a pass system) the influx of Africans into these areas; and the Native Trust and Land Act (1936) specified more fully the European and African areas. New measures enacted from the 1920s onwards restricted colored rights, and sexual liaisons between Europeans and Africans were prohibited in 1927.

Warning that prior measures were ineffective in protecting white purity, the Nationalists moved on still other fronts. Because some coloreds were 'passing' for whites, the government enacted new measures to terminate that. Under the Prohibition of Mixed Marriages Act (1949) marriage between whites and *all* nonwhite groups was prohibited. The Immorality Amendment Act (1950) outlawed extramarital sexual relations between whites and *all* nonwhites (only relations between Europeans and Africans were banned under the 1927 legislation). Finally, the Population Registration Act (1950) established racial categories, and individuals had to register their racial classification. That prevented coloreds from passing as whites or Africans passing as coloreds. The government was particularly concerned that coloreds passing for whites would 'contaminate' the latter (Henriques, 1974).

The government also sought to limit the public contacts of racial groups, doing so through legislation. It did so by building on previous legislation. The Native Land Act (1913), the Native Trust and Land Act (1936) and the Native (Urban Areas) Acts of 1922 and 1930 provided a basis for social segregation. Now the government enacted the Group Areas Act (1953) and Separate Amenities Act (1953). Under the former, residential areas were designated for specific groups (membership was determined by the Population Registration Act), and numerous individuals, particularly Cape Coloreds, were forced to move from 'white' areas. Natal in 1941 had tried unsuccessfully to isolate Indians, and now it succeeded. Under the Separate Amenities Act, parks, public toilets, post offices, railroads and other public amenities were segregated. Massive segregation became national policy, though efforts to segregate churches prompted opposition. Africans, viewed as transient workers whose homes were in the reserves, could reside in 'white' areas only if they had jobs and a legal pass book. Even their homes in such places as Soweto were regarded by the government as of a temporary nature, and the recent granting of leaseholds to residents was made contingent on their willingness to acknowledge their citizenship in the homelands.

Government measures to separate the racial groups were not always successful. Education, limited as it was, and westernization contributed to the acculturation, assimilation and acquisition by Africans of a common language (usually English) and culture, all of which forged a common identity among Africans. Early African education was in missionary schools, but that was terminated by the Nationalist government. In that manner government controlled the content of education, emphasizing African custom and tradition while de-emphasizing western culture and language. It accented traditional and technical training in place of an academic education, thereby limiting black skills and job opportunities. Funds for African education were also severely restricted. The emphasis on retribalization was underscored by the Native Laws Amendment Act (1957), described previously, and the Extension of University Education Act (1959) whereby the government took complete control of higher education, establishing separate white, black and Indian institutions. African universities were staffed with Afrikaners who could be trusted to implement the government's apartheid/separate development policies (K. Adam, 1971; Dickie-Clark, 1971). The government's allocation of educational funds favored whites. For example, by the 1970s, for every 100 rands allocated for white education, Indian education received 28, colored 26, and African education, six rands (Diamond, 1974). By controlling funds and curriculum, the government determined what skills each racial group would possess for work in the industrialized world. Few skills were taught to Africans, and they became part of the surplus, largely unskilled or semiskilled (and thereby readily interchangeable) migrant labor army competing for scarce jobs (Thomas, 1974; F. Wilson, 1972).

In the cultural sector, too, the government acted. Under the South African Citizenship Act (1949), immigration was restricted and citizenship requirements were tightened particularly for English immigrants, five years rather than two years required before they could acquire citizenship and the right to vote. By restricting English immigrant voting rights the government curtailed new voters who might support opposition political parties. The policy of accenting cultural and language differences among African groups impeded organizational efforts of African nationalists. Besides political and social structures, Nationalists utilized economic structures to curtail African power resources.

Political and social structures are significant, but it is through the *economic structures* and techniques that groups are most adeptly kept subordinate and dependent. Throughout the European era of South African history a fundamental concern of whites was whether or not Africans should be isolated or incorporated as cheap labor. Europeans opted for the second choice, and Africans were slowly incorporated within agricultural, mining, domestic and industrial sectors. All sectors, but particularly agriculture, mining and industry, prodded governments during the late nineteenth and early twentieth centuries to force reluctant Africans into the labor market. Government policies had by the 1930s contributed to the pauperization of Africans, and they were forced to work. During recessions or when employers sought to replace semiskilled white labor with cheaper black labor, white workers reacted violently. Fearing loss of their jobs, whites struck in 1913, 1914 and again in 1922, the latter Rand strike contributing to the Hertzog government's election in 1924. Similar efforts to replace white with black labor contributed to the 1948 National Party election, and it acted to protect white, especially Afrikaner, labor.

The Nationalists built on prior legislation to enhance the white (especially Afrikaner) economic position and resources while restricting the resources of blacks. The 1913 and 1936 legislation allocated to Europeans nearly 85 per cent of the country, including the most fertile lands. Forced to seek employment in the European sector, Africans were restricted in their opportunities. The government restricted African economic resources in three ways: (a) labor control, (b) work regulations and (c) protective measures for white labor.

Labor control measures included the earlier pass laws and control over African labor recruitment. The Nationalists stringently enforced or amended existing legislation, including, among others: the pass laws and influx control measures that restricted the movement of Africans in white areas; the Native Labor Regulation Act (1911) which prevented competition for African labor that would drive up wages; and the Native (Urban Areas) Acts of 1924 and 1930 which limited the number of Africans in urban areas and restricted occupations open to them.

Among the measures enacted or enforced that dealt with work regulations were: the various Masters and Servants Acts dating from the nineteenth century that set work conditions and narrowly defined the rights of domestic servants; the Native Labor Regulation Act (1911) which prohibited blacks from striking; and the Industrial Conciliation Act (1924) which established wage boards to settle disputes and determine wages of white labor. Blacks were excluded from its provisions, for they came under the Wages Act (1925) which set wages for unorganized African labor. The Native Services Contract Act (1932) compelled Africans to fulfill stipulations of any contracts they had previously signed or accepted. Other legislation protected whites from competing with nonwhite labor. The Mines and Work Act (1911), for example, restricted skilled jobs to Europeans, but during and after the First World War mine owners sought to hire and train Africans to replace semiskilled whites. That precipitated the 1922 Rand strike, where violence resulted in the death of 247 men. The strike contributed to Hertzog's 1924 election (in coalition with the Labor Party), and his government quickly enacted the Color Bar Act (1925) which reaffirmed the 1911 Act and restricted Africans from 'white' jobs. Meanwhile, Africans were impeded by the Apprenticeship Act (1922) which limited most apprenticeship programs to whites.

Nationalists built on this prior legislation, their main aim that of curtailing African economic power and resources and limiting their access to lower level positions. The most significant measures enacted were the Bantu Labor (Settlement of Disputes) Act (1953) and the Industrial Conciliation Act (1956), under which black unions were banned, strikes by Africans were prohibited and blacks were prevented from joining registered trade unions (Thomas, 1974; Horwitz, 1967: ch. 17). The purpose of these measures was to protect white workers from African competition. Although blacks constituted nearly 80 per cent of the manufacturing labor force by 1970 (H. Adam, 1975), most were unskilled or, at most, semiskilled, and without economic power. Given the shortage of white workers, employers resorted to the fragmentation of semiskilled jobs, employing black workers to occupy these fragmented positions while paying them at below-subsistence wages. Provided with limited education, often excluded from apprenticeship training programs, restricted mostly to unskilled positions as a consequence of legislation or white union opposition and job surveillance, denied the opportunity of developing skills and economic resources, and prohibited from striking or forming unions, Africans remained virtually powerless within economic structures.

Although strikes were illegal, African workers engaged in a series of wildcat strikes in Durban in 1973. They refused to appoint work committee leaders, fearful that they would be arrested. Instead, they demanded that employers and government negotiate with their homeland leaders to resolve the wage and work condition problems that prompted the strikes. Ultimately the strikes were resolved, but conditions improved very little (Institute for Industrial Education, 1974). Restrictions on the right of black workers to organize were later modified, but conditions changed little, and the 1979-80 period again witnessed a spate of strikes. Blacks remain at a decided disadvantage in the labor market (Leftwich, 1974).

Restricted in their ability to develop economic and other resources (except minimally) and prevented from effectively organizing, blacks remain subordinate. Separate development and homeland independence threaten blacks, for few of the homelands are economically viable and the government has neglected to allocate resources for developing them. Consequently, Africans must seek work in 'white' South Africa, and they and the homelands are trapped in a position of dependency. Rhoodie (1969: 65-6), a supporter of separate development, indirectly acknowledges the reality of this economic dependency:

> There are particularly two fundamental realities involved in the existing economic structure which are decisively determining the extent and tempo of the abovementioned reconstruction [independence for the homelands] scheme, viz the essential labor requirements of the White economy on the one hand, and on the other hand the inability of the Bantu areas to provide a decent economic existence for *all* their *de jure* inhabitants.

Viewed from the above perspective, the Nationalist government has used its control of political, economic and social structures to deprive Africans of power resources, enacting or implementing measures that have destroyed or curtailed African resources and mobilization capabilities. By utilizing the structures and techniques described, the Nationalists have managed to 'modernize racial domination' (H. Adam, 1971a). Even the constitutional incorporation of coloreds and Indians (but not Africans) are simply new tactics for preserving white power and privilege.

Rhodesia

In April 1980, ninety years after whites first trekked northward and settled in what later became Southern Rhodesia, elections were held in which power was turned over to Africans and the country was renamed Zimbabwe. Rhodesia whites were reluctant to see the change; indeed, they earlier unilaterally declared their independence from the British metropole (1965), endured through UN economic sanctions and fought a civil war to prevent the ascendancy of black power. The 1980 settlement and elections occurred only because South Africa, which provided extensive financial resources and war material for that war, withdrew its support. Earlier, in 1979, white Rhodesians agreed to establish a black puppet regime under the leadership of Bishop Abel Muzorewa, but in reality they retained power over that government. The civil war continued until South Africa quietly withdrew its support, though it could have prolonged the war. Rhodesia reluctantly acknowledged the necessity for a settlement.

During the preceding ninety years, whites, numbering less than five per cent of the population, held tenaciously to power. They devised a sophisticated racial system, and under the Rhodesian Front, first elected in 1962, Rhodesia 'managed to perfect its system of segregation and control without adopting the ideological baggage that accompanies the apartheid system in South Africa' (Bowman, 1973: 153). Except for the franchise and land apportionment, Rhodesia gave the appearance of being a multiracial society with 'non-racial' laws. However, as Palley (1966: 625) noted in terms of Rhodesian Front policies:

Much of Southern Rhodesian legislation is couched in non-discriminatory language and is applicable to all races. In practice however its main application is to the African population, as it results in

Africans either being subject to liabilities or unable to secure privileges whereas the majority of members of other races are not in practice subjected to the penal provisions of such measures or alternatively qualify for the privileges conferred by these Acts.

The result was that legislation adversely affected or subtly discriminated against Africans, be it in terms of land apportionment and use, commerce, education, employment or elsewhere (ibid.: 612-18). The RF adroitly manipulated existing legislation or enacted new measures to strengthen European power resources and circumscribe those of Africans (Palley, 1970a, 1970b).

Murray (1970: 370) concluded that the Rhodesian Front election and its subsequent policies went beyond 'a swing toward illiberalism' and represented the 'overturning of an established system.' Bowman (1973: 43) disagrees with that contention, arguing that the 'supposed shifts to the right' under the RF were simply reflections of 'that enduring demand that political control remain in white hands.' For him, the RF election was part of a 'continual process of white reassessment (in the context of the times) of what was needed to protect white rule' (ibid.). What is clear is that during the Central African Federation period (1953-63), black structural incorporation and black nationalism heightened white fears for their group survival, and they supported the Rhodesian Front when it promised to preserve white power and privilege. The incumbent United Federal Party exacerbated white fears, for during the 1962 election its spokesmen alluded to the possibility of broadening the structural incorporation of Africans. Subsequent UFP policies would have moved the country toward the 'British West Indian model' of black-white relations, but the electorate and certainly the Rhodesian Front embraced views and, later, policies that shifted the country toward the 'South African model.'[3] In that sense, Murray's assessment is perhaps closer to reality.

At no point during Federation did more than a few Southern Rhodesian whites support the principle of black majority rule. Indeed, a persistent theme of opposition party politics historically was the demand for greater protection of white rule (Henderson, 1972: Wetherell, 1974). White support for the Federation was based on that principle, the union of Southern and Northern Rhodesia and Nyasaland perceived as the best means for buttressing white rule (Henderson, 1972; Rogers and Frantz, 1962). When federation failed to fulfill that objective, white Southern Rhodesians searched for alternatives, rallying first behind the Dominion party which lost the 1958 elections and then the Rhodesian Front, which won in 1962. Whites viewed themselves as a racial group under siege, fighting for their survival (Leys, 1959: ch. 8; Clegg, 1960: 119-47). In 1961 they supported a new constitution that granted Africans greater representation, but virtually precluded black rule. Thereafter, when the UFP proposed giving Africans greater power, whites expressed their fears by supporting the Rhodesian Front. Continued RF victories in subsequent years transformed Rhodesia into what was virtually a one-party state.

The RF manipulated *political structures* to arrest black power and curtail black political incorporation. New legislation was not immediately necessary, for the RF realized it could utilize existing legislation and structures to achieve some of its goals. Subsequent structural changes, though, were necessary. One of the government's first moves was to withdraw from the Federation, a separation that it managed on terms highly favorable to the country's economy. Thereafter the RF took two additional major steps to protect white power and privilege: first, it declared its independence from Britain (UDI) in 1965, and second, it established a new constitution in 1969. It pursued other measures as well, but these were the most important. It also effectively applied existing security measures and legislation to arrest the development of African nationalism. Where South Africa's apartheid/separate development constituted a new society going far beyond previous segregation policies, the Rhodesian Front was caught between two alternatives: (a) that of curtailing black nationalism and power resources on a pragmatic basis, hoping to retain white rule without too many changes, or (b) that of pursuing the South African model and ideology. What it did was opt for elements of both.

The RF's initial efforts were directed toward immobilizing black nationalism and solidifying white control. During federation blacks moved upward in federal structures and increased their power resources. The RF sought to reverse this process. It moved to re-establish complete control over the political system, claiming that whites should control policy-making and administration because they were more knowledgeable about and 'concerned with making the important decisions about the resources, the investment of capital, the allocation of rewards for labor, and the access to life chances' (Mitchell, 1970: 317). The group that made these decisions could determine the distribution of power resources to itself and others. To accomplish its goal the RF enacted measures that appeared 'non-racial' but in practice strengthened their power while undermining that of Africans.

The 1961 Constitution retained power in the hands of whites, but the fact that blacks could possibly gain power under it someday threatened whites. So remote was that possibility, though, that black nationalists earlier opposed the constitution and pressured Africans into boycotting the 1962 elections.[4] Following UDI, the government in 1965 modified the constitution and changed procedures for its amendment (Palley, 1966: 751), but there remained the possibility that Africans could someday become the majority party. The RF soon removed that possibility.

Under the 1969 Constitution, the new House of Assembly included 50 Europeans and 16 African representatives. If Africans ever reached the point where they paid one-half or more of the total income tax, the Constitution stipulated that they could have equal (but never more) representation with whites. The possibility of Africans reaching parity was a chimera, for the white government, by controlling legislation and economic structures, could restrict African economic opportunities and prevent Africans from ever paying half of the total income tax (Bowman, 1973: 137-8). The government devised still other measures to restrict the power and opportunity of blacks. The RF claimed that it supported the non-racial principle and 'civilized standards' whereby people were judged on the basis of 'merit.' However, given the restrictions on African educational and employment opportunities, few could meet those 'merit' criteria. Some blacks were incorporated into higher ranks of the civil service and military during the federation period, but the RF terminated that policy. Africans were also disfranchised from local politics through stipulations in the Municipal Town Management and the Land Apportionment Acts (Palley, 1966: 625).

The Rhodesian Front utilized its control over Africans in the reserves (Tribal Trust Lands) and security measures to curtail African power resources. Historically, the government retained tight control over African reserves, 'native' or district commissioners exercising broad powers over tribal chiefs. Two approaches were used to control Africans: (a) that of designating and educating as leaders or spokesmen for their people a few blacks who remained subservient to whites or (b) that of upholding African tribal systems and placing power in the hands of the chiefs, thereby counteracting the development of African nationalism. Under Federation the government pursued the former policy, but the Rhodesian Front opted for the latter. By supporting the tribal chiefs (who were also given representation in Parliament under the 1969 Constitution), tribalism and African culture, the RF pursued a policy similar to that of the National Party in South Africa. Both governments sought to stop detribalization, curtail westernization, restrict the development of African power resources and retain tight control over the reserves (ibid.: Part I, ch. 14; Part II, ch. 5; Barber, 1967: 231-6). Tribal chiefs were accorded greater authority, but ultimate power rested with the district commissioner and the government. As in South Africa, the RF government acquired control over African education. In 1971 it assumed responsibility for missionary primary schools, but missionary groups continued to operate most African secondary schools. Through its control of curriculum, teachers and educational funds, the government shaped education in a manner that restricted the African's acquisition of resources, thereby limiting his employment opportunities and political resources.

Government policies were met by black and white opposition. Strikes, demonstrations and black nationalism threatened white control even prior to the advent of the Rhodesian Front. Governments responded by enacting security measures, including, among others: the Subversive Activities Act (1950) which enabled the government to ban meetings, prohibit or confiscate publications of 'subversive' groups, and establish a security police force; the Public Order Act (1955) under which individuals could be detained or restricted without charge or trial; the Native Affairs Amendment Act (1959) which prohibited public meetings in the reserves unless approved by the district commissioner, thereby hampering nationalist efforts to recruit members; the Unlawful Organization Act (1959, 1962) whereby groups considered a 'threat' to the country could be banned and their members arrested; the Preventive Detention (Temporary Provisions) Act (1959, 1964) whereby individuals considered a threat to public order could be detained; the Law and Order (Maintenance) Act (1960) and subsequent amendments which allowed for the banning of meetings, censorship of publications and search and arrest without warrant; and the Emergency Powers Act (1965) which provided for summary arrest and detention without trial. Other measures were also enacted, and the 1969 Constitution legalized the detention and restriction of individuals in the name of public order and safety.

Most of this legislation was enacted before the Rhodesian Front's election, but it systematically applied these measures to curb dissent. Following the Second World War, support for African nationalist movements came from urban workers, but they were joined by African farmers angered by the Land Husbandry Act (1951), a measure aimed at conservation which rural blacks considered discriminatory toward them rather than European farmers. Boycotts, strikes, demonstrations and riots prompted earlier as well as Rhodesian Front governments to clamp down on nationalist activities, and African leaders were arrested and detained and their organizations banned (Shamuyarira, 1965). By these measures the government attempted to curtail the development of African nationalism (Bowman, 1973: ch. 3).

Despite economic sanctions imposed following UDI, Rhodesia managed to survive. Indeed sanctions appeared to strengthen the resolve of whites who, perceiving themselves as a group under siege, transformed their economy into one that was largely self-sufficient, aided by South Africa which provided considerable support (ibid.: ch. 5). With many of their leaders detained or in exile, nationalist groups turned increasingly from 1973 onwards to guerrilla warfare as the only means of toppling the racial regime. The war escalated following abortive attempts to negotiate a settlement especially during the 1975-7 period; and, with their leaders released from detention and outside the country, the nationalists pursued their war more aggressively. Britain, whose numerous earlier efforts to negotiate a settlement had failed, succeeded in 1980, assisted indirectly by pressures from the Front Line States (on the guerrillas) and South Africa (on Rhodesia).

Rhodesia, in contrast to South Africa, did not opt for apartheid, but it did use its *social structures* to establish a segregated society. There was the elimination of some segregation during federation, but the Rhodesian Front reversed these developments. Rhodesian policy can be assessed by focusing on four areas: (a) interpersonal relations, (b) social relations, (c) education and (d) cultural integration. In contrast to South Africa, Rhodesia did not prohibit mixed marriages or sexual relations between the races, but the Rhodesian Declaration of Rights exempted laws relating to marriage from prohibitions against discrimination, and it could have introduced a prohibition of mixed marriages act similar to that of South Africa (Palley, 1966: 574). Nor did it enact a population registration act, but various legislative measures did define the rights or restrictions applying to specific groups, e.g. prohibitions against Africans, coloreds and others living in European areas. Rhodesia's major means for imposing racial rules was to leave municipalities free to determine their own rules for governing racial contact situations. The municipalities, then, enacted segregatory measures. The end result was similar to that in South Africa, but the Rhodesian government could claim that it did not sponsor racially discriminatory legislation.

Legislation established the pattern for social relations in Rhodesia. The Land Apportionment Act (1930) designated European and African areas, and numerous pass laws and the Native Registration Acts (1936, 1957) controlled the movement of Africans within European areas. Coming to power, the RF stringently enforced these measures. Under the Municipal Amendment Act (1967), it granted considerable autonomy to communities to determine policy concerning group contact situations. Communities responded by segregating local swimming pools, public places and amenities, recreation, athletic events and public conveniences (ibid.: 612-28). These local pressures for reimposing segregation, aided and abetted by the government, surfaced following the RF election. The government quietly terminated the incorporation of Africans into all but low level positions in the civil service, and, in Salisbury and elsewhere African professionals and businesses were ousted from European business areas. The Land Tenure Act (1969) prohibited Africans in European areas; and the 1969 Constitution and Declaration of Rights, as Palley (ibid.: 584) notes, had 'no provision prohibiting private discrimination in places to which the public resort.' Thus, business establishments had the 'right to serve' whom they pleased, a convenient technique for discriminating against non-European groups. In 1971 a Residential (Property Owners) Protection Act was introduced in Parliament but never enacted. The law was unnecessary, Palley (ibid.: 637-42) concluded, for Asians and coloreds were prevented from purchasing or living in homes within European areas by restrictive racial covenants written into most property deeds. These covenants were enforceable in the courts. Africans were excluded from living in European areas by the Land Tenure Act. Moreover, Asians or coloreds who tried to move into European areas were blocked by local property owners who appealed to the courts to rebuff their moves (*Rhodesia Herald*, 12 January 1976).

Historically, as indicated previously, the government ignored African education, and African primary and secondary schools were operated primarily by missionary groups. The government criticized their academic content, claiming that Africans should be given technical or vocational training instead. Only in 1971 did the government assume control of most primary schools, thereby gaining control over curriculum, teachers and the funds allocated to African schools. Some of the African secondary schools were also taken over, but the university remained a multiracial institution.

By emphasizing tribalism, tradition and African custom, be it in schools or elsewhere, the RF, as the South African government, tried to prevent the detribalization and westernization of Africans. Two factors motivated this policy: first, it would mean that there were fewer 'civilized' (i.e. westernized) Africans who would demand structural incorporation based on merit; and second, tribalism splintered African groups and impeded the development of African nationalism. Despite these measures, economic development and white labor shortages, resulting when whites were called to military duty from 1977 onwards, necessitated the recruitment of black labor. That led to the limited structural incorporation and acquisition of economic skills and resources by Africans.

Discrimination against Africans within *economic structures* was pervasive but more subtle in Rhodesia than in South Africa. As Murphree (1973: 7) notes, legal discrimination was more apparent in franchise and land apportionment than in employment policies. Over the years, land policies clearly contributed to the pauperization and 'proletarianization' of the peasant African (Arrighi, 1967, 1970). The African's economic condition was largely the consequence of his being undertrained, unskilled, underpaid and underemployed — all of which led to 'cumulative economic underprivilege' (Murphree, 1975: 259). The exodus of Africans from the land during the Depression and war years and the postwar influx of white immigrants reduced job opportunities and repressed wages for Africans, prompting the postwar wave of strikes. The Land Husbandry Act (1951), which imposed cattle destocking and land conservation measures, economically harmed Africans and deprived them of resources (Bowman, 1973: 45; Moyana, 1974; Shamuyarira, 1965: ch. 5). Other agricultural measures also discriminated against Africans. The land apportionment acts restricted the land available for their use; some African purchase lands were withdrawn and made part of the national reserves; and government marketing policies controlling agricultural sales of cattle and produce discriminated in favor of European farmers (Palley, 1966: 617-20).

Africans could not purchase lands in the European sector, but Europeans could establish 'non-racial' areas (for the purpose of development) within African reserves under the Tribal Trust Land Development Corporation Act (1968). Thus, government policy before and especially after the advent of the RF government impeded agricultural and resource development by Africans (Dunlop, 1974).

Government economic policy and practice had the cumulative effect upon Africans of (a) restricting their acquisition and development of economic skills and resources and (b) impeding the mobilization and organization of their members to demand better wages and benefits. Historically, Rhodesia 'possessed a web of coercive labor legislation, designed to regulate the mobility of [black] labor and stabilize employment under contract' (Van Onselen, 1973: 245). This legislation included pass laws, regulations compelling fulfillment of labor contracts, and measures that restricted the jobs available to Africans. Domestic servants, who constituted the second largest African labor group, remained under control of a Masters and Servants Act that severely restricted their rights. African labor had few organizational rights. The Industrial Conciliation Act (1934), for instance, did not apply to them, and they were excluded from its bargaining stipulations, whites being granted a *de facto* monopoly over skilled jobs. The law also integrated white unions into the negotiating machinery but ignored Africans who, as a consequence, were forced to accept whatever wages their employers paid.

Strikes during the 1950s precipitated enactment of a new Industrial Conciliation Act (1959). Classified as 'non-racial,' the bill incorporated Africans but did so in a manner that restricted their organizational powers and resources. Unions were ordered to organize on a vertical basis within each industry, incorporating all workers, black as well as white. That prevented blacks from establishing a horizontal union encompassing all their unskilled workers. Instead, they were incorporated within white-controlled unions where voting power was vested in the skilled (almost totally white) workers. Labor leaders were interested in gaining benefits for their skilled white workers and preventing blacks from taking over 'white' jobs. Agricultural and domestic workers, unskilled and black, were excluded from the provisions of the Act. Restricted by pass laws, land apportionment acts and the African (Urban Areas) Act from living in European centers, blacks had to live in areas located long distances from their work. As a consequence, they spent a disproportionate share of their limited wages for transportation, and that, along with low wages, severely curtailed their economic resources.

When it came into power the Rhodesian Front sought to restrict even further the use of Africans within the labor force. It did so by recruiting immigrant European labor to fill vacant skilled and semi-skilled jobs. During the federation period Africans were recruited for higher positions within government and the railway, but the RF terminated these programs. The RF enacted two other measures aimed at restricting African opportunities and resources. Under the Apprentice-ship Training Act (1968), an individual desirous of qualifying as a journeyman had to participate in an approved apprenticeship training program. But he had to persuade a prospective employer to accept him as an apprentice, and white employers, fearful of repercussions from white employees, seldom accepted black apprentices. Rather, they pressured government into seeking foreign white immigrants who could be trained. However, as white immigration declined and the war esca-lated, employers were forced to recruit black apprentices. Under a 1971 amendment to the Industrial Conciliation Act strikes that 'prejudice the public interest' were prohibited. This was used especially against blacks (Harris, 1974). If they attempted to strike, or struck illegally, labor leaders could be arrested and prohibited from holding union office again. That impeded the organizational activities of black work-ers. Over the years, by controlling economic structures and restricting their skill acquisition and job opportunities, the government kept Africans in an economically subordinate position.

Thus in both countries, South Africa and Rhodesia, white governments maintained control by curtailing the power resources of African groups. This they accomplished by manipulating political, economic and social structures to their own advantage, and devising policies that prevented Africans from developing their resources and mobilization capabilities. Security measures and coercive powers were employed to stifle protest and opposition. Through these techniques and devices white govern-ments modernized and preserved their racial dominance systems. Power factors, not changes in white attitudes, brought about the transformation to black rule in Rhodesia; and changing power relation-ships within South Africa now compel the National Party to pursue new measures as it seeks to preserve its racial dominance system.

Increased threat and stress transforms white South Africans into believing they are a group under siege, and that influences their perceptions and responses to the threat.

Chapter 6
Race and ethnicity: the emergence of siege groups and cultures

I

Most states are multinational or multigroup in character, composed of diverse ethnic, racial, cultural and other groups. These distinctions are muted in some societies, but elsewhere they influence and shape inter-group relations (West, 1972). Group differences surface particularly in the political arena, for it is there that crucial allocative decisions are made concerning the distribution of power, privilege and resources (Katznelson, 1972). Group characteristics, including, among others, race, ethnicity and culture, serve as the major criteria by which benefits and opportunities are allocated in 'plural' societies (Rabushka and Shepsle, 1972).

Plural society 'theory,' whether in fact theory or simply a classifi-catory scheme, posits group factors as the primary determinant of political behavior (Cross, 1971; Cox, 1971; Rabushka and Shepsle, 1972). Likewise, political conflict precipitates or sharpens group cleavages as participants contest to protect or enhance their position within society. Although these factors may not be significant initially in intergroup encounters, they become so when there is a contest for power, for group power differentials generally determine the rates of access to and incorporation within society's political, economic and social structures. Control of these structures determines who makes the distributive policy decisions thereafter (Lenski, 1966).

Numerous factors, as suggested in Chapter 1, account for the emerg-ence of group identity, that identity serving as one basis for people's behavior. A given group, whether its 'history' is real or myth, sees itself as sharing common attributes, traditions, unique experiences and modes of behavior, all of which distinguish its 'culture' or 'way of life' (DeVos, 1972). A group that so identifies itself acknowledges that specific attributes isolate it ('we') from others ('they') (Blumer, 1958). For a subordinate group, awareness and identification often occur when it recognizes that its distinctive attributes account for the differential and discriminatory treatment that it suffers (Enloe, 1973). Increased awareness of group identity may also occur in the case of a dominant group, the process initiated when its power or privilege are threatened. In either case, be it dominant or subordinate, the group mobilizes its resources and members to safeguard or enhance its wellbeing (Lenski, 1966; Blalock, 1967; Coleman, 1971).

There are situations where individuals or groups willingly discard their own culture and way of life for another, but most hold tenaciously to their group identity. Indeed, threats to its cultural survival usually heighten and intensify a group's awareness and solidarity (DeVos, 1972; Smelser, 1963: chs 9-10). When a group perceives its culture or way of life threatened, it will react in a defensive, often aggressive fashion, be it in a dominant or subordinate position (Gusfield, 1966). This mobilization process can transpire rapidly or evolve slowly, and in the process the group may transform itself into a 'value-oriented movement' (Smelser, 1963: ch. 10) which seeks to protect, restore or establish a society based on its generalized beliefs. These beliefs, defined rather amorphously initially, are thereafter sharpened and refined, assuming the characteristics of an ideology or 'belief system' (Rokeach, 1960).

The threatened group envisions a society based on its values and belief system. Depending upon society's structural arrangements and the group's power capabilities vis-a-vis the threatening group(s), the besieged group will pursue strategies it believes will protect its culture and way of life. The selection process is not always rational, for groups are swayed by emotions and stress, and conditions may be such that the options available are limited. The belief system that evolves: (a) articulates contrast conceptions which distinguish it ('we') from the threatening group ('they'); (b) serves for strengthening group solidarity in the face of perceived threats; and (c) provides a rationale or justification for mobilization efforts and group actions. The greater the perceived threat, the greater the probability the belief system of the beleagured group will become dogmatic and 'closed' (Rokeach, 1954, 1960). This 'hardening' or polarization of beliefs is reflected behaviorally by increasingly rigid and dogmatic group responses.

For purpose of illustration, the emergence and response of four specific siege groups are traced during different historical periods: white Southerners in the United States prior to and following the Civil War; Afrikaners in South Africa; white Rhodesians; and French Canadians. Different historical factors accounted for the emergence of these as siege groups, but somewhat comparable threat or stress-inducing factors transformed them into value-oriented movements. For analytical purposes, two types of siege groups are distinguished: siege cultures and racial siege groups. In reality, all were or are siege cultures, for each believed its culture and way of life were threatened. But for analytical purposes the distinction helps isolate two distinct types of threats that confronted two of the groups, white Southerners and Afrikaners: first, the presence of a competing dominant culture (the industrial North in the US; Anglo settler and British metropole in South Africa) whose assimilationist pressures threatened the cultural identity and survival of these two groups; and second, political and economic developments that threatened the racial dominance systems that protected the power, privilege and cultural identity of both groups. These two factors, lumped together in most analyses, should be separated.

Three of the groups were *siege cultures* whose way of life was threatened by the dominant cultural group: white Southerners, Boer-Afrikaners and French Canadians. White Southerners evolved a plantation-style society based in part on slavery, but they also considered their agrarian style of life as sharply different from the urban, industrial Northern culture that threatened to destroy Southern culture. Their culture and slavery threatened, white Southerners were transformed into a siege culture and a racial siege group. Both the English in South Africa and the British metropole viewed the Boer-Afrikaner culture as inferior. Consequently, they tried to anglicize Boer-Afrikaners and force them to discard their own language and culture. These assimilationist pressures, taken in conjunction with their defeat in the war, transformed Boer-Afrikaners into a siege culture. Their cultural identity, threatened initially by Anglo assimilationist pressures, was later threatened by the emergence of black groups demanding political power, that threat transforming Afrikaners into a racial siege group as well. In Canada, English settlers and the British metropole pursued similar assimilationist policies aimed at anglicizing the French. Consequently, French Canadians became a siege culture, responding defensively initially in the nineteenth century and again more recently to protect their cultural identity. The initial response of all three siege cultures was to turn inward, toward agrarianism or an agrarian *laager*, to deflect assimilationist pressures. Later, however, new strategies were employed. Two considered or attempted secession (white Southerners and French Canadians) while the other, the Afrikaners, realizing they constituted a political majority within the South African voting context, mobilized their members and in 1948 wrested political power from the prevailing Afrikaner-English coalition government. That victory catapulted nationalist Afrikaners into political power, after which they seceded from the Commonwealth, thereby assuring protection of Afrikaner culture.

The emergence of the three *racial siege groups*, white Southerners, Afrikaners and white Rhodesians, was precipitated by events that threatened the power, privilege and way of life each enjoyed under a racial dominance system. White Southerners were transformed into a racial siege group by a series of events, including, among others, a gradual loss of political and economic power to Northern states, their subordinate economic position, the Abolitionist movement, Lincoln's election and the possible termination of slavery. Boer-Afrikaners were transformed into a racial siege group by other factors: English and metropole assimilationist pressures, the Anglo-Boer War and a gradual economic incorporation of Africans that encouraged black demands for political rights under Afrikaner-English coalition governments and threatened nationalist Afrikaners. The 1948 National Party electoral victory, followed by implementation of apartheid policies, curtailed African political power, protected the Afrikaners' cultural identity and assured Afrikaners that racial privileges they enjoyed would continue. Likewise, black political demands for power under the Central African Federation (1953-63) threatened the racial privileges of white Southern Rhodesians. Consequently, they supported the Rhodesian Front, and its unilateral declaration of independence (1965) prevented the British metropole from imposing a black government on the country, thereby preserving white power and privilege.[1]

Each of these groups at some historical period believed its culture or group identity and way of life were threatened. Each mobilized its members and resources to pursue strategies aimed at assuring its cultural or group survival. Each became a value-oriented movement. The strategies each pursued were based on its assessment of structural and situational factors as well as the power capabilities of itself and the group(s) threatening its existence. Where siege groups perceived societal structures as detrimental to their group survival, they demanded structural changes. If unsuccessful in their efforts, siege groups threatened secession or war (e.g. the Civil War, the Anglo-Boer War, Rhodesia's UDI and, more recently, Quebec's secessionist threats). Fears for their cultural extinction, whether the consequence of assimilationist pressures or racial factors (or both), transformed these groups into value-oriented movements. Each group's belief system assumed more dogmatic characteristics as the perceived threats to the group's existence increased, and this influenced group behavior and policies (Rokeach, 1960: chs 17-21).

The value-oriented movement, as Smelser (1963: 83) suggests, envisions 'the reconstitution of a threatened value system,' i.e. it seeks to restore, protect or restructure a situation where a group's core values (particularly assumptions about human nature which determine social hierarchies and relationships) are threatened. The movement gains impetus when 'alternative means for reconstituting the social situation are perceived as unavailable' (ibid.: 325), and it posits values by which existing society is measured and criticized. Moreover, these values or beliefs serve as a basis for recruiting and indoctrinating members, and the group's policies and actions derive from its belief system.

Numerous factors determine the direction, the parameters and the success or failure of value-oriented movements. Among these factors are (ibid.: chs 1-3): (1) structural determinants, including the system's willingness (or unwillingness) to let the group mobilize resources and members in pursuit of its goals; (2) structural strains, most importantly those that lead a siege group to believe its culture is threatened, be these strains the consequence of government or other group actions (e.g. assimilationist policies); (3) the success or failure of the siege group's ideology and policies in mobilizing and solidifying supporters to defend or establish the 'new' society; (4) precipitating factors which, like structural strains, threaten and force the group into a defensive position; (5) strategies utilized by the siege group to protect itself, the success or failure of its strategies shaping subsequent group actions; and (6) dominant group social control measures that facilitate or impede siege group mobilization efforts.

A siege group's belief system must also be taken into account, for it is threats to a group's belief system that transform a group into a value-oriented movement. A belief system is a cognitive system that includes all beliefs, values, expectations, hypotheses and assumptions (whether conscious or unconscious, true or untrue) that an individual or group accepts as true about the world and people (Rokeach, 1960: chs 1-4). A belief system is a cognitive state 'which mediates objective reality within the person' (Rokeach, 1954: 194), and it determines how an individual or group perceives, assesses and judges the world, events, situations and experience. Belief systems are composed of two inter-dependent components, beliefs and disbeliefs, i.e. a system of beliefs that one accepts and 'a *series* of systems that one rejects' (Rokeach, 1960: 32). These can be analyzed in terms of their cognitive *content* or *structure*, and both can be measured by the degree to which they are 'open' or 'closed' (i.e. in terms of content, by the individual's receptivity to or rejection of contradictory beliefs; in terms of structure, by the individual's willingness to tolerate ambiguity and the degree of rigidity evident in his thinking processes and problem-solving capabilities).

The person with a closed belief system is characterized by dogmatism and rigidity, dogmatism reflected in his intolerance of beliefs other than his own. The *degree* of dogmatism and rigidity will vary in individuals and groups dependent on other factors discussed below, the degree expressible on a continuum ranging from 'open' to 'closed.' If the dogmatic individual or group has power, there is the probability that contradictory or competing beliefs will be prohibited or proponents punished and silenced. Rigidity refers to how a person perceives, thinks, learns and confronts or solves specific tasks and problems. This, too, can be expressed in the form of a continuum or scale. The rigid person displays limited flexibility in thinking and perceptions, and the world is generally viewed in absolutes of black or white. Nuances or ambiguities are neither recognized nor acknowledged, and the person cannot tolerate ambiguity. The greater the stress or threat that confronts an individual or group, the greater the probability that dogmatism in beliefs and rigidity and intolerance in thinking processes will result. Belief systems are held consciously or unconsciously, but stress and threat generally bring them into sharper focus. How individuals or groups respond to stress situations is influenced by the content and structure of their belief system, but stress or threat situations can decidedly influence the character (i.e. in terms of being open or closed) of belief systems (ibid.: chs 1-4).

Threats to a group's culture or power and privilege initiates a series of processes, each acting upon the other. This 'value-added process'

(Smelser, 1963), when taken in conjunction with the factors previously noted, shapes the character of an emergent siege culture. Smelser's analysis of strains and structures partly explains a siege group's emergence and development, a process that gains clarity when Smelser's analysis is taken in conjunction with Rokeach's (1960) analysis of belief systems and Festinger's (1957) cognitive dissonance theory as applied by Geschwender (1968). Together, these provide a clearer explanation below of how diverse factors precipitate siege group formation and behavior.

Whatever the precipitating factors, siege group beliefs are sharpened when the group perceives its beliefs threatened. As Geschwender indicates, when obvious inconsistencies occur between a group's belief system and conditions under which the group lives, or where conditions contradict or threaten the group's cultural beliefs, cognitive dissonance results, creating tension or threat for the individual or group. Incongruities (or dissonance) are difficult to live with, and the group seeks to reduce the dissonance or tension. One way is to discard or alter the group's beliefs to fit the situation; another is to alter the situation; while a third is to ignore the incongruity between beliefs and reality. The tenacity with which a group holds to its beliefs suggests that it will attempt to alter the situation or conditions rather than its beliefs. However, if such changes are impossible, the structural strains threaten the group's cognitive wellbeing. Since the strains cannot be ignored, group dissonance and the impossibility of altering conditions or the system leads the group to see itself as a culture under siege, i.e. its beliefs are threatened. Unable to change structures or situations, the group pursues alternative strategies. Dependent upon the degree to which the system permits, the group becomes a value-oriented movement bent on the 'reconstitution of a threatened value system' (Smelser, 1963: 83). Or, as Geschwender (1968: 133) suggests: 'One means of reducing this dissonance is to alter the environment so as to produce the desired state of affairs. Thus, dissonance-reducing activities often take the form of social protest or revolutionary behavior.' In this manner Geschwender bridges the gap between strains, belief systems, dissonance theory and the dynamics which transform a threatened group into a value-oriented or siege group.

The extremes to which threatened groups will go to protect their group or cultural identity are evident in the four siege groups: white Southerners, Afrikaners, white Rhodesians and French Canadians. All risked secession or possible war to protect their cultural identity. Southerners perceived themselves as a culture under siege prior to the Civil War, and postwar events reinforced their perceptions. Afrikaners, fearing anglicization, opted for war and lost, but altered political circumstances momentarily abated their fears. Later, however, their cultural and racial fears were exacerbated, and they turned to the National Party to protect their group identity. White Southern Rhodesians, their power, privilege and cultural identity threatened by an emergent black nationalist movement, risked war when it opted for UDI in 1965. Elsewhere, threatened by Anglo assimilationist pressures and denied equal economic opportunity even within their own province, French Canadians became a siege culture. Winning the 1976 provincial elections, the Parti Quebecois initiated a series of steps, their ultimate goal secession and establishment of an independent French Canada. The factors that transformed these four into siege groups are traced below.

II

Two distinct phases and a third, less clear, are discernible in the evolution of white Southerners as a siege culture and racial siege group. The first is the period leading up to the Civil War; the second, Reconstruction to the First World War; and the third, the period following the Second World War. Only the first two are considered here. In terms of the siege culture/racial siege group distinctions: both factors were operant in the pre-Civil War period; both were evident although the racial siege group characteristics were most pronounced during the late nineteenth century; and again racial siege group factors were most pervasive following the Second World War.

Historically, siege culture and racial siege group characteristics intermingled in the pre-Civil War period. Early American colonists, North and South, generally shared a common English heritage and culture, but a subsequent cultural bifurcation occurred, the consequence of political, economic and demographic factors. The major structural factor that accounted for the emergence of a white Southern siege culture was the political system. Earlier as separate colonies and later under the federal Constitution, Southern states retained slavery although importation of new slaves was prohibited after 1807. Federal legislation and court decisions protected the South's 'peculiar institution,' and Southern politicians in the national (metropole) government effectively blocked legislation that threatened slavery or their agrarian way of life. Even so, strains resulted from the controversies concerning slavery's possible extension to new territories that generated Southern fears and forced them to reassess their political position.

Initially there existed a North-South power parity, a parity that was maintained by the simultaneous admission of equal members of new slave and free states. However, the massive influx of immigrants primarily into the industrializing northern states convinced Southerners that free states would eventually outnumber slave states and destroy the power parity. The North's control of the country's economy further convinced Southerners that they would ultimately become subordinate economically and that the North would use its economic and political power to abolish slavery and Southern agrarianism. Added to this was another factor: an emergent Southern belief that its values, deriving from their agrarian-based society (and analytically separable from the slavery factor), were threatened by the increasingly commercial, industrial and urban culture of the North. This cultural bifurcation increased during the decades prior to the Civil War. Slavery was part of Southern culture, but had it *not* been present the North-South agrarian-urban cultural distinction would have remained.

Economic strains surfaced early. The North developed as the nation's financial, commercial and industrial center; and the South, remaining an agrarian/plantation-slave society, quickly recognized its economic dependency. Its reliance upon Northern capital and industry increased following enactment of the 1828 tariff. Although the higher tariffs protected Northern manufacturers, the higher import duties seriously hurt the South, for it relied on cheaper European-manufactured goods. Now, however, it was forced to purchase Northern goods. Led by South Carolina, the Southern states protested, threatening to 'nullify,' i.e. not recognize or obey, the tariff legislation. The metropole-state confrontation quickly ended when President Jackson threatened to use military power to force compliance. Realizing its subordinate position, the South proposed a political restructuring, including Calhoun's 'concurrent majority' doctrine, but these proposals were rebuffed by Congress. As a consequence, the South perceived its political and economic position threatened.

The tariff, nullification and state's rights controversies contributed to the South's emergence as a culture under siege. Its position as a racial group under siege was exacerbated by increasingly strident Northern abolitionist criticisms of slavery, and Southern apprehensions increased during the slavery controversy of the 1850s. Lincoln's 1860 election was the final blow, for it convinced Southern leaders that only by seceding could they protect their culture and racial system.

The Southern siege ideology evolved slowly during the pre-Civil War period. Stung by abolitionist criticisms, Southerners sought Biblical sanctions for slavery. They viewed the universe as a natural order of superior and inferior beings, whites seen as having a natural right to rule over blacks. More pragmatically, Southerners claimed that slaves were treated better than 'wage slave' industrial workers of the North. Slaves, they argued, were cared for throughout their life, while the Northern industrialist, interested solely in profit and cheap labor, inhumanely discarded wage workers who were too costly or old to work. These racial arguments, particularly the latter one, were tied closely to the Southern view that agrarianism (even without the presence of slavery) was superior to the materialist-oriented Northern culture.

The South pursued diverse strategies to protect itself. Its power parity with the North initially protected it, but enactment of the 1828 tariff signaled the South's weakening political position. Its threat to nullify metropole legislation and Jackson's response further eroded Southern power. Consequently, the South proposed a political restructuring of society, but its proposals were rejected. Southern strategy then moved on three other fronts: first, it proposed the addition of new slave states, including Mexico and Cuba, as a means of preserving its power parity with the North; second, its legislators increasingly used their power in Congress, including filibuster threats and other tactics, to defeat or weaken legislation that threatened slavery; and third, it fashioned a slave ideology geared toward mobilizing its followers and convincing the North of slavery's legitimacy. Fearing for its cultural survival, the South withdrew into its agrarian *laager* or enclave as a means of protecting itself from an 'alien' Northern culture. Persistently rebuffed in its strategies, the South grew convinced that its culture and racial system were endangered. Secession emerged as a viable alternative.

Metropole actions influenced Southern strategy. By forcing compliance to the tariff and condoning (at least in the South's perceptions) abolitionist efforts, the metropole increased Southern fears. Similarly, the refusal to consider proposals for political restructuring, followed by

Lincoln's election, convinced Southerners that the North was hostile to everything Southern. Consequently, Southern views hardened, and their belief system was increasingly characterized as closed. Southerners idealized their society to the point where all prior reservations about slavery were dismissed. Differences between whites and blacks were accented, leading to an elaborate segregation system deemed essential to prevent the 'pollution' of a presumably superior white group. Inter-group sexual liaisons and intermarriage were prohibited by law; restric-tive measures were enacted forbidding the education of blacks; the rights of free blacks in the South were restricted, whites fearful they would serve as symbols for slaves desiring freedom; and the behavior of blacks that confirmed white images of them as 'animals' or sub-human was widely publicized.

The stress and anxiety of white Southerners triggered rumors of slave insurrections, and the rumors reinforced white anxieties. Other indicators of stress were evident. Restrictive legislation was enacted that silenced critics of slavery; vigilante groups were organized to crush possible slave uprisings; harsher penalties were imposed against slaves who rebelled or were insubordinate to their masters; and the punish-ment meted out to blacks for insubordination, suspected conspiracies or rebellions were publicized widely to serve as a deterrent to blacks suspected of harboring similar thoughts. These measures were clear indicators of the increasing dogmatism of white Southerners. Rigidity came to characterize their perceptions of and responses to perceived threats. For example, people who advocated compromise, whether concerning slavery or other North-South issues, were labelled traitors, and Southerners, including Congressmen, became dogmatic and physi-cally violent in their defense of slavery. Secession and war were, under the circumstances, a logical outcome of the emergence of Southerners as a siege group.

A second phase is evident in the evolution of the Southern siege group, that extending from Reconstruction to the First World War. Although defeated in war, Southerners initially retained control of postwar state governments. Emancipation created new threats, not only to Southern culture but also to white control over blacks. White South-erners attempted to re-establish a racial dominance system in which blacks, though free, were made politically and economically subordin-ate. That was the intent of the 'Black Codes,' the debt peonage system and numerous legislative enactments. These measures, aimed at reimposing racial dominance, prompted metropole intervention. The federal government legislated the Civil Rights Acts (1866), imposed federal troops over the Southern states, ousted state governments that had enacted Black Codes, facilitated the entry of blacks into government to replace whites, and pushed through constitutional amendments which protected the civil rights of blacks and assured their incorporation within political and economic structures. White Southerners subsequently portrayed the Reconstruction South as prostrated and exploited by ignorant and corrupt blacks. Largely a distortion of reality, these views became part of a Southern mythology used to justify white retaliation and the illegal activities of such groups as the Ku Klux Klan. Events and myth intermingled, reinforcing white Southern images of themselves as a racial siege group.

Events during the Reconstruction period intensified white Southern siege perceptions. The imposition of Northern troops and civil rights legislation threatened whites and curtailed their efforts at re-establishing a racial dominance system. Despite civil rights legislation, federal troop presence and establishment of the Freedmen's Bureau to assist blacks, indifferent or lax metropole law enforcement and administration forced blacks to fend for themselves. Whites, given that lax law enforcement, tyrannized and intimidated blacks; and following withdrawal of Northern troops in 1877, Southern whites moved quickly to re-establish white hegemony. Numerous factors threatened whites during the Reconstruction period, and external (metropole policies) as well as internal (mobilization by blacks) factors prompted them to rally their members. The removal of Northern troops and subsequent Supreme Court invalidation of the Civil Rights Acts removed some of these threats, but others remained. Most threatening were the black vote and black efforts to mobilize themselves economically and politically. Numerous blacks were elected to public office during Reconstruction, but whites moved initially to undermine blacks economically. Only later, when blacks combined with poor whites to support the Populist Party in the 1890s, were major steps taken systematically to disfranchise blacks. Realizing that a black-poor white coalition threatened their power, white governments quickly disfranchised blacks, playing upon the racial prejudices of poor whites as a device to separate them from blacks. By 1900 the white racial siege group had resumed complete power, thereby allaying fears for its group survival. However, the unprecedented action of President Theodore Roosevelt inviting a black man, Booker T. Washington, to lunch with him at the White House revived Southern fears. The white siege group's hostility was vividly expressed by one Southern politician: 'the action of President Roosevelt in entertaining that nigger will necessitate our killing a thousand niggers in the South before they will learn their place again.' Roosevelt's action prompted the South to indoctrinate the North with its racial views.

Where the pre-Civil War siege group relied on Biblical justification for slavery, late nineteenth century Southerners emphasized other factors, particularly the belief that a natural order existed of superior whites and inferior blacks, this view buttressed by Social Darwinism. Two views emerged from the Darwinist argument: one held that whites were innately superior to blacks and the latter could never achieve equality; the other held that blacks represented an earlier and lower stage of development and though capable of progress could not catch up to white civilization for centuries. Either view justified white domination. Another part of this siege ideology warned that 'mixing' the races would 'pollute' or contaminate whites, reducing them to the 'animal-like behavior attributed to blacks. Proponents of this belief advocated stringent segregation of the races to protect whites. Some of these views were heard prior to the Civil War but were only fully developed in this later period as Southerners, recognizing that they could not preserve their racial system if opposed by the North, mounted a massive propaganda campaign to convince Northern whites that blacks were racially inferior. Myths about black behavior and the 'horrors' of Reconstruction were widely publicized, even in novels, and the South moved systematically to instill racial prejudice in Northern whites. Likewise, Northerners were indoctrinated with the belief that Southerners knew best how to resolve the South's 'Negro problem,' this tactic aimed at Northern acquiescence in the South's subjugation of blacks. Although it lost the Civil War, the South had by the early twentieth century won the struggle for white supremacy, supported by the North's indifference and a President (Woodrow Wilson) who espoused many of their cherished racial beliefs and used his powers to discriminate against blacks. In that way the racial siege group managed to preserve, though in modified form, its power and privilege, its racial dominance system more important at that point in time than its culture.

Historically, then, structural strains and other factors contributed to the development of the Southern siege group. Threats to its cultural survival and racial system triggered the group's emergence. Fearful of metropole policies that threatened their culture and racial wellbeing, white Southerners pursued diverse strategies which, when unsuccessful, precipitated secession and war. Although defeated, white Southerners sought to re-establish their racial hegemony, bringing upon themselves Reconstruction. Northern policies thereafter heightened their racial siege perceptions, and threats to their cultural and racial survival pushed white Southerners into holding more dogmatic racial beliefs. What emerged was a closed racial belief system, the South thereafter pursuing a policy of racial intimidation and subordination that survived (with Northern acquiescence) until the 1960s. Similar threats, either to their culture or racial beliefs (or both), prompted the emergence of Afrikaners, white Rhodesians and French Canadians as siege groups.

Two phases are evident in the evolution of the Afrikaner siege group: the period from British annexation of the Cape Colony through the Anglo-Boer War of 1899-1902, and the twentieth-century period, including the National Party's 1948 electoral victory and the subsequent implementation of its siege ideology. Perceptions by Boer-Afrikaners of themselves as a siege culture and racial siege group are evident in both periods.

The British, who annexed the Cape Colony in 1806, were regarded as intruders by Dutch colonists who, by reason of their earlier settlement viewed themselves as the legitimate possessors of the land. British-Dutch racial attitudes differed sharply. Where Dutch held that blacks were innately inferior, British policy, influenced by liberals and missionaries, moved towards according blacks equal rights, a policy that prompted an abortive Dutch uprising in 1815. Dutch-Boer resentment toward the British persisted, and British abolition of slavery in 1834 clashed with Boer racial beliefs and prompted the Great Trek, commencing in 1835, wherein the Boers moved to the frontier to escape British control and policy.

Friction, usually over 'native policy' and British metropole efforts to bring Boers under their control, persisted, culminating in two Anglo-Boer conflicts, 1880-1 and 1899-1902. The Boers, later known as Afrikaners, saw themselves as a culture under siege, this belief prompted by English settler attitudes and confirmed (in the Boers' estimation) by proposals at different times by Lords Somerset and Milner that Boers be forced to discard their own culture and language and become anglicized. These events and factors, culminating in the second Anglo-Boer War, solidified Boer fears for their cultural survival. Although defeated in the war, the Boers emerged as the majority white group under the new government (1910). However, memories of their defeat in that war along with continued metropole interference, English settler dominance in economic and cultural sectors, and English attitudes toward Boer-Afrikaner culture converged to threaten nationalist Afrikaners. Moreover, the 'native policy' of coalition liberal Afrikaner-English governments prior to 1948 led nationalist Afrikaners to see themselves as a racial siege group. The coalition governments, concerned with the country's economic development, accepted within the economy the limited structural incorporation of blacks. That policy, nationalist Afrikaners warned, would ultimately lead to black rule and be the death knell of Afrikaner culture. Growing fears for Afrikaner cultural survival led to the National Party's 1948 election.

The major structural factor that facilitated emergence of Afrikaner nationalism was the political system. Under the 1910 Act of Union, Britain established a unitary political system within which Boer-Afrikaners represented the majority white party. Moreover, Britain agreed that Africans, except in the Cape Colony, would be excluded from the franchise. In effect, the metropole sold out Africans in return for Boer acceptance of the Union. Until 1948, most governments were Afrikaner-English coalitions. Given earlier assimilationist efforts, particularly those of Somerset and Milner, Afrikaners demanded constitutional guarantees that their language and culture were co-equal with the English. Britain agreed to these demands; and Afrikaners, retaining control over their own schools, assured perpetuation of their culture and language. The English controlled major economic structures but deferred to liberal Afrikaners in the political sector. Interested in commerce, industry, profits and cheap labor, the English relied upon African labor, thereby threatening both English and Afrikaner labor. Britain earlier assumed that a massive influx of British settlers would tip the political balance away from Afrikaners, but that infusion never materialized. Consequently, Afrikaners remained the majority white group although until 1948 they split along liberal and nationalist lines, the former usually joining the English in coalition governments.

External and internal strains contributed to nationalist Afrikaner perceptions of themselves as a siege culture and racial siege group. By its policies the metropole created this threat: first, it favored the English in its policies; second, through entrenched clauses in the constitution it protected the nonwhite franchise in the Cape, an issue that distressed Afrikaners; and third, during both world wars it pressured South Africa into participating, many Afrikaners resentful since they believed the wars did not concern them.

English settler control of the economic system forced Afrikaners into a subordinate position. Motivated by the search for profits, English business and industry utilized cheap African labor, thereby ignoring the position of poor whites, most of whom were Afrikaners. This policy contributed to the explosive 1922 Rand strike where mine owners sought to replace white labor (English as well as Afrikaner) with cheaper African labor. Moreover, as society became more industrial and urban, 'poor whites,' mostly rural and poorly educated Afrikaners, found themselves competing (often unsuccessfully) in the labor market against Africans. Thus the Afrikaner was threatened culturally by the English and economically by the African. Economic incorporation of Africans contributed to the rise of black nationalism, and that group's demands for political rights frightened Afrikaners who recognized the African as a threat to Afrikaner political power, economic opportunity and culture. The cultural factor was significant, for Afrikaners recalled earlier Anglo attempts to destroy Boer Afrikaner language and culture, and they feared that if Africans acquired power they, too, would threaten Afrikaner *volk* and culture.

Afrikaner siege fears contributed to the 1948 National Party victory, and they continued to worry about metropole intervention despite the fact that the 1931 Statute of Westminster precluded intrusion in South Africa's internal affairs. The fear persisted until South Africa left the Commonwealth in 1961 and became a republic. That was a symbolic step, for by so doing South Africa shed its European ties, leaving the white minority-ruled country virtually isolated in an increasingly black-ruled continent. That fact, along with increased internal black opposition and external criticism of its racial policies, left South Africa feeling beleaguered.

The Afrikaner belief system, evolving slowly during the nineteenth century, became a full-blown cultural nationalism early in the twentieth century. The Afrikaner siege ideology emerged in response to two threats: the cultural threat that emanated from the metropole and Anglo assimilationist pressures; and the racial threat of black rule endangering Afrikaner power and group identity. Historically, Boer-Afrikaner religious beliefs assumed the group's cultural and biological superiority to Africans. British policies threatened these racial beliefs early in the nineteenth century and prompted the Boers' Great Trek. Though momentarily out from under metropole control, Boers were forced to fight Africans for possession of the land, and these conflicts accented their cultural differences. Later, reimposition of metropole control and renewed assimilationist pressures threatened the Boers. Even so, they found momentary security in the Orange Free State and the Transvaal colony late in the nineteenth century. However, the Transvaal was subsequently inundated by outsiders (*uitlanders*) who flooded into the area with the discovery of gold. *Uitlanders* quickly outnumbered Boers, and when they demanded the franchise, the Boers refused, recognizing that extension of the franchise would undermine Boer power and the group's cultural survival. British ultimatums that Boers extend the franchise were rebuffed, the Boers opting for war to preserve their power.

The bitterness of the war and the group's defeat served as a new catalyst for Afrikaner nationalism. However, a split occurred within Afrikanerdom, one group seeking reconciliation with the English, the other rejecting rapprochement and working toward establishment of an Afrikaner state that would protect the *volk*. Among the latter were a small group of nationalists who in 1914 rebelled against the government. They were quickly suppressed, their defeat leading nationalists to rally and establish an organization to articulate Afrikaner beliefs and mobilize group members in the struggle for power. From this emerged the Afrikaner Broederbond which reformulated an Afrikaner cultural ideology and politicized Afrikaners to oppose Anglo assimilationist pressures. These groups were ultimately successful in their organizational efforts, for enough Afrikaners rallied to support the National Party in 1948. Winning that election, the Nationalists moved to implement apartheid policies designed to separate the races and perpetuate Afrikaner power. Only vaguely defined at first, the group's beliefs (including separate development, establishment of homelands, etc.) were refined and modified over subsequent decades to fit new circumstances.

Stress and threat sharpen a group's perceptions of the differences between itself and the threatening group(s). The nineteenth-century Boer, his beliefs derived from his religion, considered blacks to be different and inferior to whites. These beliefs, though later modified, served as the basis for apartheid policy. By then these racial beliefs rested on three points: first, a belief that innate cultural differences separated the races; second, a belief that whites were biologically superior to blacks; and third, a fear that any form of racial mixing would lead to the 'pollution' of whites. Consequently, apartheid policies were aimed at the separation of races. But the government, determined to support policies that enhanced the economic wellbeing of Afrikaners previously discriminated against by the English, undermined its own apartheid policy by incorporating blacks as a form of cheap labor. Thus by the 1980s Afrikaner political control was used not only to protect the group's culture but also its power and privilege. Opposition, external as well as internal to its racial dominance system, increased Afrikaner siege fears.

The National Party responded to these threats with increasingly dogmatic and harsh measures. Numerous laws, including the Suppression of Communism Act, the Terrorism Act and others outlawed virtually every form of opposition or criticism. Courts became agencies for the protection of the state, and critics, whether black or white, were restricted, detained or imprisoned. This rigidity and dogmatism, resulting from stress, continued despite the absolute control wielded by Afrikaners over society. The last decade, however, has witnessed the rise of opposition, particularly among subordinate groups, though state power has kept that opposition restrained. There has also emerged within Afrikaner ranks a split of *verligte* and *verkrampte* groups, the former proposing elimination or modification of racial policies and the limited political incorporation of nonwhite groups, the latter, feeling even more insecure, demanding stricter control, continued racial domination and no real or meaningful sharing of political power with other groups. The greater the perceived stress and threat, the greater the likelihood the *verkrampte* group will be strengthened. Subsequent racial crises could result in increasingly dogmatic and authoritarian measures and possible establishment of a garrison state to protect Afrikaner power. The perception of itself as a siege culture and racial siege group constrains Afrikaners from realizing that a negotiated resolution or accommodation is feasible if the two fundamental issues are separated, i.e. a means is found for giving up privilege while working out power and structural arrangements that protect Afrikaner cultural or group identity and assure other groups the same protections and opportunities. However, increased internal conflict that threatens white South Africans (including English) most likely will prompt them to pursue the path followed earlier by white Rhodesians: internal or civil war.

What were perceived as threats to its cultural and racial survival precipitated the emergence of a Southern Rhodesia white siege group. Its secession (1965) and willingness to risk war with the metropole were reminiscent of the American South's secession and the Boers' war with Britain, extreme measures taken to assure the group's survival. Where white Southerners believed that Lincoln's election threatened slavery and their future, white Rhodesians feared that British support for black governments in Northern Rhodesia and Nyasaland indicated future metropole policy toward Southern Rhodesia. The Afrikaner as a siege group evolved slowly over a century, white Southerners over half a century, and white Rhodesians between 1945 and 1962. The Rhodesian Front Party rallied whites by promising to block black rule and preserve white power. The tactics followed were different but the goal was the same as that of Afrikaners.

Earlier factors were important, but postwar events in particular shaped the Rhodesian siege group. Whites, who constituted less than 5 per cent of the population historically, settled the area in 1890, coming into conflict with indigenous groups. These contacts precipitated conflicts in 1890 and 1896-7, but, with metropole support, the Africans were subdued and settlers claimed legitimacy over the land by virtue of conquest. Thereafter, through control of political, economic and social structures, settlers preserved their hegemony.

African opposition emerged after the Second World War, and nationalist parties were banned and their leaders arrested following a series of strikes, demonstrations and boycotts. To protect their power and privilege, Southern Rhodesian whites joined their counterparts in Northern Rhodesia and Nyasaland in the Central African Federation (1953-63). The Federation allowed for limited black participation, particularly in the two northern colonies. Britain since the 1920s had claimed that 'native interests' were paramount in its African colonies, and it supported, though often reluctantly, postwar nationalist demands for independence. Having retained closer control over the two northern colonies, Britain acceded more readily to nationalist aspirations. Southern Rhodesia was a different story. Britain retained the right to protect 'native affairs' under the 1923 Constitution, but it normally deferred to white interests. Black political incorporation in Northern Rhodesia and Nyasaland worried white Southern Rhodesians, and a series of factors prompted their support of the Rhodesian Front in 1962.

Structural factors contributed to the development of the white Rhodesian siege group. The postwar rise of African nationalism and metropole support for African independence threatened white control. Two alternatives appeared feasible for protecting white power: uniting with South Africa or joining a federation with white settlers elsewhere. Given their prejudice against Afrikaners, white Rhodesians rejected the South African option and joined the Federation.[2] When, however, economic problems and the rise of black nationalism precipitated the breakup of the Federation, Southern Rhodesia requested that the metropole grant it dominion rather than colony status, thereby eliminating Britain's right to intervene in the country's internal affairs. Britain stipulated that Rhodesia accept black political incorporation. Rhodesia refused, and later, fearful that Britain might intervene and impose black rule, Rhodesia declared UDI.

Structural strains contributed to the siege group's actions. Wartime labor shortages necessitated an increased use of African labor, but the postwar influx of white immigrants made blacks redundant. Lowered wages, restricted labor opportunities and bad working conditions prompted Africans to strike. These confrontations, along with the rapid development of black nationalism, accented the minority position of whites and raised the specter of black rule, a possibility Europeans momentarily curtailed by manipulating franchise requirements. But the rise of African nationalism to the north, followed by black rule, haunted white Rhodesians. The Federation increased their fears, for the election of black politicians from Northern Rhodesia and Nyasaland meant that Salisbury, the Federation Capital, witnessed an influx of black politicians and government workers. Many hotels, restaurants and social amenities were opened on a multiracial basis, and this exacerbated white Rhodesian racial prejudices. The result was a white backlash. It surfaced initially during 1958 in support of the Dominion Party. The party lost the election, but following its demise its supporters switched allegiance to the new Rhodesian Front Party. Their fears exacerbated by metropole policy, black nationalism, the Congo conflict, emergence of black governments to the north and increased black opposition internally, white Rhodesians rallied behind the RF, which promised preservation of white power. Subsequently, having opted for UDI, which resulted in UN economic sanctions and world opposition to its racial system, white Rhodesia perceived itself as a threatened group.

White Rhodesians pursued numerous strategies to preserve their power. They opted for Federation rather than union with South Africa; and when federalism threatened rather than protected their power, whites supported the RF, withdrew from the Federation and later declared UDI to block metropole intervention in the country's internal affairs. Internally, the RF restructured the political system to prevent black rule, and a series of new constitutions (1961, 1965, 1969) were introduced to preserve white power. This goal was clearly stated by the government when it proposed acceptance of the new 1969 Constitution: 'The (present) Constitution is no longer acceptable to the people of Rhodesia because it contains a number of objectionable features, the principal one being that it provides for eventual African rule.'

The government sought to preserve white power in two ways: first, it legislated to bring about the separation of races; and second, it silenced its critics, black as well as white. Strain and stress prompted increasingly dogmatic policies and behavior. Earlier, white Rhodesians professed a belief in multiracialism and racial partnership, but with the threat of African nationalism whites 'discovered' racial and cultural differences between themselves and blacks which they used to justify white supremacy. This view, previously held by a minority of whites, was soon espoused by most whites. Earlier proposals that had been rejected for segregated or 'parallel' development of racial groups were quietly introduced in subtle form by the government even though it espoused a policy of 'meritocracy,' i.e. advancement based on ability regardless of race. However, merit came through education and skills, and the education and economic systems were so structured that few blacks had the opportunity to develop their capabilities. Indeed, policies were enacted that restricted their opportunities, and increased segregation of groups, be it in housing, social amenities or land use, followed. Africans, restricted to low-level positions in the economy, increased their opportunities as the war intensified and a shortage of whites necessitated the increased use of blacks. That, however, was compelled by conditions, not RF policy, for the ultimate goal of the RF was a completely segregated and white-dominated society in practice if not in name.

Stress had other consequences as well. Censorship was imposed and legislative enactments (the Emergency Powers Act, Law and Order Act, Unlawful Organizations Act, etc.) stifled criticism and opposition. African political groups were banned or outlawed and their leaders detained or imprisoned. The government, viewing itself as the state rather than a political party momentarily holding power, construed criticism of its policies as conspiracy against the state. The dogmatism and rigidity of white Rhodesian perceptions and policies increased as political, economic and military pressures mounted, especially following escalation of the war in 1973. White Rhodesians remained a racial siege group. Their views did not change, but circumstances did. The threatened withdrawal of South African military and financial support forced Rhodesia to negotiate and accept a British settlement in 1980 that led to elections, black rule and the establishment of Zimbabwe.

Quebec separatist movements of recent years represent the most recent stage in French-English rivalry that has plagued Canada since France ceded Canada to Britain in 1763. Abandoned, French settlers, threatened by metropole and Anglo settler assimilationist policies, were transformed into a siege culture. In the process, they mobilized their resources and adapted diverse strategies aimed at preserving their cultural identity. Recent secessionist efforts represent the most extreme option French Canadians have pursued to assure their group survival. Following the 1763 cession, most upper-class French returned to the mother country, leaving behind trappers, farmers and clergy. Church and clergy were the major force in preserving French cultural identity. Under the Quebec Act (1774) and other measures, Britain guaranteed the French their language, law and religion, but later metropole and English settler efforts to anglicize French Canadians threatened the group's existence. French Canadians were initially accorded a degree of political autonomy within Lower Canada, but political manoeuvering and assimilationist efforts by the English exacerbated group tensions and prompted the French Canadian 1837 rebellion. Lord Durham, commissioned by Britain to assess the causes of that conflict, concluded that they derived from incompatible cultural differences. His recommended solution was the destruction of French culture and language and that group's forced assimilation into the dominant Anglo culture. Durham's proposals, although never directly implemented, further threatened the French, who responded by withdrawing more completely into their agrarian society, that seen as the most effective way of warding off assimilationist pressures and the lure of Anglo commerce, industry and materialism.

Lower and Upper Canada and other British North American colonies were united under the Canadian Confederation in 1867. A federal government was established with powers divided between federal and provincial governments. Federal-provincial jurisdictional disputes were seldom a problem, but the expansion of federal activities in recent decades has exacerbated tensions, Quebec Province in particular viewing federal policies as threatening French culture and provincial powers. Though muted initially, French-English tensions increased following Confederation, exacerbated by the execution of Louis Riel, the abolition of French language in Ontario and Manitoba schools, French opposition to Canada's support for Britain in the Anglo-Boer War (the French viewed the Boers' position as similar to their own), and the conscription crises of the two world wars. Late nineteenth and early twentieth century Canadian (Anglo) nationalism threatened French Canadians and precipitated a reactive French nationalism. Its survival endangered, French Canada resorted to whatever means necessary to protect its cultural identity, including agrarianism and, from the 1920s onwards, advocacy of an independent Laurentian Republic, that a precursor for recent proposals for secession and establishment of an independent French Canada.

French measures, including agrarianism, were essentially defensive. They had another impact, however, similar to that on white Southerners and Afrikaners. Agrarianism isolated these groups from industrialization and dominant group economic structures, leaving siege group members inadequately trained or prepared to compete in the industrial and commercial world. To force assimilation upon subordinate group members, the dominant group predicated structural incorporation on their degree of assimilation. Siege group values, including language, and the lack of training restricted the subordinate group's incorporation. Thus, whatever the source, the end result was the same: siege groups, recognizing differential rates of structural incorporation between themselves and the dominant (or other) groups, attributed that difference to the latter's discriminatory policies. Recognizing this and aware that the anglicized French enjoyed greater opportunities, nationalist French Canadians perceived Anglos as attempting to destroy French culture and language. The fact that some French willingly discarded their culture and language to enjoy the benefits of incorporation was even more threatening, and siege group leaders moved to capture political control of Quebec Province, succeeding in 1976.

As industrialization increased in Canada, including Quebec, federal government policies intruded upon such areas as welfare, taxation, education and other fields, many of which previously fell under provincial jurisdiction. Quebec vehemently protested and opposed the federal measures as a threat to provincial rights. Federal involvement in education particularly threatened Quebec, for it viewed federal measures as a device for anglicizing French Canadians. Consequently, from the 1960s onwards the polarization of French Canadians has increased, and Quebec's earlier struggle for 'provincial rights' had, by 1980, been transformed into a demand for independence. Even though the Parti Quebecois of Rene Levesque lost a 1980 provincial referendum calling for a new form of provincial-federal relations, the rebuff was only temporary. Nationalists continue to seek new ways to protect their cultural identity and limit the political powers of the metropole, their ultimate goal being secession and political independence. That, they believe, is the only means to protect the group's cultural identity.

The four siege groups in these countries — white Southerners, Afrikaners, white Rhodesians and French Canadians — have, historically and more recently, pursued diverse strategies to preserve their group identity. Differential power capabilities of siege and dominant groups, as well as the parameters of action determined by existing structures, influenced the strategies of these groups. Differential rates of structural incorporation angered white Southerners, Afrikaners and French Canadians, but what mainly precipitated the resource mobilization efforts of these groups and white Rhodesians were fears for their group (cultural and/or racial) survival. Dominant-group (or metropole) efforts to assimilate these groups or threats to their power, privilege and group beliefs precipitated siege group responses. Each evolved an ideology, mobilized its members, and transformed its organizational structure into an action-oriented movement whose goal was protection of the group's identity. In this sense, siege groups became value-oriented movements, and the strategies they adopted to protect themselves were determined by situational, structural and power factors.

Chapter 7
Ethnicity, development and power

I

Where preceding chapters have focused on the role of power as a determinant of race and ethnic relations, the concern here is with development factors as an intervening variable, for development needs, particularly though not exclusively economic, directly influence the character of intergroup relations. Examples are drawn from three Anglo fragments: the United States, Canada and South Africa. Canada and the United States are often identified by contrasting 'ethnic mosaic' and 'melting pot' metaphors, while South Africa is referred to as a racially 'segmented' society. All can be described in terms of the plural society theory or model.

Employed initially as an analytical tool to describe developing countries in Africa, Asia and the Caribbean, the plural society model can be applied to developed nations such as Canada, the USA and South Africa (Katznelson, 1972; Rex, 1971; Van den Berghe, 1970). Plural society theory concentrates on group power relationships and cleavages that emerge because of the presence of diverse cultural, ethnic, racial and other groups. These cleavages appear most sharply in (a) the types of cultural integration present in society and (b) the differential rates of incorporation of specific groups within political, economic and social structures. Plural societies can be analyzed 'as fields of social, economic and political power' (Katznelson, 1972: 143), for group power differentials significantly shape the character of cultural integration and structural incorporation.

Plural society theory and conflict theory both recognize the dominant group's primacy in determining cultural and structural policy decisions (Kuper and Smith, 1969; Schermerhorn, 1970; Lenski, 1966), but the subordinate group's role cannot be discounted. Even where differential rates of power are considerable, or asymmetrical, subordinate group behavior influences dominant group policy. So, too, do other factors, the most significant of which are development (particularly economic) factors that play an intervening role. Political and social development are important, but the emphasis here is on how economic development alters or modifies what otherwise would be the general character of cultural integration, structural incorporation and intergroup relations where power differentials are otherwise the only factor at work.[1]

Canada, the USA and South Africa were historically Anglo fragment societies, settled initially or subsequently by English settlers and controlled by them and the British metropole. Settlers and metropole, given their power, determined cultural policies and how indigenes, slaves and immigrants were structurally incorporated. Those of Anglo descent manipulated political and economic institutions to retain power for an extended historical period; but their decisions, based primarily on their cultural values and power, were tempered by one other factor: the economic or development needs and imperatives of society. Changes over time, in good part resulting from economic development, compelled the dominant group to modify cultural and structural policies to cope with these changes.

Two brief examples illustrate the importance of development factors. In pre-Civil War America, rapid economic development and the influx of European immigrants in the North threatened existing North-South power relationships. Southerners recognized that northern political supremacy threatened continuation of their slave culture; and, fearing cultural extinction (and loss of power and privilege), they supported state's rights policies and demanded political structural revisions that would preserve the North-South power parity. Having failed in these strategies, the South opted for secession, convinced that its military resources would preserve its independence should war follow. In Canada, the rapid economic development of recent decades exacerbated English-French rivalries. Development within Quebec Province was initiated by Canadian-English and US controlled corporations, and development in general prompted an increase in the federal government's involvement in health, welfare, education and other sectors. French Canadians view these as provincial responsibilities, and they considered this federal 'intrusion' a threat to their autonomy. Moreover, until recently economic advancement within these outsider-controlled industries and corporations depended upon the person's being anglicized, i.e. speaking English and accepting English work habits. Many French, wishing to advance economically, reluctantly or willingly discarded their own language and culture to win promotion. These assimilationist pressures have threatened Quebec's cultural identity and generated a cultural renascence, leading in 1976 to victory for the Parti Quebecois in provincial elections. Fearing for their group's cultural survival, the Parti Quebecois supports provincial rights and proposes structural revisions leading to special provincial status or outright independence. French-English tensions have existed since the eighteenth century, but it is these recent economic developments that have exacerbated group rivalries and transformed French-Canadians into a siege culture.

II

The preceding examples are simply illustrative of how development and power factors reciprocally influence intergroup relations. The significance of development factors is evident in an analysis of dominant group relations with three specific groups: (a) nonwhites, including indigenous and non-indigenous groups; (b) immigrant white groups; and (c) the three siege cultures analyzed in the preceding chapter: French-Canadians, white Southerners and Afrikaners. Intergroup relations are explored in two ways: first, by tracing how these relations were influenced by development factors; and second, by comparing cultural policies in the three countries, focusing again on how development factors influenced these policies.

II.1 Nonwhite groups

Among the nonwhites present in these countries are the indigenous (Amerindians in the USA and Canada, Africans in South Africa) and non-indigenous (blacks in the USA and Canada, Asians in all three countries) groups. Indigenous group subordination resulted from conquest, disruption of their economy and culture or dispossession from their land (Price, 1972; Frazier, 1957; Patterson, 1972; Fey and McNickle, 1970; MacLeod, 1928; LeMay, 1971; Van den Berghe,

1970). Non-indigenous subordination was the consequence of enslavement, indentured status or the group's entry into the country in a relatively powerless position (Davis, 1966; Stampp, 1956; Genovese, 1965, 1969; Winks, 1971; Young and Reid, 1939; LaViolette, 1945; Daniels, 1970; Kung, 1962; Barth, 1964).

In contrast to South Africa, indigenous groups in Canada and the USA were not needed for economic development, and they were as a consequence shunted to reserves or reservations where they became wards of the state. Those who left the reservations to seek employment were usually discriminated against because of their color or culture. Settlers, their descendants and white immigrants filled the major labor needs for development. If labor shortages occurred, nonwhites were imported, including some as slaves and others as indentured or migrant workers. The South's plantation economy relied upon slavery, but with its abolition share-cropping, debt peonage and migrant labor schemes were introduced to exploit black labor (DuBois, 1964; Logan, 1965; Van Woodward, 1951; Daniel, 1972). In South Africa, Dutch and English settlers used indigenous nonwhites and imported slaves because of a white labor shortage (Elphick and Giliomee, 1979). Following the abolition of slavery (1834) a head tax was imposed on indigenes to force them into working for Europeans. Later, as Natal's sugar industry developed and faced a critical labor shortage, indentured groups from India were imported. Likewise, early in the twentieth century indentured Chinese were imported, but white opposition forced their repatriation. Indians, however, remained (Huttenback, 1976; Campbell, 1971; Simons, 1969; Van den Berghe, 1970).

Slavery existed in all three countries. There were few slaves in Canada, and Britain's abolition of it had little impact (Winks, 1971). In South Africa, however, Britain's termination of slavery angered the Boers. That action along with the metropole's liberal attitudes toward blacks threatened Boer white supremacist beliefs and prompted their exodus — the Great Trek — into the hinterlands. For decades thereafter, Voortrekkers fought Bantu-speaking African groups with whom they contested possession of frontier lands, and only after British troops defeated the Zulus in 1879 was that threat to white settlers removed (Wilson and Thompson, 1969, 1971; Walker, 1930; Guy, 1979).

Slavery proved uneconomical in the northern United States, and it disappeared by 1800. Nevertheless, blacks in the North were discriminated against and their rights circumscribed, and some northern states enacted laws that prohibited their entry (Berwanger, 1967; Voegeli, 1967; Litwack, 1961). Slavery was fundamental to the South's economy, and whites justified its continuation by various rationalizations, including Biblical sanctions and the black man's supposed inferiority (Genovese, 1969; Gossett, 1965; Stampp, 1956; Jordan, 1969). Granted their freedom and enfranchised during Reconstruction, blacks participated widely in the political system. Southern white animosities intensified, and following Northern troop withdrawal in 1877, whites curtailed black political and economic power and directed their efforts toward exploiting cheap black labor (Van Woodward, 1966). By early 1900, racial policies in South *and* North had constricted black economic opportunities and forced them into a position of economic dependency, justified by a pervasive racist ideology (Logan, 1965; Trelease, 1971; Wood, 1970; Haller, 1971; Fredrickson, 1971; Newby, 1965). In viewing the North American scene, then, a number of points are obvious concerning slavery and economic development: first, the maintenance of slavery in the northern United States and Canada proved uneconomical, hence both were willing to accept its termination; second, the North, relying upon immigrant labor for economic development, felt threatened by what it saw as competition from cheap slave labor in the South, and that prompted northern opposition to the continuation or extension of slavery; and third, the South, pursuing primarily a policy of agricultural rather than industrial development, felt compelled to preserve its cheap slave labor to compensate for its economic dependence and subservience to the North.

In South Africa, slaves from West Africa and non-slave people from Malaya, India, China and, more recently, migrant labor from other African nations, were used to eliminate labor shortages (Van den Berghe, 1970; Adam, 1971a; F. Wilson, 1972). As in South Africa, shortages of white European immigrants for economic development needs in the USA and Canada, particularly for land settlement, railroad construction, mining and other enterprises, prompted the recruitment or encouragement of Asian immigration. However, because they were paid lower wages than whites, Asians threatened white labor, and subsequent strife forced both governments to exclude Chinese. Not excluded by the legislation, Japanese settled in both countries, and the strife that ensued was resolved only when the US and Canada established 'gentlemen's agreements' whereby Japan agreed to curtail the emigration of its citizens to North America (Price, 1966; LaViolette, 1945;

Daniels, 1970; Kung, 1962; Young and Reid, 1939). Latent antipathies persisted toward Asians, especially Japanese, and that contributed to the hostile reaction during the Second World War when Japanese, whether foreign or American-born, were removed from the West Coast and incarcerated in concentration camps or settled in the interior of the USA and Canada (LaViolette, 1958, 1968; TenBroek et al., 1968). Changes have occurred in the postwar period, but discriminatory treatment of nonwhites persists in both countries (Maykovich, 1975; Patterson, 1975; Himes, 1975; Scott, 1975). Institutional racism is reflected especially in the low rates of structural, particularly economic and political, incorporation of nonwhites, a rate much lower than that of immigrant whites or the dominant cultural groups (Burkey, 1971; Knowles and Prewitt, 1969; Porter, 1965; Blishen et al., 1968; Harp and Hofley, 1971; Elliott, 1971; Davis and Krauter, 1971).

In South Africa, the 1948 Afrikaner electoral victory marked a sharp change in white-nonwhite relations. The gradual incorporation of nonwhites in political structures was terminated, and as apartheid/separate development policies evolved, Africans were reclassified as migrants who possessed no political rights within 'white' South Africa. Rather, they were to exercise their political rights within the bantustans or homelands, types of internal colonies, which remained economically dependent upon South Africa. Within white economic structures blacks hold low-level or, at most, semiskilled positions, exploited as labor but deprived of political power (Brotz, 1977). Somewhat similar restrictions apply to Indians and coloreds, and what has emerged is a segmented society wherein economic and political power are in the hands of whites. Nonwhites are excluded from political structures and included within economic structures only to the extent that they are useful for economic development but do not threaten white employment opportunities.

Whites have, historically, regarded themselves as superior to nonwhites in the three countries. Their greater command over resources and technology, along with organization skills and cultural attitudes that condoned domination of nonwhites, has contributed to the perpetuation of their white dominance systems (Adam, 1971a, 1971b; Mason, 1970; Banton, 1967; Van den Berghe, 1967; Frazier, 1957: Parts III-IV; Jordan, 1969: Parts I-II, IV; Kovel, 1971). Power and dominance are viewed by superordinates as confirmation of white superiority. Although cultural differences and other factors originally contributed to this belief, the color factor ultimately emerged as the single most important criterion for distinguishing superior from inferior (Hoetink, 1971). Where needed for economic development, nonwhites have been utilized, and those who acquired white skills and behavioral patterns were more readily incorporated into lower levels within economic structures. However, the acquisition of white culture and behavior has seldom provided entry into white social structures, except in limited instances (W. Wilson, 1978). Rather, nonwhites remain segmented, 'outsiders' who are separated from white society even though, as in the case of blacks and Asians in Canada and the USA, their economic position has improved (W. Wilson, 1978; Maykovich, 1975). In the case of indigenes, then, neither Canada nor the United States needed them for economic development. They were, as a consequence, isolated on reservations. However, the shortage of white immigrants in South Africa (and, later, Southern Rhodesia) necessitated the use of some indigenes for development. They were incorporated at only the lowest, mostly unskilled levels of the economic system. All four countries relied upon Asians for filling particular development needs, but whites, by their actions, clearly indicated their cultural biases that Asians were not equal to people of European descent. Likewise, slaves were early used for development purposes in all but Southern Rhodesia. Terminated in the British colonies by metropole order and in the northern states because it was economically unviable, slavery persisted in the South until the Civil War, cheap labor essential for the South as a means of not becoming totally subservient economically to the North.

II.2 Immigrant whites

The manner in which white immigrants were culturally integrated and structurally incorporated within Canada, the United States and South Africa was determined by three major factors: (a) the historical period in which immigrants arrived; (b) the extent to which they were needed for economic development; and (c) their power, actual or potential, in terms of their resources (competitive and pressure) and mobilization capabilities.

There are three fairly distinct forms of cultural integration, and the dominant group determines how immigrants will be integrated. First, there is cultural assimilation, where the dominant group assumes the superiority of its own culture and compels other groups to discard their own culture for that of the dominant group. Second, there is cultural pluralism, where the dominant group tolerates or accepts the existence of other cultures. Thus a society may be culturally heterogeneous although there exist dominant group pressures for assimilation. And third, there is the segmented society in which the dominant group rejects another group's culture and/or somatic (color and physical appearance) characteristics as inferior. Although the dominant group may force the subordinate to discard its own culture and accept that of the dominant group, it still isolates and regards the former as inferior. That is evident in cases where there is limited structural incorporation of the subordinate group. Anglo societies were historically segmented societies, for nonwhites were — and remain so in some situations — considered inferior 'outsiders.' This is reflected in dominant group racial attitudes and behavior, and major indices for it are found in the limited structural incorporation of these outsiders. It is also reflected in discriminatory legislation and practices.

There was a degree of cultural heterogeneity in pre-Civil War American society, but the rapidly industrializing North needed assimilated workers who could be readily incorporated in economic structures. Previously, and even into the late nineteenth century cultural pluralism prevailed primarily in rural areas, Germans, Scandinavians and other European groups retaining their language and cultural identity (Fishman, 1966). Assimilationist pressures were most intense in urban areas, gaining momentum as industrialization, urbanization and the influx of South European immigrants increased, the South Europeans quite different in language and culture from anglicized Americans. Nativists, fearing 'contamination' of their 'American' (Anglo) culture, demanded 'Americanization' of these immigrants. Americanization programs were established; English was mandated as the only language in schools; legislatures restricted specific jobs to citizens, naturalized citizens or those who spoke English; and various patriotic groups assumed a vigilante role in pressuring for conformity to Anglo cultural and behavioral norms. Industry usually supported this effort because it needed workers who spoke English and accepted the Anglo work ethic. There was also a political motive. Fearing loss of political power to newer immigrant groups, Anglos believed their culture was endangered unless immigrant groups were rapidly anglicized and assimilated. Anglicized immigrants, it was assumed, would when given the vote uphold the dominant Anglo culture (Higham, 1971). The myth of the United

States as a 'new nation' reinforced these assimilationist pressures. Viewing the nation as born in revolution and free from assumed European corruptions, numerous Americans feared the country would be 'contaminated' by culturally different European groups or radical European political ideas (Sanford, 1961; Lewis, 1955; Noble, 1968; Gilbert, 1961; Rossiter, 1960). Thus, while welcoming (even encouraging) immigrant groups needed for industrial development, American society hurriedly 'purified' or Americanized immigrants before they could 'corrupt' the nation with Old World values and norms.

The greater the immigrant group's degree of assimilation, the more could it anticipate the probability of rapid structural incorporation. Thus, whether they were assimilated willingly or simply as a means of succeeding, those who assimilated were granted greater opportunities. Rates of incorporation varied, and the doors to economic or, in some cases, political, incorporation usually opened prior to those in the social realm. The melting pot was an anglicized vat, and the immigrant who melted most rapidly emerged a new man, an American whose apotheosis (in terms of assimilation) was required for access to the American dream of economic success (Gordon, 1964).

Because of the lure of America, South Africa and Canada encountered difficulties recruiting immigrants. More headed to Canada than South Africa, but even they viewed Canada as a stepping stone to the United States. British annexation of South Africa terminated Dutch emigration from Europe, but those of Dutch descent remained the majority white population in South Africa. Britain, however, retained political control over the colony, and English settlers during the 19th century controlled economic, political and social structures and established cultural policy. Later immigrants, mostly English, were assimilated into the Anglo culture and structures (Van den Berghe, 1970: ch. 2; Edwards, 1934; Thompson, 1960: ch. 1; Macmillan, 1963). Only later, after the 1948 National Party victory and South Africa's 1961 break from the Commonwealth, did non-Anglo white immigrants assimilate into Afrikaner as well as English cultures, that choice dependent partly on where they settled in South Africa. Those who settled in major urban areas more readily gravitated toward the English, but more recent pressures have been exerted to Afrikanerize immigrants (Stone, 1973).

South Africa's cultural pluralism, as that of Canada, results from the sometimes uneasy juxtaposition of two distinct white cultural or ethnic groups. In terms of racial groups, however, South Africa is a segmented society. Historically, major tensions existed between English and Boer/ Afrikaners, the split similar to that of French and English in Canada. In contrast, the United States witnessed the gradual anglicization or assimilation and incorporation of Dutch, French and other European groups. Although a degree of cultural diversity, including language, existed for a while, assimilationist forces tended to be pervasive, and only in recent decades has this changed and the society moved toward greater cultural diversity.

Canada's 'ethnic mosaic' metaphor is partly myth. As numerous studies indicate, diverse forces, particularly within the economic sector, pressure for cultural assimilation (Smith, 1970; Careless, 1969; Richmond, 1967, 1970). The presence of English and French groups contributed to the mosaic myth, and their confrontations refurbish the myth and encourage the development of cultural pluralism. Viewed historically, however, Anglo Canadian society clearly desired assimilation. It denigrated French culture and pressured for anglicization of the French. The latter's stubborn resistance to assimilationist thrusts prevented that, and within fortress Quebec the French managed to avoid the Anglo melting pot (Corbett, 1967; Cook, 1967; Careless and Brown, 1968; Mallory, 1970).

Still other factors contributed to Canada's cultural heterogeneity. Needing immigrants and concerned that those who did settle in Canada might move on to the United States, Canada embraced cultural pluralism, warning its immigrants that if they moved south of the border they would be forced to assimilate and shed their cultural identities. Canada therefore encouraged its immigrants to retain their culture and language, and they did: Ukrainians, Slavs, Doukhobors and Hutterites, among others. Most of these groups settled in isolated rural western areas, and consequently there was little need for them to assimilate. Even so, there were sporadic pressures aimed at changing their values and culture (Davis and Krauter, 1971; Elliott, 1971; McKenna, 1969). By way of contrast, most immigrants who settled in the USA during the late nineteenth and early twentieth centuries remained in cities where their advancement within the industrial work force was enhanced if they assimilated. A closer parallel with the USA at this earlier period are the immigrants who settled in Canada after the Second World War, for they, too, settled in urban areas. Though ethnic enclaves flourish in Canada and the government encourages ethnic pluralism, immigrant groups that assimilate find easier access to Anglo-dominated economic structures. They retain their own social groupings and relations, but in language and culture they adopt the characteristics of Anglo Canadians, aware that assimilation opens additional doors to economic opportunity (Richmond, 1967; Porter, 1965; Isajiw, 1968).

As plural societies, Canada and South Africa have more sharply differentiated cultural and ethnic groups than the USA, reflected especially in economic, political and social structures. In all three countries, industrialization (with its demands for uniformity) and economic development (Rostow, 1971) serve as compelling forces leading toward cultural uniformity and conformity, a fact that is evident in assimilationist pressures exerted upon white immigrant groups.

II.3 Siege cultures

Factors precipitating the emergence of siege cultures were explored in the preceding chapter. The focus here, of necessity, drawing on some of the same materials, is on how developmental factors contributed to the evolution of French Canadian, white Southerner and Afrikaner siege cultures. In each case the dominant cultural group, believing its own culture superior, used the forces of economic development in two ways: first, to enhance its own cultural position and group privilege, and second, to pressure, restrict or broaden the economic opportunities of other cultural groups dependent upon their receptivity to assimilation. These pressures and activities threatened the cultural survival of subordinate groups. Fearing cultural extinction and sharing unequally in society's benefits, the siege cultures sought initially to preserve their cultural identity by withdrawing into an agrarian enclave or laager. This had a negative effect, for in its withdrawal from the mainstream of economic development, each group put itself in a disprivileged position. Consequently, siege cultures lacked sufficient economic resources or skills to compete with the dominant cultural group.

The French in Canada and Dutch in South Africa viewed the English settlers as interlopers and themselves as legitimate claimants to the land. British metropole policies and Anglo settler assimilationist pressures, described earlier, motivated the withdrawal of these threatened groups into their agrarian laagers, but even there the metropole occasionally intruded, further threatening the groups (Hartz, 1964: ch. 7; Careless and Brown, 1968: chs 1-5; Morchain, 1967; Lower, 1946; Ossenberg, 1967, 1972; Macmillan, 1963; Walker, 1930; MacCrone, 1937; Vatcher,

1965). White Southerners similarly viewed theirs as the legitimate and superior culture, and they resented northern economic intrusion and abolitionist policies (Gossett, 1965: chs 3-4; Elkins, 1959; Fredrickson, 1971: chs 2-5; Davis, 1969). Cultural survival was the fundamental concern of all three groups, and agrarianism provided security and safety and encapsulated each group from what it considered the decadent values of commerce, industrialism and materialism (Stampp, 1956; Genovese, 1969: Part II). But agrarianism had another, not immediately recognized, consequence: it isolated siege cultures from the economic sector, and with industrialization, the dominant culture preempted control of economic structures and development. In effect, siege culture defensive policies transformed them into a position not totally unlike that of the indigenous groups isolated on reserves. All were economically dependent in some respects, constituting different forms of internal colonialism, though the analogy should not be extended too far. Each siege culture retained a greater degree of autonomy than non-whites, especially slaves and indigenous groups, though siege and non-white groups pursued similar policies and processes as they sought to break out from under dominant group control.

Among the components of a group's culture are its language, values, history, social system and symbols, all of which serve as a binding force. Initially, Southerners did not consider theirs a separate or unique culture, but one was forged from the factors and events previously noted, including agrarianism, an economy based on slavery, external opposition to slavery, northern domination of the South's economy, and increases in the North's population which contributed to its evolving political hegemony. Abolitionist threats particularly forced the South into a defensive position, and the political rebuffs it suffered while seeking structural revisions heightened group solidarity and exacerbated its siege perceptions (Davis, 1969). Secession, war, defeat, Reconstruction: all solidified the South's hostility toward the North's industrial culture. Moreover, northern industrial expansion during and following the war heightened the economic disparity between the two regions, leaving the South in an increasingly dependent position economically.

Northern industrial expansion had an unanticipated benefit for white Southerners: it hurried the termination of Reconstruction. Immersed in and enamored with its own economic development, the North tired of watching over the South. It sought and finally terminated

Reconstruction and northern rule. Totally immersed in economic expansion, the North ignored the black man's plight as Southern whites reimposed their control. Moreover, Northern attitudes were changing. As increasing numbers of blacks moved north seeking employment, they competed with white labor. The consequences were immediate: white racial prejudices surfaced and racial conflict ensued. Southern efforts to convince Northerners that blacks were inferior found increasing support, and by the First World War the myth of Anglo-Saxon and white superiority was widely held in both North and South (Logan, 1965: Parts II-III; Fredrickson, 1971; Haller, 1971; Newby, 1965).

To preserve white supremacy, the South remained agrarian and rebuffed industrialization early in the twentieth century. Only after the Second World War did it change its stance, recognizing that through industrialization its economic dependency upon the North could be broken. It openly lured northern industry south. Industrial development brought greater economic opportunity to whites; and blacks, increasingly restive, pushed for greater economic and political opportunities for themselves. Out of this emerged the civil rights movement, and the subsequent white repression precipitated Federal intervention on behalf of blacks. That, in turn, strengthened black opportunities and power resources. Again, as in the pre-Civil War and Reconstruction periods, white Southerners perceived their way of life as threatened, but at this point in time it was less their 'culture' that was threatened than it was the power and privilege they enjoyed over black Americans.

Agrarianism and white supremacy were fundamental tenets of the Boer/Afrikaner siege culture. Having imposed its control permanently over the Cape Colony in 1806, Britain and the English settlers, who regarded the Boers as culturally inferior, proceeded to implement liberal native policies that angered the Boers and precipitated the easily suppressed 1815 Boer rebellion. Subsequent metropole policies, including abolition of slavery, further alienated and threatened Boers, and many trekked inland to escape British rule. Metropole policy vacillated toward the Boers. Initially the trekkers were ignored, but when their frontier clashes with African tribes necessitated British troop intervention, Britain moved to control the Boers (LeMay, 1971: chs 2-5; Vatcher, 1965: chs 2-3; Thompson, 1960: chs 1-2).

Metropole policies precipitated the Anglo-Boer wars of 1880-1 and 1899-1902. Successfully rebuffing the British in the first, the Boers were momentarily accorded independence. However, the discovery of gold in the Transvaal changed that. Prospectors and adventurers from the USA and the Empire flooded into the area. The Boers rejected *uitlander* demands for political rights, realizing that if they acceded they would lose control of the Transvaal to the outsiders. The latter appealed to the metropole, which supported their demands. Still the Boers refused to concede, and the confrontation escalated. Rejecting a final British ultimatum, the Boers opted for war in order to protect their power and cultural identity. The cultural factor was the paramount issue, for the Boers recalled the earlier declaration of the British High Commissioner, Alfred Milner, that Britain should 'break the dominion of Afrikanerdom' by anglicizing the Boers (LeMay, 1971; Robinson and Gallagher, 1967: chs 3, 7, 14). That was his solution to the 'Boer problem,' a view reminiscent of Lord Durham's earlier proposal for eliminating English-French ethnic rivalry in Canada.

Boers had earlier fled the Cape and trekked inland to protect their culture and identity. They remained farmers, but the gold discoveries prompted British commercial and industrial intrusion in the Transvaal. Their defeat in the second Anglo-Boer war heightened the Afrikaner siege identity, and most remained on the land, struggling for their economic survival. Meanwhile, mining and industrial expansion benefited the Anglo South Africans while the Afrikaners remained poor. There emerged in the 1920s and depression years a 'poor white' problem, at its center the impoverished Afrikaner farmers whose economic plight nearly paralleled that of Africans. The war, their defeat and subsequent economic plight: all heightened Afrikaner siege perceptions. They attributed their unprivileged position to English cultural hostility. Moreover, as Afrikaners moved to urban centers seeking employment, their sense of being dispossessed was heightened when they found themselves competing with Africans for unskilled jobs. By 1948, fearful of African nationalism, angered by Anglo assimilationist pressures and the lack of economic opportunity, Afrikaners readily supported the National Party. With that election Afrikaner nationalism succeeded. Bypassed in the earlier economic development of the country, Afrikaners supported the National Party because it promised to use power in two ways: first, to bestow economic benefits upon the previously dispossessed Afrikaner group, and second, to protect the Afrikaner cultural identity — from Anglo assimilationist pressures and from the emergent African nationalism. Thus the Afrikaner cultural crisis created the necessary conditions for the emergence of a siege group; and, having mobilized its members, it proceeded to wrest power from others in order to protect its cultural identity.

Development factors also contributed to the emergence of French Canadians as a siege culture. France ceded Canada to Britain in 1763, leaving behind 70,000 French settlers, excluding the upper class which fled to France. In the 1774 Quebec Act the metropole guaranteed French settlers their language, laws and religion, but thereafter its policies and those of English settlers were directed toward assimilating the French culturally. These pressures helped precipitate the 1837 French rebellion. When Lord Durham, sent to evaluate the rebellion's causes, recommended that the French be forced to assimilate, the latter withdrew into their agrarian enclaves to preserve their way of life (Brunet, 1966; Careless and Brown, 1968; Morchain, 1967). Fortunately for the French, the metropole failed to implement Durham's recommendations. Indeed, French Canadians remained largely rural and isolated from the mainstream of Canada's economic development during the following century. Although development, especially industrial and mining, came to Quebec Province following the Second World War, it was controlled almost exclusively by Anglo Canadian and US corporations. That along with other issues and incidents exacerbated French-English tensions. Where late nineteenth century industrialization and immigration to the United States prompted assimilationist policies, within Canada a vociferous Anglo Canadian nationalism pushed for a 'Canadian nationality which . . . would be English' (Careless and Brown, 1968: 121). This frightened the French, and 'its survival openly threatened, French Canada resorted to every defensive mechanism at its disposal' (ibid.). That defensive posture took two directions: toward a continued agrarianism and isolation within Quebec Province, and toward a reactive nationalism which by the 1920s espoused an independent Laurentian Republic, that a precursor for recent independence movements.

Although it proclaims itself an ethnic mosaic, Canada, in terms of economic, political and social structures, remains Anglo controlled. Immigrants seeking economic opportunities quickly recognize that unless they assimilate their economic opportunities are limited. Within the Anglo-controlled Canadian and US industries that have moved to Quebec Province in recent decades, it is the French who speak English and have become anglicized who are the most readily incorporated

(Clark, 1971). These assimilationist pressures clearly prompted a decline in the French language and culture, and this, in conjunction with their resentment over external control of Quebec industry, revived French nationalism. A majority within Quebec Province, the French, as Afrikaners in South Africa, see themselves lacking control over their economic system. Moreover, because economic opportunities and benefits were largely withheld from those who refuse to become anglicized, French Canadians, as Afrikaners earlier, came to see themselves as locked into an economically dependent position. Fearful for their cultural survival, they have sought to gain control over the political system and their own destiny, threatening secession and possible independence if that is the only way of protecting their cultural heritage and identity.

Thus in Canada, the United States and South Africa, siege cultures have pursued diverse strategies to preserve their culture, their strategies shaped by differing political structures and power differentials. Numerous factors contributed to their emergence as siege cultures, but basic to all was the impact of economic development. Development initially bypassed all three groups, and development benefits, controlled by the dominant group, were usually withheld unless the subordinate cultural group discarded its own culture for that of the dominant group. Threats to their group identity, exacerbated by development, transformed these into siege cultures. Ethnicity and culture in society are influenced by the dominant group's cultural policies and how it incorporates other groups into economic, political and social structures. These relationships, of ethnic, development and power factors, are now traced below.

Intergroup relations and cultural policy have been shaped in these three countries by two factors: power and economic development. Power can be evaluated in two ways: relationally, in terms of group power capabilities, whether symmetrical or asymmetrical; and structurally, in terms of a given group's control over political, economic and social structures. In the former situation a group's power is determined by its resources and mobilization capabilities; in the latter, control is demonstrated by the group's ability to influence and determine cultural and structural policy decisions.

Besides power, economic development is a critical though intervening variable, for economic transformations alter the resources and mobilization capabilities of groups. Where development modifies group power capabilities, system change is possible. However, where dominant group power is extensive it uses developmental changes to its own advantage, solidifying its position of dominance. It may grant limited concessions to a subordinate group to placate it. This occurs in South Africa where Afrikaners have proffered minor concessions to Africans, Indians and coloreds as a means of modernizing racial domination while strengthening white control (Wolpe, 1970; Adam, 1971a, 1971b; Adam and Giliomee, 1979). Development, however, may serve to politicize subordinates, awakening within them a recognition of their powerlessness and exploitation, leading to responses whereby they seek to terminate the power imbalance. This occurred in the siege cultures, and similar processes, clearly aimed at breaking the patterns of domination, are evident among contemporary subordinate groups in South Africa, Canada and the USA.

Economic development, which often leaves subordinate groups in a disadvantaged position, may precipitate among subordinates organizational activities aimed at system change. This is evident among blacks and Indians in the USA and Canada, blacks in South Africa and the French in Canada. Established by South Africa to keep blacks economically dependent, the homelands have become centers for the mobilization of black opposition to government policies. Sharing unequally in the economic development of the country, blacks, particularly since the 1973 Durban strikes, have utilized — though not yet systematically — their strike power to wrest limited concessions from government. The marxian emphasis on controlling the pyramids of production has been reversed in the South African case. Blacks do not control the pyramids, but they control the base, and through strikes they can bring production and the economy to a halt. Even if that action is only momentary, it serves to reinforce the subordinate group's awareness that it is not totally powerless. Such pressure tactics have an incremental impact by reinforcing subordinate group perceptions that, despite the imposed constraints of society, they can contest against the system. They may wrest only limited concessions from the system initially, but more important than the concessions is the impact their actions have in forging group solidarity for further confrontations.

A few generalizations concerning power and development emerge from the foregoing assessment of these three countries. Present historically in all three countries was a white ethnocentrism 'exclusive' in character, i.e. nonwhites were viewed as 'outsiders.' Color served as the basis for that distinction, and nonwhites were and remain in some cases isolated or segmented from white society. Even for those who acquired the white culture, their color precluded cultural assimilation or inclusion within white social structures. There were and are exceptions. Lines of demarcation remain sharpest in South Africa, but de facto segregation in Canada and the United States, whether in schools, living arrangements, social relations, occupations or elsewhere, indicates that segments of white society wish to preserve a racially exclusive society.

Fearing eventual black rule, Afrikaners removed nonwhites from the political structure. Nonwhites in the USA and Canada were initially excluded from political structures but have since been incorporated. Despite the removal of legal barriers in the USA, problems remain. When nonwhite political mobilization activities threaten white groups or white power, the latter, whether Southern or Northern, mobilize to protect their own position. Illustrative of this is the mobilization in recent years of white ethnics (e.g. Irish, Italians, Poles and others) in the United States, each of which sees itself threatened by advances being made by blacks. Only when the subordinate group mobilizes its members is it able to break through the barriers of discrimination and opposition. Although all three countries have utilized nonwhite labor, the structural incorporation of the last has been closely regulated. To maintain control, white society established reserves, bantustans and ghettos, all of which have served as repositories for unskilled nonwhite labor should it be needed for development purposes. However, where there was or is a readily available white labor supply, nonwhites have been expendable. There are cases where a few members of nonwhite groups have acquired education and skills and have been incorporated. They have, in effect, become part of the privileged (mostly white) class, especially in the USA and Canada (W. Wilson, 1978; Scott, 1975). In South Africa, most nonwhites are restricted to low-level or semi-skilled positions, but recent government policy has been directed toward the limited structural incorporation of a few blacks into higher positions. This, as occurred earlier in Southern Rhodesia under United Federal Party rule, is an apparent attempt to co-opt middle-class blacks who might otherwise assume leadership of the black masses who oppose white society.

Another dimension of the dominant group's exclusive ethnocentrism is reflected in its response to immigrant whites. In general, the dominant group viewed immigrant group cultures as inferior to its own, but unlike nonwhites whose somatic characteristics precluded their total cultural assimilation or structural incorporation, immigrant whites could anticipate structural incorporation if they discarded their own culture for that of the dominant group. Immigrant groups were not incorporated at the same rate, and social incorporation usually lagged behind economic or political. However, the greater the cultural congruence of immigrant and dominant group cultures, the more rapidly the former group's incorporation. Assimilationist pressures varied in the three countries. Although immigrant groups were needed for development in the United States, most needed little inducement to come because the country provided economic opportunities in which they wished to share. Consequently, they were usually willing to shed their own cultural identity for that of the dominant group if it enhanced their economic opportunities. Given the shortage of settlers in Canada late in the nineteenth and early twentieth centuries, that country was forced to offer other inducements to immigrants. Most appealing to newcomers was its willingness to let them retain their cultural identity. Prior to 1948 there was less pressure on immigrants to South Africa to assimilate, though most became anglicized because it opened greater opportunities within economic structures. Once the National Party came to power in 1948, it discouraged immigration, particularly from England. Its efforts were aimed at opening up economic opportunities for Afrikaners. However, as the confrontation between black and white increased over the years, the government sought immigrants, even from Britain, desirous of expanding the size of the minority white population (vis-à-vis blacks) in that country.

Relations between dominant groups and siege cultures support the preceding assessments. Their cultural survival threatened by dominant group assimilationist policies, siege groups mobilized their resources, resorted initially to agrarianism and geographical isolation as a defensive measure, and remained outside the mainstream of economic development. This solidified dominant group control of economic structures. Left outside the mainstream of economic development the siege cultures' economic dependency increased. Geographically isolated and economically dependent, siege groups assumed a position not totally unlike that of nonwhite groups found on reserves, reservations, bantustans or in ghettos. Each represented a variant of internal colonialism (Blauner, 1972). Siege cultures possessed resources normally unavailable to nonwhite groups, and these they mobilized to contest against dominant group control. Afrikaners and white Southerners, for example, captured or used their control of political structures to broaden their economic resources, thereby strengthening their total power (political and economic) resources. By taking control of provincial political structures and moving to curtail federal powers within the province of Quebec, French Canadians now seek to mobilize economic and political resources to wrest total control from the federal government. In each case economic development played a critical role, facilitating the emergence of a subordinate group ideology, mobilization efforts and resource capabilities.

Given their political control, Afrikaners have since 1948 manipulated economic development to support racial domination. But industrialization often has unintended consequences. Desirous of broadening the economic gains of Afrikaners, the National Party hesitated in fully implementing apartheid/separate development policies. Instead, blacks were economically incorporated, though only at lower levels, but that provided them with the leverage to strike and bring the economy to a standstill, all of which suggests that they possess a competitive resource (labor) that can be utilized as a pressure resource (by striking) in support of structural change. It is a limited resource and innumerable factors work against its further use or success; however, when taken in conjunction with other mobilization activities, it can be employed by subordinate groups to force policy changes upon the dominant group. Elsewhere, in the American South, postwar industrialization slowly croded the siege culture's power and contributed to the structural incorporation (though at clearly differential levels) of blacks and whites. The slow accumulation of economic resources and increased political mobilization activities strengthened the power resources of Southern blacks, and through strikes, demonstrations and other activities they have forced changes in the system. In Quebec, economic development and external control (of government and industry) intensified nationalist sentiments, and French Canadians have mobilized to break this control.

In all three countries, group power capabilities and development needs have determined the character of cultural policy and group relations. South Africa remains a racially segmented society, and though there is a degree of cultural pluralism in terms of Afrikaner-English relations, some of their cultural differences blur and disappear under the impact of development (especially industrialization) and black nationalism. The latter, seen as a threat by both Afrikaners and

English, slowly transforms them into a racial siege group wherein cultural differences disappear in the face of a greater racial threat to their white group identity and their power and privilege. Canada and the United States are slowly losing the characteristics of racially segmented societies as nonwhite structural incorporation increases. Cultural pluralism also increases, for industrialization and development accommodate themselves to group diversity, the consequence increasingly a structural incorporation based on merit rather than ascriptive criteria.

Chapter 8
Psychological bases of white-nonwhite group encounters

I

Although group power differentials and color, culture and situational factors primarily shape the character of group encounters, psychological factors should not be discounted. Behavior is often symbolic, reflecting such psychological factors as fear, envy, anger, resentment, joy, expectation and empathy. These psychological factors are readily evident in analyses of white-nonwhite relations in the Anglo fragments, but it is examples from Canada and the United States that are drawn upon here for illustrative purposes.

The term 'nonwhite' is employed for three specific groups: indigenes and those of African and Asian descent. Of the three, only Asians were immigrants, for Africans were brought against their will and indigenes were natives of North America. Despite these differences, all three groups have been treated historically by whites as 'outsiders.' When not needed in the country's development, whites sought to 'remove' non-whites from society, color serving as the ascriptive basis for discriminatory treatment.

Descriptions of white behavior as 'racist' explain little, for racism as an ideology emerged only in late nineteenth century North America (Banton, 1967; Van den Berghe, 1967; Gossett, 1965). Racism served as a rationalization for prevailing beliefs and practices, but the term itself explains little about the more rudimentary factors that prompted historical patterns of prejudice and discrimination. To get at these one must probe the underlying psychological factors which are brought into sharper focus by drawing attention initially to the color/culture (identity) and power factors previously discussed.

Identity factors include for individuals their beliefs and attitudes concerning color, culture, social relationships and the type of society they desire. These beliefs, labelled an ideology by Elkins (1971) and a belief system by Rokeach (1960, 1968), constitute the basic identity for individuals or groups, shaping their perceptions and behavior. Jordan (1969), in his analysis of white attitudes toward slavery, demonstrates how color predispositions of white (and especially English) settlers contributed to the enslavement of Africans who were initially brought to the American colonies as indentured servants. The color black, Jordan and Kovel argue, evoked within whites negative or hostile feelings and images, black connoting, among other things, bestiality, evil, sin, irrational sexual impulses and savagery (Jordan, 1969: ch. 1; Kovel, 1971: chs 4, 7-8). Because blacks were viewed as animals or subhuman beings, their enslavement elicited within whites few moral misgivings.

Hoetink (1967: 120) labels these color factors a 'somatic norm image,' or 'the complex of physical (somatic) characteristics which are accepted by a group (or society) as its norm or ideal.' If his definition is broadened, it is possible to speak of a 'cultural norm image' that embraces a complex of cultural (religious, philosophical, political and behavioral) characteristics which are accepted by a group or society as its norm or ideal. Taken together, somatic and cultural norm images constitute a society's ideal image of itself: they are its ideology, belief system or group identity (Erikson, 1950; Shinn, 1964; Lewis, 1955). Individuals, groups and societies invariably assume that their identity and cultural/somatic norm images are superior to those of others (Shibutani and Kwan, 1965: chs 3-4; Hoetink, 1967: Part II, ch. 4), hence each group is to some degree ethnocentric. However, one must distinguish between exclusive and inclusive types of ethnocentrism. Exclusive ethnocentrism exists where a high degree of insularity exists within a group, outsiders rebuffed for fear that their entry or acceptance will threaten the group's 'purity' (DeVos, 1971). Where inclusive ethnocentrism prevails, the group, although presuming its somatic/ cultural superiority, accepts outsiders for membership or incorporation providing they reject their own culture and accept that of the purportedly superior culture or dominant group.

Both types of ethnocentrism are evident in Canada and the United States. Porter (1965), although concluding that people of Anglo and French descent constitute the 'charter groups' of Canadian society, recognizes, as do others, that the dominant Anglo group sought by numerous means to impose its cultural norm image on others, including those of French descent. In the USA, as Gordon (1964) illustrates, the dominant cultural group was composed historically of people of Anglo extraction. At least at the surface level, the historical patterns of group integration differed markedly in the two countries. Subscribing to an 'ethnic mosaic,' the dominant Anglo group in Canada allowed other immigrant groups to retain a part of their ethnic and cultural identity. In the United States, however, the dominant Anglo group virtually forced other groups to shed their cultural and ethnic identity and become anglicized in the 'melting pot.' Both cases constitute variants of inclusive ethnocentrism, though its application was limited to white groups.

Nonwhite groups encountered the opposite, an exclusive form of ethnocentrism, for their membership in society was usually rejected. Each society reluctantly acknowledged the presence of nonwhite groups it could not expel, seeking instead to isolate them in enclaves, be it reservations, ghettos or other special areas. Whites normally rebuffed nonwhite efforts at complete integration, this clearly illustrated in the case of Amerindians and Africans who sought to 'be' or 'act' white. Nonwhites thereby remained 'outsiders.'[1] In terms of a 'core culture,' both societies embraced an identity based almost exclusively on Anglo somatic and cultural norm images. This holds true for Canada as well as the United States, its 'ethnic mosaic' claims notwithstanding. There, the 'core' French group possessed limited political or economic power and was treated by Anglo Canadians as a subordinate and inferior group — except for its members who discarded their French language and culture and became anglicized. The closer an individual or group approximated the Anglo color and culture norm image, the more readily was his or its membership accepted. Nonwhites were the exception. Even if they embraced that culture, they could not fulfill the somatic norm image, hence color served as the basis for their exclusion or outsider status.

As noted previously (chapter 4), cultural rather than color distinctions precipitated initial negative white responses toward Amerindians and Africans. French and English behavior toward Indians differed somewhat, but situational factors were as important as cultural attitudes in accounting for these behavioral differences. More interested in the fur trade than colonization, the French government closely regulated settler-Indian relations in Canada. French ethnocentrism was essentially inclusive, for it assumed that Indians could be 'civilized' if they discarded their own beliefs and behavior and accepted French culture and religion. Jesuits were usually entrusted with this civilizing mission, but they sought to isolate Indians from whites, fearful that European contact would corrupt the Indian. Consequently, intergroup contacts were limited, and this contributed to what were with some exceptions generally more harmonious relations between settlers and indigenes than existed within English colonies (Goldstein, 1969; Parkman, 1902; Kennedy, 1950; Lanctot, 1963; Eccles, 1969).

For more than two centuries, from the Pequot War (1637) onwards, settlers fought Indians for control of lands within what became the United States. Britain took control of Canada in 1763, but settler-Indian conflicts never reached the same level of intensity there as existed to the south (Ellis, 1882; Jacobs, 1950; MacLeod, 1928; Prucha, 1962; Horsman, 1967; Patterson, 1972). Earlier, as in the Massachusetts colony, limited efforts were made to 'civilize' the Indians (e.g. the seventeenth century Praying Towns experiment), but most settlers viewed Indians as savages who were culturally and biologically inferior. This exclusive form of settler ethnocentrism surfaced most sharply during crises, including King Philip's War (1675-6) when settlers rounded up and incarcerated even the baptized Indians who had accepted christianity and the white man's culture. Settlers adhered to the belief — 'once a savage, always a savage' (Vaughan, 1965: ch. 12; Ellis, 1882: ch. 6; MacLeod, 1928: chs 17-18; Leach, 1958: chs 8-10). These attitudes persisted over time, accounting for white treatment of Cherokees more than a century later. Although Cherokees accepted christianity and white culture and established virtually identical political institutions, they were driven from Georgia by President Jackson because whites refused to live in close proximity to 'savages' (Weinberg, 1963: ch. 3; Foreman, 1953; Rogin, 1971). Whites wanted Cherokee lands, but cultural factors were equally significant in prompting white behavior.

Whites, as Pearce (1965: ch. 7) indicates, considered the Indian 'locked in' by a culture that compelled him to remain a savage despite his efforts to become 'civilized.' Viewed in these terms, Indian culture was considered innate or genetically transmitted. While this cultural factor was clearly important, the Indian's color also served to distinguish Indian from white (Jordan, 1969: 95-8; Keiser, 1933: chs 8, 12, 21; Pearce, 1965: ch. 7). Similar notions, though in muted form, prevailed in Canada. Indian reserves were established to protect the 'inferior' Indian from white civilization. Because indigenes were thought incapable of coping with a superior white society, a policy of separation was invoked (Patterson, 1972; Fey and McNickle, 1970). Thus in both societies the Indian was viewed as an outsider, a person and group doomed to extinction. However, Indians could not be removed as could the other two nonwhite groups who could be shipped to Africa or Asia, but they could be isolated on reserves or reservations.

Cultural rather than color factors provided the initial basis for contrast conceptions between European and African, initial 'christian-heathen' differentiations subsequently replaced by 'civilized-uncivilized' and 'white-black' distinctions. The color distinction evoked negative responses in whites (Jordan, 1969: 22-4, 91-6), and blacks, whether slave or free, were viewed as subhuman. Except for Nova Scotia, there were few blacks in Canada, and most were freed prior to Britain's abolition of slavery in its colonies (Winks, 1971). Consequently, abolition created fewer animosities there than flared up in the United States. Given their limited numbers, Afro-Canadians were seldom perceived by whites as either a political or economic threat; but in the United States, whites in the North as well as South responded aggressively to the presense of blacks during the late nineteenth and early twentieth centuries. Indeed, the cultural media became the major vehicle for perpetuating racist views and portraying blacks as inferior (Logan, 1965; Newby, 1965; Nolen, 1967; Baker, 1972, 1973). Despite some differences, whites in both countries considered themselves superior to nonwhites — and sought to preserve their 'white purity.' Their exclusive ethnocentrism was reflected in their fear that miscegenation would lead to 'contamination' or 'pollution' of the white race, a fear that was exacerbated by the late nineteenth century influx of Chinese and Japanese (Young and Reid, 1939; LaViolette, 1945, 1948; Winks, 1971: chs 9-10; Daniels, 1970; Gossett, 1965: chs 12-15; Newby, 1965; Miller, 1969: ch. 7).

Chinese were recruited or shanghaied to North America to build railroads, work the mines or perform menial labor from the 1850s onwards. Most settled along the West Coast, from California to British Columbia. Working for low wages, the Chinese immediately generated hostility among white workers, particularly the Irish (Miller, 1969: ch. 8; Lee, 1960; Kung, 1962; LaViolette, 1945). Conflicts, riots and widespread discrimination ensued; and local governing bodies, bowing to white pressures, enacted discriminatory measures. Labor was not solely responsible, for the white middle class, perceiving its culture and power threatened by the presence of Amerindians, Mexicans, Africans and Chinese, supported the anti-Chinese agitations (Barth, 1964; Miller, 1969: chs 7-9; LaViolette, 1958). Likewise, liberals and clergymen who initially defended the Chinese presence subsequently demanded their expulsion when Chinese rebuffed white assimilationist efforts (Miller, 1969: 61-75; Barth, 1964: 159-64; LaViolette, 1958: 151-3). The end result was virtually preordained: persistent public pressures forced national governments in Canada and the USA to enact Chinese exclusionary legislation (C. Price, 1966; Timlin, 1960; Young and Reid, 1939; Daniels, 1970; Kung, 1962).

The legislation, however, did not exclude other Asians, and Japanese immigrants flooded into the western states and British Columbia during the last decade of the nineteenth century. The white response was immediate: racial confrontations and demands for Japanese expulsion. White fishermen and farmers were particularly hostile, for they found themselves competing economically with the Japanese. The Japanese government protested vehemently against the treatment of its citizens. Earlier, the Chinese government had also protested, but because it was feeble and dominated by European powers, the US and Canadian governments ignored its protests. Japan, however, emerged as a world power following its defeat of Russia in the war of 1904-5, and US, Canadian and British governments listened to the Japanese protests. All took steps to curtail discriminatory practices, and the Japanese government agreed to dissuade its citizens from emigrating to North America (Huttenback, 1976).

Anti-Asian sentiments persisted, however, and following the First World War Canada and the United States enacted restrictive immigration laws that discriminated against nonwhite groups. White prejudices towards Asians, muted momentarily, surfaced again during the Second World War, and Japanese within both countries, whether aliens or citizens, were arrested and placed in concentration camps, their properties confiscated. As the war concluded, whites protested against the proposed repatriation of Japanese to their former West Coast homes, demanding instead that they, including those who were citizens of the USA and Canada, be sent to Japan. Underlying these demands were the racial prejudices of whites (LaViolette, 1958; TenBroek et al., 1968), for no such demands were made for the incarceration or expulsion of Germans and Italians in the USA or Canada even though both countries were at war with Germany and Italy.

Racial prejudice prompted the wartime detention of Japanese (Grodzins, 1949), and white demands for the 'removal' of all Japanese to Japan paralleled historical white attitudes toward other nonwhite groups: remove Indians to reservations; remove blacks by sending them to Africa; remove Chinese immigrants and prohibit the entry of others into North America; and remove Japanese to concentration camps and thereafter to Japan, including those who were citizens of the USA or Canada. This demand for the removal of nonwhite groups was motivated by a pervasive obsession of Anglo and other white groups: namely, the desire to maintain the nation's 'white identity' and protect the dominant somatic and cultural norm images.

From colonization onwards each society, Canada and the USA, forged for itself a national identity, the struggle to establish that identity being most evident in the United States where, even prior to the Revolution, society increasingly rejected the Old World heritage and proclaimed itself a 'new society' from which would emerge a 'new man' (Koch, 1964: chs 3-4; Parkes, 1959: ch. 1; Spencer, 1957: chs 1-3; Sanford, 1961: chs 1-3; Lewis, 1955). That new man, however transmogrified, nevertheless remained Anglo in his beliefs, behavior and acceptance of Anglo somatic and cultural norm images. Non-Anglo whites could be assimilated, but the melting pot meant that they must be anglicized. Consequently, culture and institutions remained essentially Anglo; and the USA, as Canada, retained the characteristics of an Anglo fragment (Hartz, 1964). Canada preserved similar characteristics despite the French presence and the rhetoric which claimed the two groups were equal (Elliott, 1971; McRae, 1964; Brunet, 1966; Porter, 1965). Hence Canada's portrayal of itself as an ethnic mosaic is misleading. Moreover, nonwhites remained outsiders in both countries, for whites were obsessed with their white identity (Porter, 1965: 66-71; Winks, 1971: 295-302, 435-7; Davis and Krauter, 1971: ch. 9).

Society's emphasis on its white or Anglo identity increased during periods that constituted types of stress situations: frontier encounters, where whites contested with Indians for land and resources; the pre-Civil War period when southerners were threatened by northern economic power and Abolitionist opposition; the postwar Reconstruction period when both southern and northern whites grew fearful as blacks increased their economic and political power; the transitional and unstable late nineteenth-century West Coast societies in both countries that witnessed a large influx of nonwhites; and numerous cultural crises during which whites feared that the nonwhite presence threatened the very 'character' of society. Stress was exacerbated by the massive infusion of other non-Anglo white immigrant groups. Although most were ultimately integrated or incorporated, their initial presence disturbed and threatened the dominant Anglo group. Once incorporated, however, these anglicized and assimilated white groups embraced, usually wholeheartedly, the dominant Anglo somatic and cultural norm images and supported or even led the opposition to nonwhite groups.

These characteristics, most evident in the United States, are also present in Canada. Similar patterns prevailed in other Anglo societies as well, including Australia, New Zealand, South Africa and Southern Rhodesia (Huttenback, 1976; Baker, 1975). The patterns are somewhat obscured under the ethnic mosaic myth of Canada, but beneath the myth the similarities emerge. Canada, fearful of being 'swallowed up' by its southern neighbor, struggled late in the nineteenth and early twentieth centuries to achieve a distinct identity, and that meant projecting itself as a contrast conception to the USA. As part of that contrast, it professed (and believed) that it treated 'its' Indians and blacks better than did the USA. However, as various observers have noted (Troper, 1972; LaViolette, 1958, 1961; Maykovich, 1975; Patterson, 1972, 1975; Winks, 1971), white behavior toward nonwhites in Canada differed little from that in the United States. Both societies clearly differentiated between white and nonwhite groups. Whites 'belonged' while nonwhites were simply tolerated and kept at a distance on reservations, reserves or in ghettos. The two societies followed somewhat divergent paths in incorporating or integrating immigrant white groups (the melting pot vs. the ethnic mosaic), but both countries, despite these variations, isolated nonwhites in a separate and subordinate category, thereby protecting the white identity of both societies. Both societies utilized power, economic, political and otherwise, to preserve white hegemony.

II

Although color and cultural factors influenced the character of white-nonwhite group relations, other — and particularly power — factors were significant. Explored more fully in previous chapters, the power factor as raised here illustrates the connection between it and psychological factors that shaped white responses to nonwhite groups.

Power, as Friedrich (1963: 160) suggests, is an ambiguous term, for it 'is to some extent a possession, and to some extent a relation.' It is, however, omnipresent: 'Every social act is an exercise of power, every social relationship is a power equation, and every social group or system is an organization of power' (Hawley, 1963: 422). Three major types of power discussed previously (chapter 2) include force, dominance and authority. The first two are usually based on coercion while the third rests on consent. Coercive power can be physical, political, economic or psychological. Three types of power contests occurred in Canada and the United States: (a) intergroup power struggles, where force (physical or otherwise) was employed for determining the power resources and capabilities of each group; (b) intergroup power contests, occurring within or outside the major structures, to determine the distribution or redistribution of the country's resources and riches; and (c) other power contests that determined who would control the political and economic structures within which policy choices are made concerning cultural and distributive decisions (Lenski, 1966).

Settler-Indian and metropole-Indian power relations, discussed more fully in chapter 4, accent the major characteristics of power relations and point to the role of psychological factors in these relations. Indians initially possessed power capabilities sufficient to expel settlers; and the latter, aware of this, sought to maintain amicable relations. Meanwhile, a concatenation of factors — metropole military intervention, diseases, trade or other factors that destroyed Indian economic systems, intertribal warfare and indigenous group disagreements that curtailed their ability to unite and fight the intruders — undermined Indian military power capabilities and curtailed their ability to thwart settler and metropole acquisition of Indian lands.

Two dates, 1637 and 1830, signify the major period of settler-Indian encounters within what became the United States. In 1637, persistent settler land encroachments precipitated the Pequot War, and colonists, taking advantage of their momentary military superiority, defeated the Pequots and their allies in southern New England. Thereafter, in a series of sporadic but significant confrontations, white troops, often in alliance with other Indian groups, defeated opposing Indian tribes or drove them westward. A series of names and dates mark the decline of Indian power: King Philip's War (1675); the French-

Indian War and the impact upon Indians of France's cession of Canada to Britain; Fallen Timbers (1794); Tippecanoe (1811); and the American military defeats of various British and Indian forces during the War of 1812. Following the termination of that war, whites, with but few exceptions (mainly the Osceola in Florida and Black Hawk in Illinois) controlled most lands east of the Mississippi or subjugated Indians remaining in that area. The Indian Removal Act of 1830 signified the supremacy of white power; and though military force was still necessary for crushing Indian uprisings west of the Mississippi, whites were able to quell disturbances and force Indians onto reservations. The reservation system helped create conditions that instilled within many Indians dependency patterns which further solidified white control (Leighton, 1959; Gurian, 1975).

Similar though usually less extreme processes were at work in Canada. Power over Indian affairs initially rested with the British metropole, but in 1867 it turned over control of 'native affairs' to the Canadian government. Given the sparseness of settlers and the extensive tracts of available land, settlers and Indians seldom came in contact with each other. But there were confrontations, and these the British and Canadian governments sought to resolve or prevent by negotiating treaties and establishing Indian reserves. Although Indians retained some of their previously held lands (in contrast to the USA, where Indians were often removed from their original lands and given others), the reserve system and contact with whites undermined Indian economic systems and cultures. That left Indians in an increasingly dependent position, economically as well as psychologically. On the West Coast, however, the Canadian government refused to recognize Indian land claims. Instead, it imposed its control over Indians and sought to destroy their cultures (i.e. to 'civilize' them), thereby precipitating subsequent Indian protest movements (LaViolette, 1961).

The reserve or reservation system proved highly effective in perpetuating white control over indigenous groups. Physical force, if necessary, could be readily utilized, for metropole troops were usually stationed nearby. Normally, though, the reservation itself stifled rebellion by creating dependency behavior among Indians. The reserve was a form of colony, and white officials, whether government administrators, missionaries or others, sought to 'civilize' Indians by destroying indigenous cultures and imposing upon Indians the white man's culture. These acts contributed to the social disorganization of Indian tribes; and whites, by withholding economic goods necessary for survival, coerced Indians into obeying the former's dictates and commands. Indian disobedience invariably prompted reprisals, economic, political or physical.

Canadian practises, though on the surface more humane, had a similar psychological impact, for the reserve system tended to 'make the Indians economically and politically dependent on the white man's government; to utterly destroy the Indian spirit' (Waubageshig, 1970). By imposing white values and cultures upon Indians, officials destroyed the Indian way of life (LaViolette, 1961; Patterson, 1975; cf. Gurian, 1975). What emerged were dependency relationships and behavior (Mannoni, 1964), with whites utilizing diverse forms of power, coercive, political, economic and psychological, to keep Indians in a dependent and subordinate position. Indians who left the reserves or reservations often manifested this dependency behavior; and for them as well as others, their color, culture and behavior reinforced white perceptions of Indians as inferior and powerless people. Thus it was seldom the threat of Indian *power* that prompted hostile white behavior; rather it was other, often psychological, factors which precipitated white responses.

White-black relations similarly illustrate the intertwining of power and psychological factors. Blacks, historically, were also powerless. There was the potential for blacks exercising power in some situations, but they, as Indians, were closely controlled. Consequently, given the limited nature of even a potential black threat to white power, whites should not have — in terms of the power factor — responded to blacks in a strident manner. Explanations for white behavior must be found elsewhere, primarily in psychological factors. These emerge in assessments of the character of black-white relations. Brought initially to the American colonies as indentured servants, Africans were quickly enslaved because of the white man's 'ability to do so with impunity' (Ruchames, 1970: 15). Predisposed against Africans because of their color and culture, whites, who esteemed power, viewed the blacks' powerlessness with contempt. Blacks, as slaves, had limited opportunity to rebel. Nevertheless, white fears of black insurrections were pervasive, and rumors of possible rebellions created near-paranoia among whites. Cases of black rebelliousness prompted harsh if not brutal reprisals from whites. Slaves who sought to survive by adopting what Elkins (1959) labelled 'Sambo' behavior (i.e. of appearing docile, slow-witted and happy-go-lucky) fulfilled white stereotypes of blacks as dependent and inferior beings. Blacks, whether in Canada or the USA, slave or free, were not considered the equal of whites; and whites in the North and Canada openly discriminated against them (Berwanger, 1967; Litwack, 1961; Winks, 1971).

Following the Civil War, blacks in the South and North sought to enhance their economic and political position. That threatened whites. There emerged a pervasive racist ideology which, while alluding to the black political and economic threat, focused on white fears of racial miscegenation and the possible 'pollution' of the white race through interracial marriage. That pollution, it was feared, would 'contaminate' whites and transform them into subhumans whose animal-like behavior would be uncontrollable. Whites would fall prey to uncontrollable emotions and sexual passions, the very qualities that whites accused blacks of possessing (Kovel, 1971; Wood, 1970; Newby, 1965; Stember, 1976). These white fears were further exacerbated by the influx of other nonwhite groups into the country, especially Chinese and Japanese.

Neither the Chinese nor Japanese represented a political or economic threat to Canada or the USA, but white society's color and cultural biases and fears prompted their hostile response to Asians. Chinese, to avoid conflicts with whites, sought jobs which whites did not want. Even so, whites responded with hostility, for the Chinese response was viewed as a sign of weakness or powerlessness. The Japanese, however, organized, confronted local authorities and protested to the US, Canadian and Japanese governments about their treatment. The situation was momentarily resolved, but white resentment toward the Japanese persisted, surfacing later in the prejudice and discriminatory practises directed against this 'yellow peril,' exploding finally during the Second World War when both North American governments, prodded by white citizens, incarcerated Japanese in concentration camps (Daniels, 1970; TenBroek et al., 1968; LaViolette, 1948).

Although power and power differentials influenced the character of white responses to nonwhite groups, the virtual powerlessness (except for momentary periods) of these groups suggests that it was not fear of the others' power that solely accounted for white behavior. Nor can white reactions, reflected in racist views and policies, be attributed solely to the white rationalizations used to justify exploitation of these groups. Nor can white behavior be attributed totally to white somatic and cultural norm images or to color/culture biases. A key factor can be discerned in the persistence with which whites expressed their fears of

the 'black peril,' the 'yellow peril' and the possibility of racial miscegenation, these fears conjuring for whites images of 'racial pollution'
or the 'contamination of the white race.' These fears motivated whites
to isolate nonwhite groups — on reserves, reservations and in ghettos —
through legislation, segregatory measures and even laws against interracial marriage. What these actions indicate is an obsessive fear within
whites of these other groups, all of which had one attribute in common: they were not white.

However, the color factor in itself does not explain white responses
to nonwhites. Color was simply the symbol of other factors. Although
cultural and power factors partly explain white behavior toward nonwhites, the preceding analysis suggests that neither they nor color
factors fully explain white behavior. Rather, another possible source for
their behavior must be explored: underlying psychological factors.

III

The almost feverish attempt by early nineteenth-century white America
to rid itself of blacks by shipping them to Africa was, as Jordan (1969:
567) suggests, 'so persistent while so preposterously utopian' that it
constituted 'a compelling fantasy.' Similar efforts, though less extensive, occurred in Canada, particularly in Nova Scotia where the largest
number of blacks resided (Winks, 1971). Jordan attributes these efforts
to psychological factors, Kovel (1971: ch. 1) to psychohistorical ones.
Hartz (1964) and his colleagues trace white motivations toward nonwhites to massive cultural changes that occurred earlier in European
history and subsequently influenced people's beliefs and perceptions
as well as events in the New World. Most significant among these were
religious, cultural and scientific transformations that significantly
restructured European thought during the fifteenth to eighteenth
centuries (Kovel, 1971: chs 6-7; Butterfield, 1960; Whitehead, 1967;
Reichenbach, 1951; Bury, 1955). The discovery of the New World also
had a major impact, for it dramatically altered European perceptions of
the world (Jones, 1968). These various changes had an ambivalent
impact, however. Protestantism and secular thought emphasized (in
part) man's self-reliance and free will, but religious thought in general,
whether Protestant or Catholic, continued to believe in the duality of
man's nature, i.e. that he was simultaneously the son of God and a

creature of uncontrollable passions and aggressions. The latter, portrayed in religious thought as man's 'animal nature,' were feared as attributes or impulses that had to be rigidly regulated in man.

Within European society the church and other institutions could closely and rigidly regulate individual human behavior. This was less true in the colonies, for settlers, traders and adventurers often found themselves in situations where they could give freer reign to their impulses. However, the church and, indeed, the society itself, tried to impose constraints and restrict colonial people in their newly found freedom. That created tension and anxiety within individuals, be it those seeking greater freedom or those who, fearful of what would transpire if their passions were unleashed, sought to impose their will upon others. Both secular and religious authorities struggled to regulate behavior, fearful that individuals would otherwise become creatures of impulse and revert to 'uncivilized' or 'animal' behavior. People were, as Jordan (1969: 40; cf. Baudet, 1965) concludes, caught in their own minds and in society between the dual forces of 'adventure and control.' Despite the freedom that it afforded, the frontier demanded of individuals a high degree of self-discipline, restraint and control, for without these attributes the individual could not survive. The frontier pitted individuals against the elements and, in many instances, hostile groups, the persistent presence of potential danger creating for individuals a high degree of stress. Individuals who could not control their impulses were suspect, considered by others to be uncivilized. Power over others was thereby deemed essential, for if people were not controlled they might revert to uncontrollable impulses or savagery. Individuals who believed they were civilized either denied the existence within themselves of these impulses or lauded their impulse control and self-discipline. In either case, they projected upon others these 'animal' impulses, attributing irrational behavior and aggression to individuals considered a threat (e.g. Indians) or thought to be powerless (slaves). Obsessed with the image of themselves as civilized, whites projected upon others their own aggressive and sexual impulses. As Jordan (1969: 579) suggests: 'White men were attempting to destroy the living image of primitive aggressions which they said was the Negro but was really their own.'

Implicit in Jordan's analysis is the premise that a culture imposes particular demands and constraints upon an individual. These cultural demands and constraints influence or shape his perceptions, beliefs and behavior. Beyond this, there are an individual's own psychological needs, including the need or feeling for safety, security, affection, affiliation, belonging, and esteem (Maslow, 1954; Knutson, 1972). These needs likewise influence an individual's perceptions, beliefs and behavior. Societal demands and constraints and the individual's needs may conflict or complement each other, as Freud (1962) and Fromm (1941) among others have noted. The particular interplay of these factors is partly determined by the specific situation in which an individual finds himself, situational factors thereby serving as a precipitant for an individual's behavior (Aronoff, 1967; Yinger, 1965; Lewin, 1951).

Jordan and Kovel focus on these diverse factors, including societal demands/constraints, individual needs and situations. Religious, particularly protestant thought, and other cultural demands stressed in individuals the necessity of rigid behavior patterns (e.g. impulse control, denial restriction, sobriety, and industriousness), emphasizing particularly self-control and self-discipline. Individuals or groups whose culture and characteristics differed markedly were viewed as a threat, for it was feared that they and their culture might induce people to reject impulse control and revert to 'animal-like' behavior. Thus it was presumed that indigenous or Indian cultures might 'contaminate' civilized people and entice whites to 'go native' (Vaughan, 1965: 208-9; Jordan, 1969: 573-82). The basis for this fear is obvious: 'going native' threatened the entire belief system of the white group. Power became significant in this context, for the dominant white cultural group felt compelled to control the 'animal behavior' it feared present in its own members and in those it classified as savages or slaves. Power was deemed vital for controlling what were seen as almost uncontrollable impulses, passions and aggressions latent in human nature.

Psychological needs are another determinant of behavior (Fromm, 1941; Maslow, 1954), and these needs or need deprivation can have political implications (Fromm, 1941; Knutson, 1972; cf. Davies, 1963; Greenstein, 1969; Wolfenstein, 1969). Maslow (1954) concludes that all human beings have particular needs that must be fulfilled, including among others, the need for safety, security, affection, belonging, self-esteem and self-actualization. Early and particularly severe need deprivation, whether of one or more needs, influences an individual's later behavior even if the need has since been filled. For example, individuals who early in life feel threatened or lack security will often later in life become anxiety-ridden, intolerant and dogmatic. They perceive the world as threatening and chaotic, and they view with suspicion and hostility others who are different or seen as threatening. Anxiety-ridden people often seek to impose order, sameness and consistency upon others and the world, for ambiguities, differences and contra-dictions create for them additional anxiety (Knutson, 1972: 28).

Individuals who early in life are deprived of affection or who believe they do not 'belong' often become distrustful of others (ibid.: 36). Despite that distrust they have an intense need for affiliation or belong-ing, a need sometimes filled by subordinating themselves to a leader or cause. Willing to be dominated by a leader, they may, in turn, seek to dominate or exercise power over others (ibid.: 40; Fromm, 1941: chs 3-4; Neumann, 1960). The individual who lacks self-esteem will often seek out causes, support social movements or accept belief systems that denigrate others (Knutson, 1972: 50), that denigration of others providing a degree of status and self-esteem. Such individuals, Rokeach (1956: 5-6; cf. Rokeach, 1960: chs 1, 4, 7) claims, willingly accept 'closed belief systems,' particularly if they 'feel alone or isolated in the world they live in . . . [and are] fearfully anxious of what the future holds.' Thus feelings of inadequacy or insecurity lead some individuals 'to overcome such feelings by becoming excessively con-cerned with the need for power and status' (Rokeach, 1956: 6).

Adulthood experiences can also precipitate feelings of psychological deprivation. For example, stress situations create anxiety within indi-viduals, and previously filled psychological needs (e.g. security, safety, belonging) are no longer fulfilled, thereby creating insecurity and anxiety. Individuals, for example, who previously felt secure may as a consequence of new encounters or experiences fear for their safety or security. New experiences may create still other need deprivations — of affection, affiliation or self-esteem. Consequently, if new situations or experiences create stress for individuals, the situations must be scruti-nized as determinants of behavior.

Stress for individuals, often situationally determined, can be extern-ally or internally induced. If externally induced, the stress derives directly from the situation (e.g. a specific event, pressures from society to conform to particular behavior patterns, etc.); if internally induced, the stress, though possibly precipitated by the situation, emanates from within the individual (e.g. need fulfillment, a feeling or belief that he must act in a particular manner or suffer guilt or the opprobrium of society, etc.). Whatever the source, external or internal, the consequent stress precipitates within individuals particular forms of behavior. Of concern here are the types of situations that create stress for individuals or groups.

Diverse types of new experiences may, whether recognized or not, create stress for individuals or groups. Frontier type situations, for example, created stress for numerous individuals. Previously secure people encountered a harsh, often hostile and threatening frontier environment, the threat deriving from the elements or hostile groups. Frontier-type conditions usually prevailed for an extended period, perpetuating stress for individuals while reshaping their perceptions, beliefs and behavior and creating various forms of insecurity. The need, then, for security and safety was because of changed conditions no longer fulfilled, and that affected the perceptions, feelings and behavior of people, leaving them feeling insecure and unsafe. New forms of patterned behavior usually emerged, and these patterns persisted long after the original source of stress (i.e. the situation) changed. The frontier was one such stress situation. Slavery was another. Domination and exploitation were based on white power; and violence, where necessary, was ruthlessly employed to preserve the system. But violence was a two-edged sword, for slaves, too, could rebel. Slave uprisings and insurrections, whether real or rumored, intensified the fears of whites. They, as frontier settlers, imagined themselves surrounded by hostile, nonwhite enemies. Their fears were exacerbated by Northern abolitionists who threatened to free the slaves, a situation that would enable the latter to visit retribution on Southern whites. As a consequence, whites grew increasingly insecure, perceiving themselves as a group under siege. What evolved, in effect, was a siege or *laager* mentality,[2] whites viewing themselves as surrounded by a hostile environment. In both situations, frontier and slavery, adult rather than childhood experiences created within people psychological need privations that prompted the new forms of behavior described.

Psychological as well as situational factors shaped white responses to nonwhites, and the two factors are closely linked. Both factors shaped white perceptions of nonwhites, transforming perceptions into highly rigid, polarized 'contrast conceptions' of 'we' and 'they,' with whites attributing to Indians and blacks the negative qualities which they refused to admit existed in themselves (Copeland, 1939; Blumer,

1958). The psychological processes by which this occurred can be readily illustrated. Frontier situations, where settlers encountered physical and other threats to their wellbeing, created within individuals a high level of stress. Moreover, cultural demands, whether self- or societally-imposed, added to an individual's stress, for previously held beliefs and practises were of necessity modified or discarded on the frontier: the individual had to adapt to survive. Some individuals welcomed these changes, but the lack of externally imposed controls created anxiety among others. In effect, individuals in frontier situations were starting anew, forced to create their own guidelines for behavior. That freedom threatened some, for without control or discipline they feared that they or others would fall prey to aggressive or other impulses, including irrational forces that could lead to chaos, anarchy and a reversion to savagery (Jordan, 1969: 578-82; Jones, 1968: chs 2, 5, 8). Religion, particularly Protestant religions, sought to keep tight rein over people; and early revivalist movements were in part motivated by efforts to bring these feared impulses under control.

Frontier conditions necessitated similar control, for the harsh environment demanded of individuals who hoped to survive a high level of self-discipline, impulse control, denial, industriousness and perseverence. There was little opportunity for revelry or relaxation, for frontier conditions compelled a struggle for survival. The environment was usually harsh and hostile; and the Indian, increasingly belligerent as his lands were taken, was viewed as part of a hostile environment that had to be conquered. If simple subduing was ineffective, then the Indian's extermination was deemed necessary, that view rationalized on the ground that the Indian's demise was part of an ineluctable law of progress or survival of the fittest (Pearce, 1965). The rationalization itself is not the significant factor: what is are the psychological factors that predisposed many whites to embrace or believe such rationalizations.

The linkages of these factors can be untangled and traced only in part, but the psychological factors, including the importance of stress, that prompted white responses to nonwhites, be they Indians, blacks or Asians, are fairly evident. Given the persistence of stress situations (frontier, slavery, Reconstruction, economic competition, immigration, struggles to achieve the American goal of success, etc.), white reactions to nonwhites occurred at diverse levels. Cultural demands, proscriptions and prohibitions (whether externally or internally imposed) vied with an environment and conditions which increased individual opportunities for freedom. Caught between adventure and control, individuals moved uneasily. Viewing for whatever reasons nonwhites as different and inferior, and denying within themselves the attributes or impulses the culture considered debased, whites attributed these negative qualities to nonwhites. When whites acted impulsively they blamed not themselves but others — the outsiders, the nonwhites. Thus Indians were held 'responsible' for precipitating aggressive white behavior toward them, and black women were blamed for desiring sexual relations with and seducing white males. Consequently, whites did not hold themselves responsible for their actions: others were blamed for prompting them to act in that manner. In this fashion whites were thereby absolved of guilt or responsibility.

Stress-inducing situations also prodded various individuals into adhering tenaciously or more rigidly to their culture, contributing to cultural dogmatism.[3] Basically, Canada and the United States were Anglo cultures, and Anglo somatic/cultural norm images prevailed. Stress situations intensified polarized perceptions: generally, the greater the disparity between Anglo somatic/cultural norms and the somatic/cultural attributes of another group, the greater the dominant group's hostility toward the perceived threatening (and different) group. The massive infusion of non-Anglo immigrants into North America, particularly the United States, during the late nineteenth century, including South Europeans and Asians, threatened the dominant Anglo group's power and culture. This prompted hostile responses, including discriminatory behavior, the enactment of restrictive immigration measures and the emergence of nativist groups (e.g. the American Protective Association) which sought to preserve '100% Americanism' (Higham, 1971).

Legislative prohibitions and restrictions, immigration laws and demands for the assimilation and 'Americanization' of foreigners were the dominant group response to non-Anglo white immigrants. Black economic competition and population movements, along with the influx of Asians, accounted for the emergence of racism as an ideology and the white response to these groups. Moreover, the nonwhite presence precipitated the increase in white racial violence, the attempt to 'civilize' indigenes, and the enactment of measures that restricted Asian immigration. Some of these policies appear contradictory, but their basic intent was that of 'protecting' whites, especially the dominant Anglo group, from 'contamination' by 'outsiders.' Two methods for accomplishing this were segregation − the isolation of nonwhite groups, be they Indians, blacks or Asians, to reservations or ghettos,[4] and the expulsion of blacks and Asians from the country. Non-Anglo white immigrant groups could be assimilated and incorporated, thus making them charter members, but the color difference of nonwhites precluded their incorporation. They remained outsiders, lacking the necessary power and somatic attributes to demand admittance. Racial intermarriage and miscegenation, possible means for incorporation, were usually prohibited by law, nonwhites serving as contrast conceptions for whites and symbolizing the supposedly debased part of man's nature which whites refused to acknowledge as present within themselves. Because interracial contact could lead to contamination, whites utilized every possible measure to isolate or expel from the American garden of Eden those who were viewed as serpents.

The above circumstances and conditions apply almost equally to Canada and the USA. Moreover, the freedom and opportunity found within both societies prompted still another type of stress. To varying degrees each society emphasized the goal of achievement, and the individual's worth was determined by what he made of himself rather than by ascriptive criteria (Lipset, 1963: ch. 5, 1964; Hartz, 1964: chs 1-2). Material success was therefore a significant factor in determining self-esteem, and that prompted among individuals competition for riches or resources. Nonwhites, and particularly Indians, became obstacles to the realization of these goals, and their possession of land necessitated their removal. The African, initially as a slave and subsequently as cheap labor, could contribute to the whites' material advancement, but when emancipated blacks became a competitive threat they had to be dealt with. That necessitated new efforts at subordinating these groups, be it the isolation of these groups in ghettos or on reservations or the expulsion of Asians and Africans from the country.

Nonwhites were not pawns or powerless. Indians represented a threat until late nineteenth century; blacks during and following Reconstruction acquired some political and economic power, thereby threatening white control and privilege and prompting a backlash; and Asians, though politically powerless, achieved a modicum of economic power. Consequently, all three groups at one point or another were perceived as threats to white power, privilege and culture. Color, not initially a significant factor, emerged as the symbol of white fears, and this was translated into the late nineteenth-century racist ideology. Hence specific situations and amorphous racial fears precipitated white racial violence during the late nineteenth and early twentieth centuries.

The convergence of the preceding factors, exacerbated by the continued infusion of immigrants, unsettled the dominant group, created stress and prompted cultural crises in both countries. The dominant Anglo group feared that 'its' society was being overrun by inferior people. Nativist groups sought to impose a cultural dogmatism, particularly (though not exclusively) in the United States. Newcomers were pressured into discarding their own culture and becoming anglicized, the melting pot identifying this process in the United States. Less stress was placed upon cultural uniformity in Canada, but under the ethnic mosaic myth and particularly during periods of stress the dominant Anglo group sought to anglicize others, especially urban immigrants. White groups that most closely approximated or accepted Anglo norms were more readily embraced, but nonwhites, even when anglicized, remained outsiders, their color ruling against their acceptance or total incorporation.

Although many of the stress-creating situations noted above disappeared by the 1920s, racial prejudice and discrimination were prevalent. Racism, as an ideology, persisted largely independent of the historical factors which contributed to its emergence, now deeply engrained in the beliefs, perceptions and behavior of people and reinforced by institutional practices. Psychological factors, precipitated or exacerbated by stress situations, significantly influenced white responses toward nonwhites, as evident in the historical situations noted. No single factor fully explains or accounts for the enduring hostile white responses to nonwhites, but the three noted — identity (color and cultural norm images), power and psychological factors — together were and are among the most important.

PART III

Chapter 9
Race, ethnicity and power

I

Race-ethnic-power linkages have been emphasized in preceding chapters, but demographic, situational and psychological factors were also considered. Anglo countries were examined from both comparative and analytical perspectives: comparative, in terms of their similarities and differences; analytically, in terms of the processes and dynamics that shape the character of intergroup relations. When the cultural factor is held constant, the role of other variables is more sharply focused, as is the cultural factor itself. Cultural variations in these societies result from diverse factors, including, among others: the different time periods when British groups settled the colonies; demographic factors that resulted in cultural variations; specific events and situations unique to each country; and group power differentials. Despite the differences attributable to these and other factors, the six countries represent subvariants of a common Anglo cultural tradition that shaped ethnic and race relations. The dynamics and processes undoubtedly have their counterpart in non-Anglo countries, but that possibility has not been explored. What is evident is that intergroup relations fluctuate between two conditions or poles: those of equilibrium, or stasis, and change; the character of race/ethnic relations at any moment results from the variables noted, including group power differentials and capabilities.

The three points explored below provide a synthesis and conclusion for the study. They are: (1) the factors which shape the character and dynamics of group relations; (2) the major configurations of ethnic and race relations in the six Anglo countries; and (3) the role of power as a determinant of intergroup relations. Cultural and power factors are usually the most important, but demographic, situational and psychological variables often intervene and modify group relations. The importance of each factor depends upon particular conditions, hence the historical specificity of situations. No single factor, be it economic, political, psychological, cultural or otherwise, fully accounts for the dynamics and character of intergroup relations. Were it necessary to specify a rank order to the importance of variables as determinants of intergroup relations, the following designation (in descending order of importance) would appear most appropriate:

1 The relative power capabilities of groups, whether in an objective sense or as perceived subjectively by each group.
2 The cultural predispositions of individuals and groups, including (a) their cultural and somatic norm images and (b) the intensity with which these norms and beliefs are held.
3 Situational events, historical as well as contemporary, that influence the perceptions, values and behavior of individuals and groups.
4 Specific conditions, including but not limited to those of a demographic and development nature.

These factors were explored in preceding chapters, but the following observations illustrate their linkages. Anglo fragments were settled during different historical periods, but settlers shared roughly similar Anglo cultural traditions and predispositions. They established 'little Englands,' colonial replicas of the mother country, and perceived indigenes, slaves and most non-Anglo groups as culturally different or inferior to themselves. Where possible settlers established political, economic and social institutions that closely replicated those in England, but local conditions necessitated minor variations in structures and patterns. Despite structural modifications adopted in the newly independent United States, and even though the dominant Anglo group considered itself different from England, it nevertheless imposed upon others (i.e. through assimilation) what were fundamentally Anglo values, norms and modes of behavior. 'Americanism' and the 'melting pot,' as indeed the Canadian 'ethnic mosaic,' were simply facades, for in both settings the dominant Anglo group sought to anglicize others.

Situational, particularly demographic and development factors, necessitated alterations in Anglo cultural policy in South Africa and Southern Rhodesia. The politically dominant Anglo group imposed its culture over Afrikaners and some indigenes, but the latter, unlike their counterparts in North American and Pacific fragments, were not totally shunted aside because their labor was needed. Not all Africans were anglicized, but those who discarded their culture believed they would be incorporated within white structures. Few were, and what incorporation occurred was limited to the lowest of levels within economic and political structures, whites aware that extensive African political incorporation would threaten their control. Consequently, Anglos initially and then Afrikaner-Anglo political coalitions after 1910 restricted African political incorporation. The fear of possible black rule so threatened Afrikaners that most supported the National Party in 1948, while similar fears prompted white Rhodesians to support the Rhodesian Front in 1962. Both parties allayed white fears by promising to perpetuate white minority rule. Indigenous groups remained the numerical majority in both African fragments, but white settlers and immigrants quickly outnumbered indigenes in North American and Pacific fragments. Consequently, indigenes posed a continuing political threat to whites only in the African fragments. Had native groups remained the numerical majority in North American and Pacific fragments, whites in all likelihood would have pursued policies similar to those that characterized South Africa and Rhodesia in recent decades. Circumstances and conditions, not superior moral virtues, shaped racial policies in all six Anglo countries. Group power differentials, actual or potential, significantly shaped intergroup relations, but what the above examples suggest is that situational factors also play a role.

The role of values cannot be discounted in historical assessments, for they are also important. The United States provides the most obvious example. Myrdal (1944), for instance, traced the impact of 'American Creed' in shaping American behavior. This creed he described as a set of principles found in the Declaration of Independence which claims that all people are created equal and deserve equal treatment and opportunity. The creed was initially applied to whites, not slaves. The Declaration was a political weapon, justifying the American Revolution, and in subsequent years its principles were embraced by subordinate groups, white as well as black, demanding equal treatment, rights and opportunities. Thus the creed and its principles serve as a political weapon for subordinate groups seeking equal rights. However, the creed is usually effective only if subordinate groups possess power resources as well. The two, creed and power, are used to wrest concessions from dominant Anglo groups. Values unsupported by power are not effective in correcting power imbalances.

The six Anglo fragments were or remain variants of racial dominance systems, situational and power factors accounting for their differences. Slavery was most pervasive in three countries: the USA, Canada and South Africa. Arguments that colonization was motivated solely by one group's desire to subjugate and exploit other groups are historically inaccurate. Various factors prompted settlers' colonization efforts, including, among others: (1) their search for physical security and wellbeing; (2) their quest for economic gain and opportunity; and (3) their desire to preserve their cultural identity and values. Specific individuals and groups differed in their motivations, but few had as their initial intention that of exploiting and oppressing others. Given their power and cultural beliefs, however, many whites came to view indigenes as impediments to their personal advancement and others, including slaves, as vehicles for economic gain and privilege. The lack of countervailing power among subordinate groups enabled the dominant group to misuse its power and position, a view that should not be construed as an attempt to 'blame the victim' for his position. Rather, it accents the importance of power as a determinant of intergroup relations. Beyond the power dimension, cultural and somatic factors, not simply capitalism, shaped the historical development of race and ethnic relations. The capitalist factor cannot be discounted, but it must be put in proper perspective — as only one of the situational factors that influenced intergroup relations.

The relationship between situational and cultural factors emerges in comparisons of Anglo and French/Iberian settler-indigenous relations. Most important was whether the dominant cultural group was exclusive or inclusive in its cultural/somatic beliefs, its position on that issue reflected in whether or not it (a) would accept and incorporate as equal a group that discarded its own culture for that of the dominant group, or (b) would reject another group it considered inferior, classifying the group as an 'outsider' unworthy of incorporation within dominant group structures (or, if incorporated, at only the lowest of levels). Historically, most European groups — Anglo, Dutch, French and Iberian — were inclusive in their willingness to assimilate and incorporate groups that were culturally different but white (providing the other group discarded its own culture for that of the dominant group), but Anglo and Dutch groups were clearly exclusive in their refusal to incorporate groups that were nonwhite. Here the somatic factor determined the character and degree of structural incorporation.

The exceptions to these generalizations occurred where situational, including demographic, factors tempered the impact of somatic factors on group relations. For example, whether a colony was settler or sojourner influenced group relations. In English settler colonies, for instance, entire families settled. Intent on replicating the metropole society, most Anglo families were endogamous and tightly knit socially, seldom associating with indigenes or nonwhite groups. But French and Iberian settler colonies usually suffered from a shortage of European women. This resulted in interracial liaisons, miscegenation and, later, interracial marriages (Degler, 1971). Sojourner colonies, Anglo or otherwise, closely paralleled interracial patterns found in Iberian and French settler colonies, for they usually lacked European women. Thus interracial liaisons between European males and nonwhite females were commonplace. In these cases situational and demographic factors served as intervening variables, reducing the impact of cultural and somatic factors as determinants of intergroup relations.

The importance of power as a determinant of intergroup relations is reflected in the church's and metropole's role in colonial situations. Given their power to excommunicate members who treated natives or slaves harshly and contrary to church policy, the Catholic church and clergy thereby influenced intergroup relations. In contrary fashion, neither Protestant church nor clergy exercised similar control over their members. Clergy were usually selected or appointed by church members, and if their racial views differed sharply they were replaced. Here, then, is an example of how the power of specific religious groups influenced intergroup relations. Similar variations are evident in the metropole's role. Where possible the British metropole imposed itself between indigenes and settlers and thereby protected them from each other, but Britain's geographical distance from its colonies made such intervention difficult. Unsuccessful in restricting settler land intrusions in the American colonies despite the 1763 Proclamation, the British government exercised stricter control in Canada, New Zealand and later South Africa and Southern Rhodesia. Even so, unless the metropole stationed troops in the colony, settlers treated natives as they pleased. Possibly more important for the indigenes (and, later, other subordinate groups) than the metropole's role was their own power capability and whether or not their coercive and pressure resources could be used for protection from the dominant group. The less the subordinate group's countervailing power, the greater the probability was its exploitation and domination.

The preceding comments suggest the importance of historical specificity in analyzing intergroup relations, but beyond that the importance of power, cultural, situational and other factors is evident. What can be deduced from the preceding observations and chapters are a series of generalizations concerning race and ethnic relations in Anglo societies.

II

The following generalizations, treated as propositions and statements, emerge from the study. All trace relationships that exist between two or more variables, but at the root of the first three propositions is the factor of congruence:

Proposition 1
The closer or more congruent in cultural characteristics (beliefs, norms and behavior) the Anglo to the non-Anglo group, the more readily is the latter accepted and incorporated by the former. Indices of that acceptance are the types and degrees of incorporation of the non-Anglo group into dominant group structures (economic, political and social).

Proposition 2
The closer or more congruent in somatic characteristics the Anglo to the non-Anglo group, the more readily is the latter accepted and incorporated by the former. Indices of that acceptance are the types and degrees of incorporation of the non-Anglo group into dominant group structures (economic, political and social).

Proposition 3
In terms of incorporation, the group that is more congruent to the Anglo group in somatic characteristics will be more readily accepted than the group which differs markedly in somatic characteristics but is closer in cultural characteristics. Indices of that difference and acceptance are the types and degrees to which the two groups are differentially incorporated within dominant group structures (economic, political and social).

The exceptions to these generalizations, particularly the third, are attributable to power, situational and demographic variables. Historical examples cited in previous chapters substantiate these propositions. In general, non-Anglo white groups were initially incorporated at lower levels within Anglo economic structures, moving upward as they were anglicized. Upward movement within political and social structures followed. Some white groups remained outside Anglo social structures, doing so because they wished to retain their separate cultural and social identities (e.g. Jews, Greeks, and others). The Irish in the USA are a graphic example of this incorporation process. Discriminated against initially, the Irish gained economic access slowly, followed by limited political incorporation. Anglo politicians and bosses initially mobilized the Irish for bloc voting, but thereafter Irish political bosses wrested control, mobilized fellow Irishmen and wrested political (as well as other) concessions from Anglo leaders. The 'ethnic factor' consequently loomed large in politics. Having mobilized their members, Irish leaders used their power to broaden economic opportunities for the group. The Irish, particularly those who were anglicized, were then incorporated within social structures. There were variations and exceptions, but a pattern is discernible among Irish as well as other white immigrant groups within these countries. Public schools were a vehicle for assimilation, and immigrant parents and children quickly recognized that economic opportunities were closely tied to how quickly they discarded their own language and culture and became anglicized. Assimilationist pressures and policies contributed to this process, for governments restricted specific professions and vocational opportunities to those who spoke English and were anglicized. Again, there were exceptions, but these patterns prevailed in most fragment societies.

The somatic factor in the second and third propositions can be readily illustrated. White groups were more rapidly incorporated than nonwhites. Even where nonwhites were economically incorporated they were pushed aside by newly arrived white immigrants as occurred among blacks in New York City during the nineteenth century. In North American and Pacific fragments, immigrant whites were usually incorporated within economic structures at higher levels than were nonwhites, including indigenes. Moreover, late nineteenth-century industrialization prompted industrialists and governments to encourage white immigration despite the fact that indigenes and, in some cases, blacks were available as a labor source. A few blacks were employed, but they were used primarily as strikebreakers or as a means of forcing lower wages on white workers.

Indigenes were usually barred from economic structures or restricted to low-level positions. Likewise, even anglicized indigenes were excluded from white political structures until the twentieth century except in New Zealand. There, Maoris were politically incorporated but had no power. Australian Aborigines, though granted the ballot in recent decades, are not encouraged to participate even though other Australians are required to vote. In South Africa and Rhodesia, the gradual although limited political incorporation of Africans precipitated a white backlash that led to Nationalist and Rhodesian Front victories and the curtailment of African political power.

What the foregoing assessment indicates is that the dominant Anglo group imposed its cultural and somatic norm images on society, its belief system and values determining the type and degree of structural incorporation of other groups. The following observation is thus in order:

Statement 1

Historically, Anglo fragments were monocultural rather than poly-cultural societies, Anglo cultural and somatic norm images considered superior to others. Threatened by the presence of these somatically and/or culturally different groups, the dominant group tolerated their presence only because situational or development factors intervened, but it used its control over structures to maintain its position of dominance.

Anglo societies were exclusive in two respects: first, they viewed Anglo culture as superior; and second, they viewed somatically different people as inferior. Other groups were tolerated only out of necessity. Steps were taken to anglicize them, particularly those who somatically resembled the dominant group. In that sense, then, the Anglo group was inclusive, for it would incorporate somatically similar groups that were anglicized. But somatically different groups were, even if anglicized ('civilized' in Anglo terms), regarded as inferior. At most, their incorporation was limited to the lowest of structural (economic and political) levels, and socially they were isolated or removed from society. If it was physically impossible to remove the group from the country (witness efforts to send blacks 'back to Africa' or expel Asians), they were segregated. The motivation was obvious: the dominant group desired a society based on its cultural and somatic norm images: one color and one culture, Anglo (anglicized) and white. Exceptions to these principles resulted from factors previously cited. Thus Canada's ethnic mosaic resulted from its need to retain immigrant groups that otherwise would emigrate to the USA if Canada sought to anglicize them. Likewise, efforts to anglicize French Canadians and Afrikaners failed because these groups encapsulated or isolated themselves within agrarian laagers, their territorial isolation momentarily helping them preserve their cultural identity.

Anglo groups tolerated culturally and somatically different groups only when they could not be expelled or when their labor was needed. Caught between contradictory impulses to expel the 'outsiders' or use their labor, the dominant group invariably retained them. This created ambiguity and frustration within the dominant group, and it vented its frustrations in specific ways: it anglicized indigenes but treated them as inferiors; it sought to ship blacks 'back to Africa;' it harassed Asians, hopeful that they would leave the country when their labor was no longer needed, or it enacted legislation forbidding future entry of other Asians; it enacted legislation that curtailed employment opportunities of aliens who were not anglicized; and it ignored or indeed encouraged citizens' discriminatory practices against foreigners. Intent on expanding its privileged position, the dominant group tolerated and used these outsiders, their behavior closely paralleling that of contemporary whites toward blacks in South Africa. However, subordinate groups gradually acquired competitive and pressure resources within Anglo fragments, and having done so they were able to wrest limited concessions from the dominant group. Asymmetrical power relations continued, but Anglo power was in the process of being eroded. These observations suggest two additional propositions:

Proposition 4
The more symmetrical the power equation between dominant and subordinate groups, the more likely the dominant group will accept some form of intergroup accommodation; conversely, the more asymmetrical the power relationship, the more likely the dominant group will seek to destroy the power resources and mobilization capabilities of the subordinate group, thereafter utilizing control of structures and resources to perpetuate its control, privilege and interests.

Proposition 5
The more committed the dominant group to the need for economic development (for whatever purposes), the more likely it will tolerate a subordinate group's cultural and/or somatic differences if the latter's presence helps the dominant group reach its economic goals.

The importance of power is evident in numerous situations. In colonial situations, for example, settlers negotiated treaties if indigenes were perceived as powerful. If conflict ensued, settlers demanded metropole military support for destroying indigenous military capabilities — a situation that occurred in the American colonies, the United States, Canada, New Zealand, South Africa and Southern Rhodesia. In New Zealand, the threatened withdrawal of metropole troops prodded settlers into making concessions, including the limited political incorporation of Maoris in the settler Parliament. Earlier, fearful of Indian power, the US government proposed establishment of an Indian state that would send representatives to Congress, a proposal quickly discarded when white military superiority was achieved. Having conquered the indigenous groups, Anglo groups established indigenous enclaves that were relatively easily policed and controlled. Coercive control, taken in conjunction with the destruction of indigenous cultures, effectively destroyed subordinate group solidarity.

Slaves and ex-slaves possessed virtually no power resources, and free blacks were systematically discriminated against in a manner that perpetuated their subordination. Early repressive measures were of an ad hoc nature, but when blacks and poor whites converged briefly in the American South under Populism, the dominant white group moved quickly to disfranchise all blacks. Although blacks could have been incorporated within industries, thereby increasing their competitive resources, industrialists instead encouraged European immigration, thereby thwarting black economic development.

Other groups, including Asians, French Canadians, Boer/Afrikaners and European immigrants, were initially restricted to economically and politically subordinate positions. Group power differentials influenced the character of Anglo relations with these groups. If the latter were needed for development purposes or possessed competitive and pressure resources, they could increase their opportunities and resources. However, the dominant group restricted subordinate group resource development by playing one group off against another, as it did when using blacks for strikebreakers. Whites in South Africa and Rhodesia utilized still another technique, that of recruiting African workers from other countries, a device that prevented indigenous Africans from increasing their competitive and pressure resources. European immigration was encouraged and skilled as well as semi-skilled occupations were reserved for whites. Because they occupied unskilled positions and could be easily replaced by foreigners, indigenous black workers found it difficult to organize or withhold their labor. However, the 1973 Durban strikes indicated that Africans could withhold their labor and wrest concessions, a pressure tactic the white government thereafter sought to restrict.

Usually it is the dominant group's desire for development and economic privilege that accounts for its willingness to temporize in imposing its cultural and somatic beliefs or expelling the 'outsider' from society. Because indigenes in North American and Pacific fragments were not needed for development they were shunted aside, but white labor shortages in the African fragments prompted whites to utilize some indigenous labor. However, other Africans were restricted to the reserves. Africans who were incorporated economically were kept in unskilled positions. When labor shortages occurred, Asians and Africans from other countries were recruited for unskilled positions while Europeans were recruited for the skilled and semi-skilled positions. When there was less need for nonwhite labor, the Chinese were expelled or Africans were returned to the reserves. These efforts, however, were at most perfunctory, and as a consequence many Africans remained in urban areas, objects of discriminatory measures whenever the dominant group felt threatened by their presence.

Using as an inducement the possibility of greater structural incorporation, Anglo groups sought to anglicize European immigrants, French Canadians and Afrikaners. The tactic succeeded in some cases, but French Canadians and Afrikaners, their cultural identity threatened, mobilized their members to thwart the assimilationist pressures. Their power base and resources (they constituted a numerical majority among whites in Quebec and South Africa) contributed to their success. What these examples indicate is that Anglo efforts to anglicize or exclude groups who were culturally and/or somatically different were tempered by development needs or, more significantly, the relative power capabilities of groups. These intervening factors precipitated still another condition: namely, dominant group fears that its cultural identity and power were threatened. This threat perception prompted Anglo groups to hold more dogmatically and rigidly to their cultural beliefs and behavior, a condition that is explained in terms of the following proposition:

> *Proposition 6*
> The greater the perceived threat to the dominant group, dependent upon the sources of that threat, the greater the probability of cultural/somatic closure, that closure measured in terms of dogmatism in beliefs and rigidity in thinking and behavior. Indices of that closure are evident in policies the group pursues to protect its cultural identity from the threatening group.

Threat perception, which creates within individuals or groups a high degree of stress, was examined earlier. Various types of threats can create stress, but most basic for an individual or group are: (a) threats to its physical security and wellbeing; (b) threats to its cultural identity, including its cultural and somatic beliefs; (c) threats to its material interests, including its economic status and privilege; and (d) threats to its power, including its resources, mobilization capabilities and position vis-à-vis groups. Among the most prominent of historical situations that created threats for individuals and groups have been: frontier situations; sudden encounters or confrontations between groups; industrialization; sociocultural changes; and specific events that disrupt the status quo and alter group power capabilities and differentials. Each of these situations can prove threatening to either dominant or subordinate groups. Threatening situations create stress and result in psychological responses, including that of closure, the process whereby individuals or groups protect themselves through encapsulation or drawing inward or together to protect themselves from a threatening object. If the threatened group possesses greater power than its opponent, it may strike out and use power to destroy or similarly encapsulate or segregate the enemy.

Dominant Anglo group behavior during the late nineteenth and early twentieth centuries in the United States illustrates the impact of such threats. Anglos feared that the massive influx of immigrants threatened their power and cultural beliefs and would 'swamp' and destroy 'the American way of life.' Their fears prompted concerted measures to 'Americanize' or expel immigrants; gave rise to nativist protectionist groups; and prompted restrictive legislation aimed at aliens. The presence of these groups, taken in conjunction with rapid industrialization, urbanization and sociocultural changes in society, triggered a 'symbolic crusade' that led to the Prohibition Amendment and anti-immigration legislation (Gusfield, 1966; Higham, 1971; Hofstadter, 1956). Perceiving itself as a culture under siege, the dominant Anglo group utilized its power to respond in dogmatic fashion.

Threats to their cultural identity also transform subordinate groups into siege cultures, as evident in the case of French Canadians and Afrikaners. Recent years have also witnessed the transformation of indigenous groups into siege cultures. Having fashioned or re-established a 'cultural identity' to mobilize their members against the dominant group, indigenous groups now see their culture and identity threatened by past or present cultural policies of the dominant group. Consequently, they perceive themselves as cultures under siege (Manganyi, 1977). Amerindians, Maoris, Aborigines and Africans, in moving from group awareness to group consciousness, have mobilized themselves to break dominant group control over their lives. Power emerges as the significant factor, and group power capabilities and differentials are presently undergoing change. The foregoing observations lead to the following conclusion:

Statement 2
Roughly parallel sequences or processes have characterized intergroup relations, past and present, in Anglo countries, the sequences and processes originally followed as Anglos dominated other groups now being followed in roughly comparable reverse order as those previously subordinate groups break the patterns of domination.

The sequences and processes that resulted in Anglo dominance still prevail although in muted form in North American and Pacific fragments. Anglo dominance ended in South Africa when Afrikaners wrested control in 1948, and Africans dislodged white power in Rhodesia during 1979-80. Despite the massive influx of immigrants, primarily European, people of Anglo descent preserved their political and cultural control in the USA, Canada, Australia and New Zealand well into the twentieth century. Other ethnic groups, particularly those who were anglicized, were structurally incorporated, but not until the 1960s, influenced by the Black Power movement, did other groups mobilize to break the iron grip of Anglo cultural control. The effect of this confrontation was to assert the legitimacy of cultural pluralism in place of an Anglo monocultural society. The French Canadian presence contributed to the image of a culturally plural society, but most groups recognized that people of English descent and those who were anglicized enjoyed greater power and opportunity. Australia and New Zealand remained politically and culturally Anglo well into the 1970s, and only recently has there been a move toward cultural diversity. Maoris and Aborigines, however, have little voice or power in the system and still encounter assimilationist pressures, and European immigrants recognize that structural opportunities are closely linked to being anglicized. Even so, pressures for greater cultural diversity do exist.

The historical sequences and processes that led to Anglo dominance and hegemony can be distinguished in terms of the techniques or modes of control by which Anglos gained and preserved their power. The initial control form was that of conquest or imposition, and under it the Anglo group, whether by military conquest, the destruction of indigenous economies, the enslavement of blacks or the exercise of power (through control of structures and resources), imposed its rule over other groups. The second form was coercive/reward control, the dominant group utilizing its coercive (military, police, the withholding of benefits, etc.) and reward (granting benefits, opportunities, etc.) powers to elicit from others desired forms of behavior. The third form, dependency control, relied upon coercive-reward techniques, for the dominant group used its control of structures to force others into a position of dependence. Examples of this were or are: forcing indigenes on to reserves where, unable to provide for themselves, they become wards of the state, their compliance necessary if they are to receive basic services including food and shelter; the denial of jobs to immigrants who are not anglicized; the use of the welfare system to restrain or placate dispossessed and subordinate groups; and the co-optation of subordinate group leaders as a means of curtailing the mobilization capabilities of these groups. Finally, there was thought control, the most sophisticated form of control because subordinate group members discard their cultural identity, believe they are inferior to the dominant group and accept as their own the dominant group's culture and beliefs. Individuals where this cultural imposition has occurred control themselves in the manner desired by the dominant group because they think like the dominant group.

These modes of control were and are the major means used for subordinating and controlling indigenes and immigrants. Anglo settlement usually led to conquest or the imposition of Anglo control over indigenes, the dispossession of their lands, and enforcement of measures aimed at destroying indigenous cultures. Among other nonwhite groups, including Africans in the USA and Canada and Asians in all six countries, similar steps were followed. Africans, enslaved and powerless, were forced to shed their cultural identity and accept the identity imposed upon them by the dominant group. Following the abolition of slavery blacks remained virtually powerless because whites controlled structures and circumscribed black opportunities. Asians also suffered from limited structural incorporation. These patterns prevailed for most nonwhites through the Second World War, and only thereafter, incrementally and slowly, were nonwhites able to build their economic resources, this leading to group mobilization. Subordinate group mobilization efforts and confrontations against dominant group power were often unsuccessful — until the advent of Black Power. Asserting their cultural and group identity, blacks effectively mobilized themselves to contest against discriminatory policies and practices. Their efforts, although not always successful, nevertheless provided the impetus for similar movements particularly among indigenous groups. Crucial to Black Power's success was its emphasis on group consciousness, the group's cultural identity serving as the rallying point for group mobilization efforts.

Similar processes are evident in the analysis of how Afrikaners and French Canadians broke the prevailing modes of Anglo control. They, too, were the object of Anglo assimilationist pressures, but they reasserted their cultural identity and mobilized to break Anglo dominance. Similar processes are evident in the experience of white immigrant groups which, with but few exceptions, found themselves pressured to shed their culture and language. Some groups, even though anglicized, retained close ties with their ethnic group, and when the group's position in society was threatened by still other groups seeking to advance their opportunities (e.g. blacks seeking jobs), they emerged as 'unmeltable white ethnics' seeking to protect their position.

Viewed from a historical perspective, the processes leading to Anglo dominance are evident: conquest or the imposition of Anglo control; the use of coercive-reward techniques for controlling groups; and the utilization of political, economic and social structures to limit subordinate group resources and mobilization capabilities while preserving Anglo hegemony. Structural controls were crucial, but most effective was thought control. A subordinate group that believes it is inferior to the dominant group and accepts its subordinate position controls itself. Cultural imposition, resting upon the destruction of a group's cultural identity, provides the means for achieving this condition. Subordinate groups often tried to break Anglo control but were unsuccessful, their failure less the consequence of Anglo control of structures than of the subordinate group's inability to mobilize and sustain the solidarity of its members. Subordinate group members who do not recognize themselves as a group or who believe they are inferior to the dominant group cannot be counted upon for support. Only when they recognize and acknowledge their group identity and accept the fact that they are oppressed or exploited because of their group characteristics will they mobilize for action. Mobilization and confrontation may result in a subordinate group's momentary defeat, but even that defeat, as in the case of Afrikaners, can provide the impetus for more intensive mobilization efforts.

The Black Power movement is the most graphic example of how a group's consciousness and psychological awareness facilitate its organizational efforts. Through the reaffirmation of the group's cultural and somatic identity (e.g. Black is Beautiful), the psychological basis existed for rallying blacks to oppose the system. This same factor can be discerned in the emergence of recent indigenous group political activities — the Red Power movement in the US and Canada; Brown Power in New Zealand; Black Power in Australia; and Black Consciousness in South Africa. At the root of power is the psychological factor — that of self-awareness, self-affirmation and self-assertion. Domination is maintained by structural *and* psychological means, and the use of these evolved slowly over time. Both are fundamental to the perpetuation of dominance, but psychological power represents a more subtle and sophisticated — and thereby enduring — mode of control or power. If domination rests upon thought control, subordinate group onslaughts directed against structural or coercive/reward modes of control will often fail. Unless the subordinate group comes to grips with its beliefs or feelings of inferiority and incompetency (vis-à-vis the dominant group), it cannot successfully break the hold of the oppressor. Domination, from conquest through structural and psychological techniques of control, is a process, that process composed of a sequence of events or steps, all of which must be reversed. Where thought control is present, the subordinate group must concentrate initially on the psychological components of dominance in order to mobilize its members and contest against domination. The breaking of dominance begins when the subordinate group reaffirms and reasserts its cultural or group identity. That is a critical first step if resources and mobilization capabilities are to be developed. Thus self-affirmation is necessary for the breaking of thought control, dependence behavior and dependency relationships.

III

Power as a factor in intergroup relations is usually viewed from two perspectives: substantively, as resources and mobilization capabilities, and relationally, as reflected in the interaction of groups. Intergroup power contests normally occur within political, economic and social structures, where groups mobilize their resources to contest against each other in quest of desired goals. Power, viewed from either of these perspectives, is primarily a sociological phenomenon, even if, as in marxist analyses, the emphasis is on economic forces or modes of production. Implicit if not explicit in most sociological (including marxist) approaches is the assumption that structures and forces outside and beyond individual control shape or determine human action. The individual is, in large measure, considered a pawn or puppet whose behavior results from external forces of which he is unaware or over which he has no control. That being the case, changes in structures or forces precipitate changes in human behavior. For marxists the abolition of capitalism and establishment of a socialist system will end dominant group oppression and exploitation of subordinate (including ethnic and racial) groups, racism and ethnocentrisms viewed as simply rationalizations or justifications for exploitation under the prevailing capitalist system.

The critical factor in this sociological or structural approach is that human behavior is a dependent variable. Human beings are, in good measure, *acted on*; they are not actors or participants who, in making choices, shape history. Power from this perspective rests *outside* individuals or groups, and change, including changes in power relations, comes from outside people. This approach accounts for the character of intergroup relations in some settings, but it does not explain all situations or phenomena. What must be considered in addition to this sociological or structuralist approach is a psychological approach that takes human action into consideration — not as a consequence of changed resources, structures or situations but as a factor in itself. Structures, situations, resources and the mobilization capabilities of groups may change but that does not invariably lead to change in people, be it in their beliefs or behavior. The failure of people to respond as predicted is in marxist terms attributed to people's false consciousness, to their being blinded or misguided by ideology. Change the mode of social consciousness, the marxists claim, and behavior will parallel changes in structures and situations. What is implied in this view and, indeed, in the notion of a 'false consciousness' is that cognitive changes occur *within* individuals or groups. That is a psychological, not a sociological or structural, factor. What transpires within the individual is a cognitive restructuring: the individual or group moves from one form of social consciousness to another. That occurs within people, not in modes of production. The transition of a group from being a group in itself (awareness) to being a group for itself (consciousness) is a psychological act. Changes in perceptions lead individuals or groups to act, and that is a psychological factor. Whether the precipitating source of an individual's actions is labelled initiative, incentive or motivation, it has its derivation from two sources: new cognitions and, at another level, the individual's or group's response to those new cognitions — anger, resentment (for example, at being exploited), etc. These are all psychological factors. Ultimately, then, it is psychological, not sociological or structural, factors that induce individuals or groups to act. The act of volition, the transformation of individuals or groups into participants and actors, occurs within individuals, not in structures or forces. The latter may induce people to act, and there may be occasions when people act without recognizing all the forces prodding them to act, but behavior is not simply a programmed response to specific stimuli. Marx recognizes but neglects these psychological factors in his analysis (McMurtry, 1978), but many of his followers cavalierly ignore it.

Objective conditions, marxists contend, determine class, economic conditions and group relations. But how these conditions are perceived and judged by individuals or groups is a subjective or psychological factor. How individuals or groups perceive situations influence and shape their response. Structures or conditions may change but people do not necessarily change in conformity with new structures and conditions. What must first change are their images and perceptions, and that is a psychological rather than a sociological or structural factor. Changes in individual or group resources do not invariably lead to the mobilization of these resources. Mobilization implies action, and for individuals that is a conscious act that flows from changes in their cognitions, perceptions and motivations – all of which are psychological factors. Thus, while one form of power, the sociological or structural, usually receives the greatest attention, the other – psychological – is of equal importance.

Sociological types of power (resources and resource mobilization; coercive-reward techniques; structural control) were of major importance in establishing and preserving Anglo dominance, but their application and use, in terms of manpower and expense, was costly and not totally effective in preserving control. More sophisticated and effective, the psychological modes of control were and are less costly, for if individuals or groups believe (through cognitive restructuring) they are inferior or less competent than the dominant group, they accept their subordinate position. A belief in one's incompetence effectively erodes or destroys an individual's or group's incentive or motivation for bringing about change, confronting an oppressor or building power resources. A situation may change and objective conditions may be such that a subordinate could achieve independence, but if he perceives himself as incompetent, inferior and incapable of acting, what prevails is a form of dependency behavior. What is necessary is a cognitive restructuring (in Marx's terms, a transformation in forms of social consciousness) whereby the subordinate realizes his capabilities. What is necessary is an act of self-affirmation and self-assertion, for only when these steps are taken can there be a breaking of thought control.

The use of these modes of control, sociological and psychological, has been traced in preceding chapters. Blacks, indigenes and white ethnics all sought on occasion to prevent or break Anglo control, only to fail. Two groups, Afrikaners and French Canadians, succeeded, partly because they could isolate themselves from dominant group assimilationist pressures, partly because they fought tenaciously to preserve their cultural or psychological identity. Other groups were less successful, and control of structures meant that the dominant group could destroy or restrict the resources and mobilization capabilities of other groups while destroying their cultural or group identity. Hence early subordinate group efforts to break dominant group control usually floundered or failed. Only when subordinate groups recognized or addressed the psychological components of power did they achieve any success in breaking thought control. Examples of this — Black Power, Red Power, Brown Power and Black Consciousness — have previously been cited. The breaking of the dominant group's psychological hold over the subordinate group is a critical first step if the latter is to build resources, mobilize its members and achieve a degree of solidarity in contesting against dominant group power.

Historically, Anglo groups resorted to sociological and psychological forms of power to achieve and preserve their hegemony. Sociological forms were initially employed, but subordinate group efforts to preserve their identity prompted the Anglo group to devise increasingly sophisticated forms of power and dominion, these forms almost inevitably given Anglo cultural and somatic norm images and the conflict-type and stress-inducing situations that brought these groups into contact. Thereafter, subordinate group attempts to break Anglo control failed for numerous reasons. Anglos controlled structures and resources; Anglos co-opted or removed leaders of subordinate groups, preventing group mobilization; and Anglos destroyed the cultural identities of groups. Subordinate groups that accepted the premise of Anglo cultural superiority (and thereby their own cultural inferiority) could not effectively contest against Anglo power. That power was built on psychological modes of control. Where and when groups reasserted their cultural or group identity, they transformed (or are in the process of doing so) themselves from groups in themselves to groups for themselves, this transformation providing the basis for building resources, mobilizing members and confronting dominant group control. This process is an ongoing one and is transforming what were once Anglo monocultural societies into polycultural ones. Polyculturalism, however, remains largely a goal rather than a reality, but elements for this change are emerging in North American and Pacific fragments. The African fragments, no longer Anglo controlled, move in other directions. Previously, however, they followed comparable paths, and Africans, Asians and coloreds in South Africa presently pursue these same paths in contesting against white domination.

Notes

Introduction

1 Three points should be noted in clarification of these statements:
   (a) 'settlement' is used in terms of European intrusion or occupation of these lands, as all were occupied by indigenous groups when the Europeans came; (b) the term 'British' should perhaps be employed, as in many instances settlement included others besides the English from the British Isles. However, it was the English who exercised power, and this power they used to impose their culture and values upon or over others, including other groups of British descent. And (c), these countries earlier consisted of colonies established by Britain or others, and only later were they unified to become the six countries noted.

2 The cultures of indigenous groups in these countries were vastly different, but the central point here is how the dominant Anglo group used its power to impose its culture and control over other groups. Differences in the cultural backgrounds of the indigenous and other groups, as well as situational factors, resulted in the different patterns of responses of these groups to the dominant Anglo group.

3 Effective British control over South Africa terminated with the 1910 Act of Union, but South Africa remained a member of the British Empire, then Commonwealth, until it became a republic in 1961.

4 Analyses of both individuals and groups are, in a sense, abstractions from reality, but while it is possible to isolate individual motivations, as suggested, there is no such thing as a 'group mind.'

5 One recent – and notable – exception is Fredrickson's (1981) study of white supremacy in South Africa and the United States.

6 As noted previously, the Afrikaner National Party wrested complete control from the English-Afrikaner coalition in 1948, and in 1961 South Africa left the British Commonwealth. It is included in this study, however, for two reasons: first, because of the pervasive influence of the English in shaping the culture and institutions of South Africa during the pre- and even post-1948 period; and second, to provide somewhat of a comparison with the other Anglo settler societies.

Chapter 2 Power and group relations

1 The following relies largely on Blalock (1967: ch. 4).

2 The notion of a 'cultural norm image' derives from Hoetink's (1967) analysis of what he terms a 'somatic norm image,' and it constitutes part of a broader 'belief system' embracing the positively and negatively viewed cluster of attributes that Rokeach (1960) describes as a 'belief-disbelief system.' This is treated more fully in later chapters.

3 There are two exceptions to this: first, where the subordinate group, despite a sharply different culture, possesses power or pressure resources that could threaten the dominant group, or, second, where the subordinate possesses competitive resources, e.g. skills needed by the dominant group for the economic development of the country. This is explored in Chapter 7.

4 Although the dominant group may tailor the educational system to perpetuate the subordination of another group, 'unintended consequences' may result from it, elements of that education actually serving to liberate the subordinate, be it in terms of creating within the latter a sense of opposition to the system or providing him with skills he can withhold from the dominant group, using that threat of withholding as a device for extracting concessions from the superordinate (Murphree, 1976: 15-19).

5 Structures themselves serve as agents of socialization, shaping the psychological state, the predispositions and the perceptual field of the individual. This does *not* imply that the individual is simply a robot who responds unthinkingly to socialization forces, for as an actor he determines for himself the meaning of these experiences (Blumer, 1969; Barbu, 1960).

6 The characteristics described here are different from the 'culture of poverty' or similar concepts often used to explain the behavior of subordinate groups. See Ryan (1976).

7   The European, claimed Fanon (1970: 70) *made* the Malagasy *feel* dependent and inferior: 'If he is overwhelmed to such a degree by the wish to be white, it is because he lives in a society that makes his inferiority complex possible, in a society that proclaims the superiority of one race . . . .'

8   The sequential approach suggested should not be construed as comparable to the rigid stages of Park's (1949) 'race relations cycle.' But they do constitute, in Schermerhorn's (1970) terms, 'intergroup sequences' or 'recurrent patterns' of group relations. These sequences closely parallel Allport's (1954) 'event-structures,' and the processes or factors which contribute to the movement from one sequence to another closely approximate what Smelser (1963) and others have defined as a 'value-additive' process.

9   Welfare benefits became an integral component of a dependency system, i.e. they provided limited benefits to the poor, a type of pacification program especially for those who might otherwise oppose a society that denied them access to opportunities.

10 Both the social ideology and educational system helped perpetuate notions of white superiority in *all* people, including the dominant white group.

11 For whites, apparent compliance by most nonwhites seemed to acknowledge the legitimacy of white power, white superiority and the greater worth of white culture.

12 This same process, it should be noted, also applies to women and the subordinate position they have generally occupied in most societies.

Chapter 3 Race relations: North American and Pacific fragments

1   The terms sojourner and settler are employed by Price (1963: 48-52). Romantic images of the native Indian in America are explored in Kraus (1949) and Pearce (1965). Pearce traces changes in white perceptions of Indians from the pre-contact period through the Civil War in American literature, illustrating how literature became a subtle means for rationalizing white policies of Indian extermination.

2   The United States, no longer under British control, felt this influence less, though some American groups were concerned. Efforts to correct abuses normally fell on the deaf ears of a society indifferent toward the Indian's plight. See, for example, Helen Jackson's (1969) study, first published in 1881, documenting

mistreatment of the native population. The British government possessed a degree of control and restraint over Canada, Australia, New Zealand and South Africa (Southern Rhodesia was not established until later). British power over its Dominions and Colonies served as a leavening influence against the harsh attitudes of settlers who desired native lands. As long as the British government retained control over native affairs, which it did for part of the century, it could influence native policy. This aspect of British power is discussed more fully later.

3 Price's (1972) study carried only through the Second World War. The new directions he perceived were slowed by the war, and postwar economic developments further diverted attention from native group problems. Some of the changes Price envisaged have since occurred, but they result less from government initiative than from indigenes mobilizing their members and demanding control over their own affairs and development.

4 Fredrickson's (1981) study of the United States and South Africa focuses primarily on those of *African* descent in both countries: hence, his emphasis is on *color* rather than other factors. It could be argued that his study would be more comparative had he focused on Africans in South Africa and indigenous Indians in the United States, the emphasis thus on the two as *indigenous* groups. See Hartz (1964: Part I), Hoetink (1967), Van den Berghe (1967: chs 1, 6), Tannenbaum (1968) and Hanke (1970).

5 This difference is also reflected in the attitude of the French and the Catholic Church toward Indians in Canada, as noted later. See especially Price (1972), Mellor (1951) and Stanley (1960).

6 See Hoetink (1967), Hartz (1964), Tannenbaum (1968), Hanke (1970) and Davis (1966). Where the Catholic Church played this intervening role, i.e. tempering white encounters with and treatment of the native in Iberian settlements, the British Imperial government, until it relinquished control over native affairs in its colonies, played a somewhat comparable though less immediate or effective role with the Anglo settler societies.

7 Kovel (1971) explores the bases of these color or racist notions. In his view, the Anglo tradition compels the individual to think of people as objects to be controlled. Western man, he claims, is an obsessive-compulsive personality, the inculcation of these traits leading to punctuality, orderliness and cleanliness. Rationality is also part of the traits. Given his obsession with accumulating power and property, and lacking a religious tradition that accepted indigenes or nonwhites as fellow beings, western man

and Anglos in particular perceived indigenes and nonwhites as inferior and less than human. These notions were reinforced for the settler when natives denied him access to coveted lands or resources. Superior weapons enabled the Anglo to conquer natives just as he dominated the physical environment with his machinery. Given these factors, suggests Kovel, the belief that slaves were a form of chattel represented a logical development in Anglo thought.

8 Hoetink (1967: 120) proposes the term 'somatic norm image' for the complex of physical (somatic) characteristics which are accepted by a group as its norm or ideal. He considers this a more 'value-free' term when discussing a group's acceptance of its own physical attributes as more highly esteemed. These characteristics come into sharp focus when members of groups whose physical characteristics differ come in contact. Color, or physical characteristics, are part of broader ethnocentric beliefs. The culture itself constitutes yet another component of these beliefs. One can speak of a 'cultural norm image,' a composite of social, political and economic values that represent (paraphrasing Hoetink) 'the complex of cultural characteristics which are accepted by a group as its norm or ideal.' In psychological terms, these somatic (SNI) and cultural norm images (CNI) provide the perceptual and motivational base for a group's behavior in its interaction with others.

9 Somewhat similar patterns are observable in slave societies (Blassingame, 1972; Elkins, 1959; Genovese, 1974).

10 Mannoni (1964) describes these emergent dependency patterns, but as indicated previously, Fanon (1967) takes issue with Mannoni's analysis. Elsewhere Fanon (1968) acknowledges that domination had a psychological impact on the native but claims that the dependency patterns which emerged were the direct consequence of superordinate policies. See, too, Mason's (1970) analysis.

11 See especially Huttenback (1976). Similar statements are applicable to South Africa and Southern Rhodesia, be it in terms of indigenous or other nonwhite groups. The major Asian group that settled there came from India. A few Chinese indentured workers were introduced early in the twentieth century by the British government, but white opposition was so intense that they were soon repatriated.

12 In appraising the response to Asian immigration, including Chinese, Japanese and Indians, see as illustrative: Mellor (1951);

Huttenback (1966, 1976); Keith (1928: vol. II); Kung (1962); Daniels (1970); TenBroek et al. (1968); La Violette (1945, 1948); Berger (1970); Timlin (1960); Fong (1959); and Yarwood (1964, 1968).

13 A few people from India settled in the four countries. Most, however, went to Natal as indentured workers in the sugar cane fields, moving outward into other South African colonies and Southern Rhodesia. Indians also emigrated to Britain's numerous other colonies or possessions. In South Africa anti-Indian hostility prompted discriminatory measures, and by 1911 the importation of Indian indentured workers was terminated. Efforts to repatriate Indians from South Africa and elsewhere were largely unsuccessful, and sporadic conflicts in British colonies led to racial violence during the twentieth century. Following The Afrikaners assumption of power in 1948, Indians, Cape Coloreds and others were restricted in their freedom and opportunities. Indians earlier emigrated to British colonies in East Africa, and during the 1970s they were forced to flee to England. There, too, they encountered prejudice and discrimination. See Tinker (1974, 1978).

14 In the American case, Hawaii has been somewhat of a model in terms of racial harmony. There were conflicts historically, but in recent decades that society, composed of Hawaiians, Japanese, Chinese, those of European descent and others, has managed to achieve a high degree of racial harmony. The discriminatory treatment of Japanese during the Second World War was an exception to this.

15 Through a series of rulings the federal courts constricted the meaning of constitutional amendments and congressional legislation protecting blacks, thereby limiting the rights of Afro-Americans. The courts declared the 1875 Civil Rights Acts unconstitutional, and in 1896 the Supreme Court upheld 'separate but equal' facilities in Plessy v. Ferguson, thereby permitting southern states to segregate public facilities that were seldom equal. That doctine was overturned by the 1954 Brown v. Bd. of Education and subsequent Court decisions, the Brown case holding that separate but equal educational facilities were by definition unequal because they placed a stigma of inferiority on the group (Afro-Americans) separated from whites.

Chapter 4 Color, culture and power: the USA and Canada

1 Compare Josephy (1958: 35-52); Ruchames (1970, Introduction);

Hanke (1970: x); and the earlier study of MacLeod (1928).
Vaughan (1965: 62-3) is critical of historians who attribute
Indian-white conflicts to racial or color factors. This, he suggests,
is prompted by their 'moral indignation at the plight of the
Indian.' His own somewhat overly sympathetic treatment of
New England settlers is brought into question by Jennings's
(1971) analysis which illustrates that settlers weren't as con-
siderate in their relationships with Indians as Vaughan suggests.
Vaughan continually rationalizes the settlers' brutal treatment
of Indians, a brutality that was obvious during the Pequot conflict and King Philip's War, as evident even in Vaughan (1965:
122-50 and ch. 12).

2 Hoetink, a sociologist, suggests that the ambiguities attached to
the term 'race' necessitate use of a more value-free term. He
suggests 'somatic norm image,' which can be defined as 'the
complex of physical (somatic) characteristics which are accepted
by a group as its norm and ideal' (1967: 120). The somatic norm
image (SNI) of a society, as a value, can be analyzed (ibid.:
120-60) in the same way as are other societal values. In some
respects, Jordan's (1969) analysis of white attitudes toward color
(especially black) is comparable to what Hoetink would term
white society's somatic norm image.

3 Van den Berghe (1967: 11) defines racism as: 'any set of beliefs
that organic, genetically transmitted differences (whether real or
imagined) between human groups are intrinsically associated with
the presence or absence of certain socially relevant abilities or
characteristics, hence that such differences are a legitimate basis
of invidious distinctions between groups socially defined as races.'
It should be noted that one group may consider the inferiority of
the other group as innate and thereby unchangeable or as the
consequence of other factors which, if corrected, could lead to
equality. Schermerhorn (1970: 73) traces modern racism to
European expansion and colonization since the fifteenth century.
He distinguishes between 'minimal' and 'maximal' racism. 'In its
minimal form, racism defined darker peoples as backward or less
evolved, different in degree but not in kind from their masters,
therefore, capable with training and education, to rise. . .to a
status of equality with the ruling group.' And: 'The key notion in
maximal racism becomes the inherent superiority of peoples with
lighter color, together with its obverse, the inherent inferiority of
the darker colored. In this view, the rule of the former over the
latter is therefore inevitable, not arbitrary' (ibid.: 73-4). Scher-

merhorn's distinctions are noted at length because of their rele-
vance to the conclusions reached in this analysis. However, it can
be argued that his terms need not be defined simply as applying
to white treatment of blacks. Similar beliefs could be held by
blacks of nonblacks, be they white, brown, red or otherwise. In
that sense Schermerhorn's definition is too restrictive and needs
to be broadened: racism, whether minimal or maximal, is not
simply the property of whites. Given their position of power,
however, over the centuries, white racism could more readily
manifest itself in the world. But given power, blacks, browns or
other nonwhite groups could also manifest forms of racism and
racist behavior.

4 Josephy (1958: 12, 16-17, 20ff, and ch. 10). Even Vaughan
(1965:20), who disputes the racial interpretations of Indian-white
conflicts, acknowledges that after King Philip's War 'New Eng-
landers were more inclined. . . to consider Indians as a race apart.'

5 Jordan (1969: 27; cf. 22, 162, 241-2). The colonists, he states
(ibid.: 162), 'did not consider Indians as being in any sense pale
replicas of Negroes.'

6 See Gossett's (1965: 238-42) comments on Cooper, and those of
Pearce (1965: ch. 7).

7 Jordan (1969: 97-8). Religion, as a characteristic, could be included as part of the culture category, but given its significance in
this particular context, it is isolated for the moment.

8 This ethnocentrism has manifested itself throughout American
life as the dominant English group attempted to anglicize or assimilate other immigrant groups, forcing them to shed their own
culture and accept the Anglo or American culture. This is the
'Americanization' process (Gordon, 1964).

9 Adding credence to this view is the comment of the US Senate
Committee in its Report on Indian Education made in 1969. In
its appraisal of the nation's programs for Indians, it concluded:
'At the root of the assimilation policy has been a desire to divest
the Indian of his land and resources' (quoted in Fey and Mc-
Nickle, 1970: xii). The assimilationist policy initiated by the
Dawes Act of 1887, although enacted at the instigation of humanitarians, was manipulated to accomplish an end totally repugnant
to humanitarians: namely, divesting the Indian of his land. This
is discussed below.

10 Vaughan (1965: 20). See Josephy (1958: 35) and Gossett (1965:
20). Vaughan (1965: 319) notes that Indian prisoners taken in
King Philip's War were sold into slavery in the West Indies. It was

not their color but their potential threat, he argues, which prompted the colonists' 'removal' of them to the West Indies. Thus the power factor emerges as a major theme. Indians were, for numerous reasons, more difficult to enslave than blacks (Jordan, 1969: 22, 66-92, 227; Crane, 1959). See also concerning settler-Indian relations: Leach (1966) and Jacobs (1950).

11 See W.J. Wilson's (1973: ch. 3) discussion of cultural racism as being biological or inherent.

12 Gossett (1965: 239-46) explores this in detail. The ongoing nineteenth-century discussions over 'race' and 'color' were prompted in part by whites' efforts to find rationalizations for their domination and exploitation of nonwhite groups.

13 Most of the color-culture argument to this point has drawn upon the American experience. The differences between the two societies will emerge in the analysis that follows.

14 Shibutani and Kwan (1965: ch. 5) refer to these as 'recurrent patterns of transformation.' They distinguish between 'incorporation' (of immigrants) and 'domination and conquest' (where an outside group, such as English settlers, intent on permanent colonization, oust or conquer an indigenous population). Schermerhorn (1970: ch. 3) refers to these as 'recurrent historical patterns' or 'intergroup sequences.' and he argues for comparative studies of racial encounters.

15 Fey and McNickle (1970: 82-90), Fritz (1963) and the US Senate Committee's 1969 comment concerning the assimilation policy, cited in n. 9. See also Hagan (1961), Levine and Lurie (1970), Sorkin (1971) and Washburn (1971).

16 There were, of course, exceptions to this, as LaViolette (1961) notes. But see Honigman (1968: 816-825), Leighton (1959: ch. 9) and, for an earlier example Bailey (1969: ch. 9).

17 See Schermerhorn's definition in n. 3.

Chapter 5 Race and power in South Africa and Rhodesia

1 The Natal Colony Charter of 1856 granted the franchise to all males on the basis of property and income, but whites quickly found means, especially after 1865, to disfranchise blacks.

2 During 1947-8, Afrikaners for the first time outnumbered English living in urban areas (Ford, 1971).

3 In the British West Indies, blacks emerged with political power and control of political structures in the 1960s, but whites re-

tained (at least initially) considerable control over economic structures. That is still in the process of changing. Viewing themselves as culturally superior to Afrikaners, Anglo Rhodesians deplored the apartheid policies of their southern neighbors. Consequently they rejected apartheid as a policy, fearful of being compared with Afrikaners. In terms of practice, however, they wanted to achieve something similar that would preserve white dominance.

4 The irony, as Bowman (1973: 36) suggests, is that had they participated, black voters might have swung enough votes and elected enough black representatives that they and the UFP would have a majority rather than the RF. Africans then might have played a determining role in legislation, including the use of their power to demand further changes leading toward black majority rule long before it was finally achieved.

Chapter 6 Race and ethnicity: the emergence of siege groups and cultures

1 Although they did not initially see themselves as having a separate or distinct culture or way of life, white Rhodesians, particularly in the years following UDI, did come to view themselves as different from Britain, as 'preserving' Anglo cultural traditions that had been 'lost' in the mother country. That may have been a rationalization for their actions, but they thought of themselves as the upholders of the British tradition. In that sense there was a parallel with the process of transformation that evolved earlier where American colonists saw themselves as preservers of Anglo traditions which they claimed Britain had abandoned, thereby justifying (in the colonists' minds) the American Revolution (Hartz, 1964).

2 A small percentage of whites in Southern Rhodesia were Afrikaner, and there were other European immigrants as well. However, most whites were from England or of English descent.

Chapter 7 Ethnicity, development and power

1 On development aspects, see Enloe (1973); on power and development, Schermerhorn (1970: chs 4-5) and Lenski (1966: chs 2-4). Gordon (1964: ch. 3) distinguishes between cultural (behav-

ioral) and structural assimilation. The terms, though, are confusing, for assimilation is but one form of cultural integration. For example, the dominant group may demand that other groups discard their culture and accept the dominant group culture (assimilation), may accept the presence of other cultures as equals (pluralism) or may reject other cultural groups as of less worth and, while it forces the latter to reject its own culture and accept that of the dominant group it still does not structurally incorporate or accept the latter (segmentation). In terms of plural society analysis, the term structural incorporation, rather than structural assimilation, more clearly distinguishes how and to what extent various groups are incorporated into the dominant group's political, economic and social structures, or whether they retain their own structures willingly (pluralist) or as a consequence of being forced to remain outsiders (segmented).

Chapter 8 Psychological bases of white-nonwhite group encounters

1   The ongoing nineteenth century dialogue or debate, often quite acrimonious, over whether the human race derived from one or numerous species (the monogenetic vs. the polygenetic debate) in part was concerned with whether or not Africans were similar to or different from whites. The acrimony of this debate loses perspective unless these racial implications are considered. See especially Gossett (1965: chs 3-5, 7), Jordan (1969: chs 6, 8) and Banton (1967: chs 2-4).
2   This siege or laager mentality characterized the encounters of Dutch (Afrikaners) with indigenous groups in South Africa. The Afrikaner term 'laager' describes the feeling of being surrounded by hostile forces. See especially Vatcher (1965).
3   The compulsive and ritualistic implementation of British manners and behavior (morning and afternoon teas, dressing as if in Britain rather than in tropical climates, etc.) characterized British (and often other European) colonials, their efforts to establish 'little Britains' overseas in part induced by the uncertainties and stress of their new environment.
4   The Indians could not be expelled, but by putting them on reservations they could be isolated from whites. The late nineteenth century witnessed concerted efforts by white society to push blacks into ghettos, where they too could be isolated from whites, these attempts increasing after efforts to ship blacks to

Africa had largely failed and blacks steadily organized themselves politically and economically to break out from under subordination. Chinese and Japanese, too, usually ended up in enclaves, either pushed there by white society or opting to isolate themselves as a means of protecting themselves from white hostility and discrimination.

Bibliography

Abel, Annie (1907), 'Proposals for an Indian State: 1778-1878,' *Annual Report*, American Historical Association, 1.

Adam, Heribert (1971a), *Modernizing Racial Domination*, Berkeley: University of California Press.

Adam, Heribert (ed.) (1971b), *South Africa: Sociological Perspectives*, London: Oxford University Press.

Adam, Heribert (1971c), 'The South African Power Elite,' in Heribert Adam (ed.), *South Africa: Sociological Perspectives*, London: Oxford University Press.

Adam, Heribert (1975), 'Conflict and Change in South Africa,' in Donald G. Baker (ed.), *Politics of Race: Comparative Studies*, Westmead: Saxon House.

Adam, Heribert and Giliomee, Hermann (1979), *Ethnic Power Mobilized: Can South Africa Change?*, New Haven: Yale University Press.

Adam, Kogila (1971), 'Dialectics of Higher Education for the Colored,' in Heribert Adam (ed.), *South Africa: Sociological Perspectives*, London: Oxford University Press.

Allport, Floyd (1954), 'The Structuring of Events: Outline of a General Theory,' *Psychological Review*, 61: October.

Aronoff, Joel (1967), *Psychological Needs and Cultural Systems*, Princeton: Van Nostrand.

Arrighi, G. (1967), *The Political Economy of Rhodesia*, The Hague: Mouton.

Arrighi, G. (1970), 'Labour Supplies in Historical Perspective: A Study of the Proletarianization of the African Peasantry in Rhodesia,' *Journal of Development Studies*, 6: April.

Bailey, Alfred (1969), *The Conflict of European and Eastern Algonkian Cultures, 1504-1700*, Toronto: University of Toronto Press.

Baker, Donald G. (1972), 'From Apartheid to Invisibility: Black

Americans in Popular Fiction,' *The Midwest Quarterly*, 13: July.

Baker, Donald G. (1973), 'Black Images: The Afro-American in Popular Novels, 1900-1945,' *Journal of Popular Culture*, 6: Winter.

Baker, Donald G. (ed.) (1975), *Politics of Race: Comparative Studies*, Westmead: Saxon House.

Banton, Michael (1967), *Race Relations*, New York: Basic Books.

Barber, James (1967), *Rhodesia: The Road to Rebellion*, London: Oxford University Press.

Barbu, Zevedi (1960), *Problems of Historical Psychology*, New York: Grove.

Barth, Fredrik (1969), *Ethnic Groups and Boundaries*, Boston: Little, Brown.

Barth, Gunther (1964), *Bitter Strength: A History of the Chinese in the United States, 1850-1870*, Cambridge: Harvard University Press.

Baudet, Henri (1965), *Paradise on Earth: Some Thoughts on European Images of Non-European Man*, New Haven: Yale University Press.

Berger, Carl (1970), *The Sense of Power: Studies in the Ideas of a Canadian Imperialism, 1867-1914*, Toronto: University of Toronto Press.

Berlin, Ira (1974), *Slaves Without Masters: The Free Negro in the Antebellum South*, New York: Pantheon.

Berwanger, Eugene (1967), *The Frontier Against Slavery: Western Anti-Negro Prejudice and the Slavery Extension Controversy*, Urbana: University of Illinois Press.

Billington, Ray (1967), *Westward Expansion: A History of the American Frontier*, New York: Macmillan.

Blalock, Hubert (1967), *Toward a Theory of Minority-Group Relations*, New York: Wiley.

Blassingame, John (1972), *The Slave Community*, New York: Oxford University Press.

Blau, Peter (1964), *Exchange and Power in Social Life*, New York: Wiley.

Blauner, Robert (1972), *Racial Oppression in America*, New York: Harper & Row.

Blishen, Bernard *et al.* (eds) (1968), *Canadian Society: Sociological Perspectives*, Toronto: Macmillan.

Blumer, Herbert (1958), 'Race Prejudice as a Sense of Group Position,' *Pacific Sociological Review*, 1: Spring.

Blumer, Herbert (1969), *Symbolic Interactionism*, Englewood Cliffs, New Jersey: Prentice-Hall.

Bowman, Larry (1973), *Politics of Rhodesia*, Cambridge: Harvard University Press.

Brookes, Edgar (1974), *White Rule in South Africa, 1830-1910*, Pieter-maritzburg, University of Natal Press.

Brotz, Howard (1977), *The Politics of South Africa*, London: Oxford University Press.

Brunet, Michel (1966), 'The French Canadians' Search for a Father-land,' in Peter Russell (ed.), *Nationalism in Canada*, Toronto: McGraw-Hill.

Burgess, M. Elaine (1978), 'The Resurgence of Ethnicity,' *Ethnic and Racial Studies*, I: July.

Burkey, Richard (1971), *Racial Discrimination and Public Policy in the United States*, Lexington, Mass.: D.C. Heath.

Bury, J.B. (1955), *The Idea of Progress*, New York: Dover.

Butterfield, Herbert (1960), *The Origins of Modern Science*, New York: Macmillan.

Campbell, Persia (1971), *Chinese Coolie Emigration to Countries within the British Empire*, London: Frank Cass, first published 1923.

Careless, J.M.S. (1969), 'Limited Identities in Canada,' *Canadian Historical Review*, 50: March.

Careless, J.M.S. and Brown, R. (eds) (1968), *The Canadians, 1867-1967*, New York: St Martin's Press.

Carnoy, Martin (1974), *Education as Cultural Imperialism*, New York: David McKay.

Carstens, Peter (1966), *The Social Structure of a Cape Colored Reserve*, New York: Oxford University Press.

Carter, Gwendolyn (1962), *The Politics of Inequality: South Africa Since 1958*, New York: Praeger.

Clark, S.D. (1971), 'The Position of the French-Speaking Population in the Northern Industrial Community,' in Richard Ossenberg (ed.), *Canadian Society: Pluralism, Change and Conflict*, Scarborough, Ont.: Prentice-Hall.

Clarke, Duncan (1974a), *Contract Workers and Underdevelopment in Rhodesia*, Salisbury: Mambo Press.

Clarke, Duncan (1974b), *Domestic Workers in Rhodesia*, Salisbury: Mambo Press.

Clegg, Edward (1960), *Race and Politics: Partnership in the Federation of Rhodesia and Nyasaland*, London: Oxford University Press.

Cohen, Abner (ed.) (1974), 'Introduction: The Lesson of Ethnicity,' *Urban Ethnicity*, London: Tavistock.

Coleman, James S. (1971), *Resources for Social Change: Race in the United States*, New York: Wiley.

Comas, Juan (1958), *The Race Question in Modern Science*, Paris: M. Blondin.

Connor, Walker (1978), 'A Nation is a Nation, is a state, is an ethnic group, is a. . . .,' *Ethnic and Racial Studies*, I: October.

Cook, Ramsey (1967), *Canada and the French-Canadian Question*, Toronto: Macmillan.

Copeland, Lewis (1939), 'The Negro as a Contrast Conception,' in Edgar Thompson (ed.), *Race Relations and the Race Problem*, Durham: University of North Carolina Press.

Corbett, Edward (1967), *Quebec Confronts Canada*, Baltimore: Johns Hopkins University Press.

Cox, Oliver (1971), 'The Question of Pluralism,' *Race*, 12: April.

Crane, Verner (1959), *The Southern Frontier, 1670-1732*, Ann Arbor: University of Michigan Press.

Cross, Malcolm (1971), 'On Conflict, Race Relations and the Theory of the Plural Society,' *Race*, 12: April.

Dalton, B.J. (1967), *War and Politics in New Zealand, 1855-1870*, Sydney: Sydney University Press.

Daniel, Peter (1972), *The Shadow of Slavery: Peonage in the South, 1901-1969*, New York: Oxford University Press.

Daniels, Roger (1970), *The Politics of Prejudice*, New York: Atheneum.

Davies, James (1963), *Human Nature in Politics*, New York: Wiley.

Davis, David B. (1966), *The Problem of Slavery in Western Culture*, Ithaca: Cornell University Press.

Davis, David B. (1969), *The Slave Power Conspiracy and the Paranoid Style*, Baton Rouge: Louisiana State University Press.

Davis, Morris and Krauter, Joseph (1971), *The Other Canadians*, Toronto: Methuen.

Degler, Carl (1971), *Neither Black Nor White: Slavery and Race Relations in Brazil and the United States*, New York: Macmillan.

DeLoria, Vine (1970), *Custer Died for Your Sins: An Indian Manifesto*, New York: Avon.

Deutsch, Karl (1970), 'Research Problems on Race,' in George Shepherd and Tilden LeMelle (eds), *Race Among Nations*, Lexington, Mass.: D.C. Heath.

DeVos, George (1971), 'Conflict, Dominance and Exploitation,' in Nevitt Sanford and Craig Comstock (eds), *Sanctions for Evil*, Boston: Beacon Press.

DeVos, George (1972), 'Social Stratification and Ethnic Pluralism: An Overview from the Perspective of Psychological Anthropology,' *Race*, 13: April.

Diamond, Charles (1974), 'Economic Perspectives on Organized Labor and Socio-Economic Development,' in Wolfgang Thomas (ed.), *Labor Perspectives on South Africa*, Cape Town: David Philip.

Dickie-Clark, H.F. (1971), 'The Dilemma of Education in Plural Socie-
ties,' in Heribert Adam (ed.), *South Africa: Sociological Perspec-
tives*, London: Oxford University Press.
Dorsey, B.J. (1975), 'The African Secondary School Leaver,' in Mar-
shall Murphree (ed.), *Education, Race and Employment in Rhodesia*,
Salisbury: Artca Publications.
Doyle, Bertram (1937), *The Etiquette of Race Relations in the South*,
Chicago: University of Chicago Press.
DuBois, W.E.B. (1964), *Black Reconstruction in America, 1860-1880*,
Cleveland: World Publishing.
Dunlop, Harry (1974), 'Development in Rhodesian Tribal Areas,' *The
Rhodesian Journal of Economics*, 8: December.
Eccles, W.J. (1969), *The Canadian Frontier, 1534-1760*, New York:
Holt, Rinehart & Winston.
Edwards, Isobel (1934), *The 1820 Settlers in South Africa*, New York:
Longmans.
Elkins, Stanley (1959), *Slavery: A Problem in American Institutional
and Intellectual Life*, Chicago: University of Chicago Press.
Elkins, Stanley (1971), 'Slavery and Ideology,' in Ann Lane (ed.),
The Debate Over Slavery, Urbana: University of Illinois Press.
Elliott, Jean (ed.) (1971), *Minority Canadians*, Scarborough, Ont.:
Prentice-Hall.
Ellis, George (1882), *The Red Man and the White Man in North Ameri-
ca*, Boston: Little Brown.
Elphick, Richard and Giliomee, Hermann (eds) (1979), *The Shaping of
South African Society, 1652-1820*, Cape Town: Longman.
Enloe, Cynthia (1973), *Ethnic Conflict and Political Development*, Bos-
ton: Little, Brown.
Erikson, Erik (1950), *Childhood and Society*, New York: Norton.
Fanon, Frantz (1967), *Black Skin, White Masks*, New York: Grove.
Fanon, Frantz (1968), *The Wretched of the Earth*, New York: Grove.
Fanon, Frantz (1970), *Black Skin, White Masks*, London: Granada.
Festinger, Leon (1957), *A Theory of Cognitive Dissonance*, Evanston:
Row, Peterson.
Fey, Harold and McNickle, D'Arcy (1970), *Indians and Other Ameri-
cans*, New York: Harper & Row.
Fishman, J.A. (1966), *Language Loyalty in the United States*, The
Hague: Mouton.
Fong, Ng Bickleen (1959), *The Chinese in New Zealand*, Hong Kong:
Hong Kong University Press.
Ford, Richard (1971), 'The Urban Trek,' in Heribert Adam (ed.), *South
Africa: Sociological Perspectives*, London: Oxford University Press.

Foreman, Grant (1953), *Indian Removal: The Emigration of the Five Civilized Tribes of Indians*, Norman: University of Oklahoma Press.

Forster, John (1975), 'Maori-White Relations in New Zealand,' in Donald G. Baker (ed.), *Politics of Race*, Westmead: Saxon House.

Frazier, E. Franklin (1957), *Race and Culture Contacts in the Modern World*, Boston: Beacon Press.

Fredrickson, George (1971), *The Black Image in the White Mind: The Debate on Afro-American Character and Destiny, 1817-1914*, New York: Harper & Row.

Fredrickson, George (1981), *White Supremacy: A Comparative Study in American and South African History*, New York: Oxford University Press.

Freire, Paulo (1974), *Pedagogy of the Oppressed*, New York: Seabury.

Freud, Sigmund (1962), *Civilization and Its Discontents*, New York: Norton.

Friedrich, Carl (1963), *Man and His Government*, New York: McGraw-Hill.

Fritz, Henry (1963), *The Movement for Indian Assimilation: 1860-1890*, Philadelphia: University of Pennsylvania Press.

Fromm, Erich (1941), *Escape from Freedom*, New York: Holt, Rinehart & Winston.

Fromm, Erich (1947), *Man for Himself*, New York: Holt, Rinehart & Winston.

Gann, L.H. (1965), *A History of Southern Rhodesia, Early Days to 1934*, London: Chatto &Windus.

Geertz, Clifford (1963), 'The Integrative Revolution: Primordial Sentiments and Civil Politics in the New States,' in Clifford Geertz (ed.), *Old Societies and New States*, New York: Free Press.

Genovese, Eugene (1965), *The Political Economy of Slavery*, New York: Vintage.

Genovese, Eugene (1969), *The World the Slaveholders Made*, New York: Vintage.

Genovese, Eugene (1974), *Roll, Jordan, Roll: The World the Slaves Made*, New York: Pantheon.

Geschwender, James (1968), 'Explorations in the Theory of Social Movements and Revolutions,' *Social Forces*, 47: December.

Gilbert, Felix (1961), *To the Farewell Address: Ideas of Early American Foreign Policy*, Princeton: Princeton University Press.

Glazer, Nathan and Moynihan, Daniel (1974), *Beyond the Melting Pot*, Cambridge: MIT Press.

Goldstein, Robert (1969), *French–Iroquois Diplomatic and Military Relations, 1609-1701*, The Hague: Mouton.

Gordon, Milton (1964), *Assimilation in American Life*, New York: Oxford University Press.

Gossett, Thomas (1965), *Race: The History of an Idea in America*, New York: Schocken.

Greenstein, Fred (1969), *Personality and Politics*, Chicago: Markham.

Grodzins, Morton (1949), *Americans Betrayed: Politics and the Japanese Evacuation*, Chicago: University of Chicago Press.

Gurian, Jay (1975), 'Psycho-Political Power Patterns in Native American-White Conflicts,' in Donald G. Baker (ed.), *Politics of Race*, Westmead: Saxon House.

Gusfield, Joseph (1966), *Symbolic Crusade*, Urbana: University of Illinois Press.

Guy, Jeff (1979), *The Destruction of the Zulu Kingdom*, London: Longmans.

Hagan, William (1961), *The American Indian*, Chicago: University of Chicago Press.

Hall, Raymond (ed.) (1979), *Ethnic Autonomy: Comparative Dynamics*, New York: Pergamon.

Haller, John (1971), *Outcasts from Evolution*, Urbana: University of Illinois Press.

Halpern, Manfred (1970), *Applying a New Theory of Human Relations to the Study of Racism*, Denver: University of Denver Monograph Series.

Hanke, Lewis (1970), *Aristotle and the American Indians: A Study in Race Prejudice in the Modern World*, Bloomington: Indiana University Press.

Harp, John and Hoflcy, John (eds) (1971), *Poverty in Canada*, Scarborough, Ont., Prentice-Hall.

Harris, Peter (1974), *Black Industrial Workers in Rhodesia*, Salisbury: Mambo Press.

Hartz, Louis (1964), *The Founding of New Societies*, New York: Harcourt, Brace & World.

Hawley, Amos (1963), 'Community Power and Urban Renewal Success,' *American Journal of Sociology*, 68: January.

Henderson, Ian (1972), 'White Populism in Southern Rhodesia,' *Comparative Studies in Society and History*, 14: September.

Henriques, Fernando (1974), *Children of Caliban: Miscegenation*, London: Secker & Warburg.

Higham, John (1971), *Strangers in the Land: Patterns of American Nativism, 1860-1925*, New York: Atheneum.

Himes, Joseph (1973), *Racial Conflict in American Society*, Columbus, Ohio: Merrill.

Himes, Joseph (1975), 'Black-White Relations in the United States Since World War II,' in Donald G. Baker (ed.), *Politics of Race*, Westmead: Saxon House.

Hoetink, Hermannus (1967), *The Two Variants in Caribbean Race Relations*, London: Oxford University Press.

Hoetink, Hermannus (1971), *Caribbean Race Relations: A Study of Two Variants*, New York: Oxford University Press.

Hofstadter, Richard (1956), *The Age of Reform*, New York: Macmillan.

Holleman, J.F. (1969), *Chief, Counsel and Commissioner*, London: Oxford University Press.

Honigman, John (1968), 'Social Disintegration in Five Northern Communities,' in Bernard Blishen *et al.* (eds), *Canadian Society*, Toronto: Macmillan.

Horrell, Muriel (1973), *The African Homelands of South Africa*, Johannesburg: South African Institute of Race Relations.

Horsman, Reginald (1967), *Expansion and American Indian Policy, 1783-1812*, East Lansing: Michigan State University Press.

Horwitz, Ralph (1967), *The Political Economy of South Africa*, London: Weidenfeld & Nicolson.

Huttenback, Robert (1966), *The British Imperial Experience*, New York: Harper & Row.

Huttenback, Robert (1976), *Racism and Empire: White Settlers and Colored Immigrants in the British Self-Governing Colonies, 1830-1910*, Ithaca: Cornell University Press.

Institute for Industrial Education (1974), *The Durban Strikes: 1973*, Durban: Raven Press.

Isajiw, Wesevolod (1968), 'The Process of Social Integration: The Canadian Example,' *Dalhousie Review*, 48.

Jackson, Helen (1969), *A Century of Dishonor*, New York: Harper & Row; first published in 1881.

Jacobs, Wilbur (1950), *Diplomacy and Indian Gifts: Anglo-French Rivalry along the Ohio and Northwest Frontiers, 1748-1763*, Stanford: Stanford University Press.

Jenness, Diamond (1932), *The Indians of Canada*, Ottawa: National Museum of Canada.

Jennings, Francis (1971), 'Virgin Land and Savage People,' *American Quarterly*, 23: October.

Johnson, R.W. (1978), *How Long Will South Africa Survive?*, London: Macmillan.

Jones, Howard M. (1968), *O Strange New World: American Culture, the Formative Years*, New York: Viking.

Jordan, Winthrop (1969), *White Over Black: American Attitudes Toward the Negro, 1550-1812*, Baltimore: Penguin.

Josephy, Alvin, Jr (1958), *The Patriot Chiefs*, New York: Viking.

Katznelson, Ira (1972), 'Comparative Studies of Race and Ethnicity,' *Comparative Politics*, 5: October.

Keiser, Albert (1933), *The Indian in American Literature*, New York: Oxford University Press.

Keith, Arthur (1928), *Responsible Government in the Dominions*, Oxford: Clarendon Press, 2 vols.

Kelly, George (1963), *A Theory of Personality*, New York: Norton.

Kennedy, J.H. (1950), *Jesuit and Savage in New France*, New Haven: Yale University Press.

Kerner Commission (1968), *Report of the National Advisory Commission on Civil Disorders*, New York: Bantam; hereafter referred to as the Kerner Report.

Knowles, Louise and Prewitt, Kenneth (eds) (1969), *Institutional Racism in America*, Englewood Cliffs: Prentice-Hall.

Knutson, Jeanne (1972), *The Human Basis of the Polity*, Chicago: Aldine-Atherton.

Koch, Adrienne (1964), *Jefferson and Madison*, New York: Oxford.

Kovel, Joel (1971), *White Racism: A Psychohistory*, New York: Vintage.

Kraus, Michael (1949), *The Atlantic Civilization*, Ithaca: Cornell University Press.

Kung, S.W. (1962), *Chinese in American Life*, Seattle: University of Washington Press.

Kuper, Leo and Smith, M.G. (eds) (1969), *Pluralism in Africa*, Berkeley: University of California Press.

Lanctot, Gustav (1963), *A History of Canada: Origins to Royal Regime, 1663*, Cambridge: Harvard University Press, vol. I.

Lanternari, Vittorio (1963), *The Religions of the Oppressed*, New York: Knopf.

LaViolette, Forrest (1945), *Americans of Japanese Ancestry*, Toronto: Canadian Institute of International Affairs.

LaViolette, Forrest (1948), *The Canadian Japanese and World War II*, Toronto: University of Toronto Press.

LaViolette, Forrest (1958), 'Canada and Its Japanese,' in Edgar Thompson and Everett Hughes (eds), *Race*, Chicago: Free Press.

LaViolette, Forrest (1961), *The Struggle for Survival: Indian Cultures and the Protestant Ethic in British Columbia*, Toronto: University of Toronto Press.

LaViolette, Forrest (1968), *The Canadian Japanese and World War II*,

Toronto: University of Toronto Press.

Leach, Douglas (1958), *Flintlock and Tomahawk: New England in King Philip's War*, New York: Macmillan.

Leach, Douglas (1966), *The Northern Colonial Frontier: 1607-1763*, New York: Holt, Rinehart & Winston.

Lee, Rose Hum (1960), *The Chinese in the United States of America*, Hong Kong, Hong Kong University Press.

Leftwich, Adrian (ed.) (1974), *South Africa: Economic Growth and Social Change*, London: Allison & Busby.

Leighton, Alexander (1959), *My Name is Legion*, New York: Basic Books.

LeMay, G.H.L. (1971), *Black and White in South Africa*, New York: American Heritage Press.

Lenski, Gerhard (1966), *Power and Privilege: A Theory of Social Stratification*, New York: McGraw-Hill.

Levine, Stuart and Lurie, Nancy (eds) (1970), *The American Indian Today*, Baltimore: Penguin.

Lewin, Kurt (1951), *Field Theory in Social Science*, New York: Harper & Row.

Lewis, R.W.B. (1955), *The American Adam*, Chicago: Phoenix Books.

Leys, Colin (1959), *European Politics in Southern Rhodesia*, Oxford: Clarendon Press.

Lifton, Robert (1961), *Thought Reform and the Psychology of Totalism*, New York: Norton.

Lippmann, Lorna (1970), *To Achieve Our Country: Australia and the Aborigines*, Melbourne: Cheshire.

Lippmann, Lorna (1973), *Words or Blows: Racial Attitudes in Australia*, Harmondsworth: Penguin.

Lipset, Seymour (1963), *The First New Nation*, New York: Basic Books.

Lipset, Seymour (1964), 'Canada and the United States: A Comparative View,' *Canadian Review of Sociology and Anthropology*, I.

Litwack, Leon (1961), *North of Slavery: The Negro in the Free States, 1790-1860*, Chicago: University of Chicago Press.

Logan, Rayford (1965), *The Betrayal of the Negro*, New York: Collier-Macmillan.

Lower, Arthur (1946), *Colony to Nation: A History of Canada*, Toronto: Longmans, Green.

MacCrone, Ian (1937), *Race Attitudes in South Africa*, Johannesburg: Witwatersrand University Press.

McKenna, Marian (1969), 'The Melting Pot: Comparative Observations on the United States and Canada,' *Sociology and Social Re-*

search, 53: July.
MacLeod, William (1928), *The American Indian Frontier*, New York: Knopf.
Macmillan, W.M. (1940), *Complex South Africa*, London: Faber & Faber.
Macmillan W.M. (1963), *Bantu, Boer and Briton: The Making of the South African Native Problem*, Oxford: Clarendon.
McMurtry, John (1978), *The Structure of Marx's World-View*, Princeton: Princeton University Press.
McRae, Kenneth (1964), 'The Structure of Canadian History,' in Louis Hartz, *The Founding of New Societies*, New York: Harcourt, Brace & World.
Mafejo, Archie (1975), 'Religion, Class and Ideology in South Africa,' in M. Whisson and M. West (eds), *Religion and Social Change in Southern Africa*, Cape Town: David Philip.
Mallory, J.R. (1970), 'The Canadian Dilemma: French and English,' *Political Quarterly*, 41: July-September.
Manganyi, N. Chabani (1977), *Mashangu's Reverie*, Johannesburg: Ravan Press.
Mannoni, O. (1964), *Prospero and Caliban: the Psychology of Colonization*, New York: Praeger.
Mansergh, Nicholas (1962), *South Africa: 1906-1961*, New York: Praeger.
Marks, Shula (1970), *Reluctant Rebellion*, Oxford: Clarendon Press.
Maslow, A.H. (1954), *Motivation and Personality*, New York: Harper & Row.
Mason, Philip (1970), *Patterns of Dominance*, New York: Oxford University Press.
Maykovich, Minako (1975), 'Japanese and Chinese in the United States and Canada,' in Donald G. Baker (ed.), *Politics of Race*, Westmead: Saxon House.
Meer, Fatima (1971), 'African Nationalism — Inhibiting Factors,' in Heribert Adam (ed.), *South Africa: Sociological Perspectives*, London: Oxford University Press.
Melling, J. (1966), 'Recent Developments in Official Policy Toward Canadian Indians and Eskimos,' *Race*, 7: April.
Melling, J. (1967), *Right to a Future: The Native Peoples*, Ontario: Anglican and United Churches of Canada.
Mellor, George (1951), *British Imperial Trusteeship: 1783-1850*, London: Faber & Faber.
Memmi, Albert (1965), *The Colonizer and the Colonized*, Boston: Beacon Press.

Metge, Joan (1964), *A New Maori Migration*, London: Athlone Press.
Miller, Harold (1966), *Race Conflict in New Zealand, 1814-1865*, Auckland: Blackwood and Janet Paul.
Miller, J.D.B. (1966), *Britain and the Old Dominions*, Baltimore: Johns Hopkins University Press.
Miller, Stuart (1969), *The Unwelcome Immigrant: The American Image of the Chinese, 1785-1882*, Berkeley: University of California Press.
Mitchell, J.C. (1970), 'Race, Class and Status in South Central Africa,' in A. Tuden and L. Plotnicov (eds), *Social Stratification in Africa*, New York: Free Press.
Mol, Hans (1966), *Religion and Race in New Zealand*, Christchurch: National Council of Churches.
Moodie, T. Dunbar (1975), *The Rise of Afrikanerdom*, Berkeley: University of California Press.
Morchain, Janet (1967), *Search for a Nation: French-English Relations in Canada Since 1759*, Toronto: Dent & Sons.
Moyana, Henry (1974), 'Land Apportionment in Rhodesia, 1920-1960,' unpublished PhD thesis, Columbia University.
Murphree, Marshall (1973), *Employment Opportunity and Race in Rhodesia*, Denver: Studies in Race and Nations, University of Denver.
Murphree, Marshall (1975), 'Race and Power in Rhodesia,' in Donald G. Baker (ed.), *Politics of Race*, Westmead: Saxon House.
Murphree, Marshall (1976), *Education, Development and Change in Africa*, Johannesburg: South African Institute of Race Relations.
Murray, D.J. (1970), *The Government System in Southern Rhodesia*, Oxford: Clarendon Press.
Myrdal, Gunnar (1944), *An American Dilemma*, New York: Harper & Row.
Nammack, Georgiana (1969), *Fraud, Politics and the Dispossession of the Indians*, Norman: University of Oklahoma Press.
Neame, L.E. (1962), *The History of Apartheid*, London: Pall Mall.
Neumann, F. (1960), 'Anxiety and Politics,' in M.R. Stein *et al.* (eds), *Identity and Anxiety*, Chicago: Free Press.
Newby, I.A. (1965), *Jim Crow's Defense: Anti-Negro Thought in America, 1900-1930*, Baton Rouge: Louisiana State University Press.
Noble, David (1968), *The Eternal Adam and the New World Garden*, New York: Braziller.
Noel, Donald (1968), 'A Theory of the Origin of Ethnic Stratification,' *Social Problems*, 16: Fall.
Nolen, Claude (1967), *The Negro's Image in the South: The Anatomy*

of White Supremacy, Lexington: University of Kentucky Press.

Nordlinger, Eric (1968), 'Political Development, Time Sequences and the Rates of Change,' *World Politics*, 20: April.

Novak, Michael (1971), *The Rise of the Unmeltable Ethnics*, New York: Macmillan.

Ossenberg, Richard (1967), 'The Conquest Revisited: Another Look at Canadian Dualism,' *Canadian Journal of Sociology and Anthropology*, 4: November.

Ossenberg, Richard (1972), 'Social Pluralism in Quebec,' in Richard Ossenberg (ed.), *Canadian Society: Pluralism, Change and Conflict*, Scarborough, Ont.: Prentice-Hall.

Palley, Claire (1966), *The Constitutional History and Law of Southern Rhodesia, 1888-1965*, Oxford: Clarendon Press.

Palley, Claire (1970a), 'Law and the Unequal Society: Discriminatory Legislation in Rhodesia: Part I,' *Race*, 12: July.

Palley, Claire (1970b), 'Law and the Unequal Society: Discriminatory Legislation in Rhodesia: Part II,' *Race*, 12: October.

Palmer, R.H. (1968), *Aspects of Rhodesian Land Policy, 1890-1936*, Salisbury, Central African Historical Association, Local Series no. 22.

Park, Robert (1949), *Race and Culture*, Chicago: Free Press.

Parkes, Henry (1959), *The American Experience*, New York: Vintage.

Parkman, Francis (1902), *A Half Century of Conflict*, Boston: Little, Brown.

Patterson, E. Palmer (1972), *The Canadian Indian: A History Since 1500*, Don Mills, Ont.: Collier-Macmillan.

Patterson, E. Palmer (1975), 'Indian-White Relations in Canada,' in Donald G. Baker (ed.), *Politics of Race*, Westmead: Saxon House.

Pearce, Roy (1965), *The Savages of America: A Study of the Indian and the Idea of Civilization*, Baltimore: Johns Hopkins University Press.

Phimister, I.R. (1971), 'The Shamva Mine Strike of 1927,' *Rhodesian History*, 20.

Pittock, A. Barrie (1975), 'Politics and Race in Australia,' in Donald G. Baker (ed.), *Politics of Race*, Westmead: Saxon House.

Pitt-Rivers, George (1929), *The Clash of Cultures and the Contact of Races*, London: Routledge.

Pocock, J. (ed.) (1965), *The Maori and New Zealand Politics*, Auckland: Blackwood and Janet Paul.

Porter, John (1965), *The Vertical Mosaic: An Analysis of Social Class and Power in Canada*, Toronto: University of Toronto Press.

Price, A. Grenfell (1963), *The Western Invasions of the Pacific and Its Continents*, Oxford: Clarendon Press.

Price, A. Grenfell (1972), *White Settlers and Native Peoples*, Westport, Conn.: Greenwood Press; first published in 1950, Melbourne: Georgian House.

Price, Charles (1966), '"White" Restrictions on "Coloured" Immigration,' *Race*, 7: January.

Prucha, Francis (1962), *American Indian Policy in the Formative Years*, Cambridge: Harvard University Press.

Rabushka, Alvin and Shepsle, Kenneth (1972), *Politics in Plural Societies: A Theory of Democratic Stability*, Columbus, Ohio: Charles Merrill.

Ranger, T.O. (1966), 'Traditional Authorities and the Rise of Modern Politics in Southern Rhodesia,' in E. Stokes and R. Brown (eds), *The Zambezian Past*, Manchester: Manchester University Press.

Ranger, T.O. (1967), *Revolt in Southern Rhodesia*, London: Heinemann.

Ranger, T.O. (1970), *The African Voice in Southern Rhodesia*, London: Heinemann.

Reichenbach, Hans (1951), *The Rise of Scientific Philosophy*, Berkeley: University of California Press.

Rex, John (1971), 'The Plural Society: The South African Case,' *Race*, 12: April.

Rhoodie, Nic (1969), *Apartheid and Racial Partnership in Southern Africa*, Pretoria: Academica.

Richmond, Anthony (1967), *Post-War Immigrants in Canada*, Toronto: University of Toronto Press.

Richmond, Anthony (1970), 'Immigration and Pluralism in Canada,' in W.E. Mann (ed.), *Social and Cultural Change in Canada*, Toronto: Copp Clark, vol. 1.

Robinson, Ronald and Gallagher, John (1967), *Africa and the Victorians*, New York: St Martin's Press.

Rogers, Cyril and Frantz, C. (1962), *Racial Themes in Southern Rhodesia*, New Haven: Yale University Press.

Rogin, Michael (1971), 'Liberal Society and the Indian Question,' *Politics and Society*, 1: May.

Rokeach, Milton (1954), 'The Nature and Meaning of Dogmatism,' *Psychological Review*, 61: May.

Rokeach, Milton (1956), 'Political and Religious Dogmatism,' *Psychological Monographs*, 70.

Rokeach, Milton (1960), *The Open and Closed Mind*, New York: Basic Books.

Rokeach, Milton (1968), *Beliefs, Attitudes and Values*, San Francisco, Jossey-Bass.

Rossiter, Clinton (1960), *Marxism: The View from America*, New York: Harcourt, Brace.

Rostow, W.W. (1971), *Politics and the Stages of Growth*, Cambridge: Cambridge University Press.

Rowley, C.D. (1972), *The Destruction of Aboriginal Society*, Sydney: Penguin.

Rowley, C.D. (1972), *Outcasts in White Australia*, Sydney: Penguin.

Ruchames, Louis (ed.) (1970), *Racial Thought in America*, New York, Grosset & Dunlap (1969, University of Massachusetts Press).

Ryan, William (1976), *Blaming the Victim*, New York: Vintage.

Sanford, Charles (1961), *The Quest for Paradise: Europe and the American Moral Imagination*, Urbana: University of Illinois Press.

Schapera, Isaac (ed.) (1967), *Western Civilization and the Natives of South Africa*, New York: Humanities Press.

Schattschneider, E.E. (1961), *The Semisovereign People*, New York: Holt, Rinehart & Winston.

Schermerhorn, R.A. (1970), *Comparative Ethnic Relations*, New York: Random House.

Schwimmer, Erik (ed.) (1968), *The Maori People in the Nineteen-Sixties*, Auckland: Blackwood and Janet Paul.

Scott, Nolvert (1975), 'The Black Peoples of Canada,' in Donald G. Baker (ed.), *Politics of Race*, Westmead: Saxon House.

Shamuyarira, Nathan (1965), *Crisis in Rhodesia*, London: Andre Deutsch.

Shibutani, Tamotsu and Kwan, Kian (1965), *Ethnic Stratification: A Comparative Approach*, New York: Macmillan.

Shinn, Roger (1964), *The Search for Identity: Essays on the American Character*, New York: Harper & Row.

Simons, H.J. and R.E. (1969), *Class and Colour in South Africa, 1850-1950*, Harmondsworth: Penguin.

Sinclair, Keith (1961), *The Maori Wars*, Wellington: New Zealand University Press.

Smelser, Neil (1963), *Theory of Collective Behavior*, New York: Free Press.

Smelser, Neil (1973), 'The Methodology of Comparative Analysis,' in Donald Warwick and Samuel Osherson (eds), *Comparative Research Methods*, Englewood Cliffs, New Jersey: Prentice-Hall.

Smith, Allan (1970), 'Metaphor and Nationality in North America,' *Canadian Historical Review*, 51: September.

Sorkin, Alan (1971), *American Indians and Federal Aid*, Washington: Brookings.

Spencer, Benjamin (1957), *The Quest for Nationality*, Syracuse:

Syracuse University Press.

Stampp, Kenneth (1956), *The Peculiar Institution*, New York: Vintage.

Stanley, George (1960), *The Birth of Western Canada: A History of the Riel Rebellions*, Toronto: Toronto University Press.

Stanton, William (1960), *The Leopard's Spots: Scientific Attitudes Toward Race in America, 1815-1859*, Chicago: University of Chicago Press.

Stember, Charles (1976), *Sexual Racism*, New York: Harper.

Stevens, Frank (ed.) (1972), *Racism: The Australian Experience*, Sydney: Australia and New Zealand Book Company, vol. 2.

Stone, John (1973), *Colonist or Uitlander: A Study of the British Immigrant in South Africa*, New York: Oxford University Press.

Sundkler, Bengt (1961), *Bantu Prophets in South Africa*, London: Oxford University Press.

Swanson, Maynard (1968), 'Urban Origins of Separate Development,' *Race*, 10: July.

Tannenbaum, Frank (1968), *Slave and Citizen: The Negro in the Americas*, New York: Vintage.

Tatz, Colin (1962), *Shadow and Substance in South Africa*, Pietermaritzburg: University of Natal Press.

TenBroek, Jacobus *et al.* (1968), *Prejudice, War and the Constitution*, Berkeley: University of California Press.

Thomas, Wolfgang (1974), 'The Economics of Changing Labor Relations in South Africa,' in Wolfgang Thomas (ed.), *Labor Perspectives on South Africa*, Cape Town: David Philip.

Thompson, Leonard (1960), *The Unification of South Africa, 1902-1910*, Oxford: Clarendon Press.

Timlin, Mabel (1960), 'Canada's Immigration Policy, 1896-1910,' *Canadian Journal of Economics and Political Science*, 26: November.

Tinker, Hugh (1974), *A New System of Slavery: The Export of Indian Labor Overseas, 1830-1920*, London: Oxford University Press.

Tinker, Hugh (1978), *India and the Indians in the Commonwealth, 1920-1950*, Vancouver: University of British Columbia Press.

Trelease, Allen (1971), *White Terror: the Ku Klux Klan Conspiracy and Southern Reconstruction*, New York: Harper & Row.

Troper, Harold (1972), 'The Creek-Negroes of Oklahoma and Canadian Immigration,' *Canadian Historical Review*, 53: September.

Van den Berghe, Pierre (1964), *South Africa*, Middletown: Wesleyan University Press.

Van den Berghe, Pierre (1967), *Race and Racism*, New York: Wiley.

Van den Berghe, Pierre (1970), *South Africa: A Study in Conflict*, Berkeley: University of California Press.

Van der Horst, Sheila (1942), *Native Labour in South Africa*, London: Oxford University Press.

Van Jaarsveld, F.A. (1964), *The Afrikaner's Interpretation of South African History*, Cape Town: Simondium.

Van Onselen, Charles (1973), 'Worker Consciousness in Black Miners: Southern Rhodesia, 1900-1920,' *Journal of African History*, 14.

Van Woodward, C. (1951), *Origins of the New South, 1877-1925*, Baton Rouge: Louisiana State University Press.

Van Woodward, C. (1966), *The Strange Career of Jim Crow*, New York: Oxford University Press.

Vatcher, William (1965), *White Laager: The Rise of Afrikaner Nationalism*, New York: Praeger.

Vaughan, Alden (1965), *New England Frontier: Puritans and Indians, 1620-1675*, Boston: Little, Brown.

Voegeli, V. Jacque (1967), *Free but Not Equal: The Midwest and the Negro During the Civil War*, Chicago: University of Chicago Press.

Walker, Eric (1930), *The Frontier Tradition in South Africa*, London: Oxford University Press.

Walker, Eric (1957), *A History of Southern Africa*, London: Longmans, Green.

Washburn, Wilcomb (1959), 'The Moral and Legal Justification for Dispossessing the Indians,' in James Smith (ed.), *Seventeenth Century America*, Chapel Hill: University of North Carolina Press.

Washburn, Wilcomb (1971), *Red Man's Land, White Man's Law*, New York: Scribner.

Waubageshig, Harvey McCue (ed.) (1970), *The Only Good Indian*, Toronto: Toronto University Press.

Weber, Max (1947), *The Theory of Social and Economic Organization*, Oxford: Oxford University Press.

Weinberg, Albert (1963), *Manifest Destiny: A Study of Nationalist Expansion in American History*, Chicago: Quadrangle Books.

Weiner, Myron (1965), 'Political Integration and Political Development,' *The Annals*, 358: March.

Weinrich, A.E.H. (1971), *Chiefs and Councils in Rhodesia*, London: Heinemann.

Welsh, David (1972), 'The Cultural Dimension of Apartheid,' *African Affairs*, 71: January.

Welsh, David (1973), *The Roots of Segregation*, London: Oxford University Press.

West, Katherine (1972), 'Stratification and Ethnicity in "Plural" New States,' *Race*, 13: April.

Wetherell, Iden (1974), 'Continuity and Change in Opposition Politics in Southern Rhodesia, 1923-1962,' MPhil, University of Rhodesia.

Whitehead, Alfred (1967), *Science and the Modern World*, New York: Macmillan.

Williams, Eric (1966), *Capitalism and Slavery*, New York: Capricorn.

Williams, John (1969), *Politics of the New Zealand Maori*, Seattle: University of Washington Press.

Williams, Loretta (1975), 'Black Subordination in Colonies and Nation, 1619-1945,' in Donald G. Baker (ed.), *Politics of Race*, Westmead: Saxon House.

Williamson, James (1967), *A Short History of British Expansion*, New York: St Martin's Press.

Wilson, Francis (1972), *Migrant Labour in South Africa*, Johannesburg: Spro-Cas.

Wilson, Monica (1961), *Reaction to Conquest: Effects of Contact of Europeans on the Pondo of South Africa*, London: Oxford University Press.

Wilson, Monica and Thompson, Leonard (eds) (1969, 1971), *The Oxford History of South Africa*, Oxford: Clarendon Press, 2 vols.

Wilson, William J. (1973), *Power, Racism and Privilege*, New York: Macmillan.

Wilson, William J. (1978), *The Declining Significance of Race*, Chicago, University of Chicago Press.

Winks, Robin (1971), *The Blacks in Canada*, New Haven: Yale University Press.

Wolfenstein, E. Victor (1969), *Personality and Politics*, Belmont, California: Dickenson.

Wolpe, Harold (1970), 'Industrialism and Race in South Africa,' in Sami Zubaida (ed.), *Race and Racialism*, London: Tavistock.

Wood, Forrest (1970), *Black Scare: The Racist Response to Emancipation and Reconstruction*, Berkeley: University of California Press.

Yarwood, A.T. (1964), *Asian Migration to Australia: The Background to Exclusion, 1896-1923*, Melbourne: Melbourne University Press.

Yarwood, A.T. (ed.) (1968), *Attitudes to Non-European Immigration*, Melbourne: Cassell.

Yinger, J. Milton (1965), *Toward a Field Theory of Behavior*, New York: McGraw-Hill.

Young, Charles and Reid, Helen (1939), *The Japanese Canadians*, Toronto: University of Toronto Press.

Young, Crawford (1976), *The Politics of Cultural Pluralism*, Madison: University of Wisconsin Press.

Index

In this index the following abbreviations are used:
Rh — Rhodesia, SA — South Africa, USA — United States